XML and SQL Server™ 2000

John Griffin

New Riders

www.newriders.com

201 West 103rd Street, Indianapolis, Indiana 46290
An Imprint of Pearson Education
Boston • Indianapolis • London • Munich • New York • San Francisco

XML and SQL Server™ 2000

Copyright © 2002 by New Riders Publishing

FIRST EDITION: July 2001

International Standard Book Number: 0-7357-1112-7

Library of Congress Catalog Card Number: 00111659

05 04 03 02   7 6 5 4 3 2 1

Interpretation of the printing code: The rightmost double-digit number is the year of the book's printing; the rightmost single-digit number is the number of the book's printing. For example, the printing code 02-1 shows that the first printing of the book occurred in 2002.

Composed in Bembo and MCPdigital by New Riders Publishing

Printed in the United States of America

Trademarks

Warning and Disclaimer

Publisher
David Dwyer

Associate Publisher
Al Valvano

Executive Editor
Stephanie Wall

Managing Editor
Gina Brown

Product Marketing Manager
Stephanie Layton

Publicity Manager
Susan Nixon

Development Editor
Rubi Olis

Senior Editor
Lori Lyons

Copy Editor
Amy Lepore

Indexer
Christopher Morris

Manufacturing Coordinator
Jim Conway

Book Designer
Louisa Klucznik

Cover Designer
Brainstorm Design, Inc.

Cover Production
Aren Howell

Composition
Amy Parker

❖

*To my wife Judith, who, when I told her I was going
to write a book said, "And exactly WHERE
are you going to find the time to write a book!?!?"
Then she found me the time.*

❖

Table of Contents

About the Author

John Griffin is currently Senior Applications Developer for Iomega Corp. in Roy, UT. He has worked in the computer industry in one form or another since 1969. Previous experience includes contract work for Sprint-Paranet of Houston, TX, systems administration for the Department of Defense, and serving in the U.S. Navy for nine years. He holds the MCNE, MCSE, MCP+I and A+ certifications. John lives in Layton, Utah with his wife, Judith, and Australian Shepherd, Maggie.

About the Technical Reviewers

These reviewers contributed their considerable hands-on expertise to the entire development process for *XML and SQL Server 2000*. As the book was being written, these dedicated professionals reviewed all the material for technical content, organization, and flow. Their feedback was critical to ensuring that *XML and SQL Server 2000* fits our reader's need for the highest quality technical information.

Rick Shelton is a professional Web developer with more than 18 years of experience, working for top companies such as Space Dynamics Laboratory, Iomega Corporation, and PacifiCorp. He has designed and implemented a variety of Web sites involving B2B and B2C e-commerce using ASP/ADO, DHTML, XML, VBScript, JavaScript, using several different back-end databases. An experienced CPA, Rick understands the practical business application of Web development and e-commerce solutions.

Scott Fitchet is a software developer, technology writer, and travel photographer based in Cambridge, Massachusetts. He specializes in application framework design using technologies such as XML, SQL Server, and Macromedia Flash, although his favorite development environment continues to be a unique mixture of ballpoint pens and cocktail napkins. Scott can be reached at scott@figital.com or through his Web site at www.figital.com.

Tell Us What You Think

As the reader of this book, you are the most important critic and commentator. We value your opinion and want to know what we're doing right, what we could do better, what areas you'd like to see us publish in, and any other words of wisdom you're willing to pass our way.

As the Executive Editor for the Web Development team at New Riders Publishing, I welcome your comments. You can fax, email, or write me directly to let me know what you did or didn't like about this book—as well as what we can do to make our books stronger.

Please note that I cannot help you with technical problems related to the topic of this book, and that due to the high volume of mail I receive, I might not be able to reply to every message.

When you write, please be sure to include this book's title and author as well as your name and phone or fax number. I will carefully review your comments and share them with the author and editors who worked on the book.

Fax: 317-581-4663
Email: stephanie.wall@newriders.com
Mail: Stephanie Wall
       Executive Editor
       New Riders Publishing
       201 West 103rd Street
       Indianapolis, IN 46290 USA

Introduction

This book is intended for SQL Server 2000 developers and project managers who need to build solid XML applications on Microsoft's database platform.

Experienced SQL Server developers who have been building desktop and distributed applications in a client/server environment can read the book to assess the new XML capabilities of SQL Server 2000 and then employ them in a very short time. This book provides sample code, guidelines, and sample templates to help developers utilize XML wherever this new technology is needed.

Who Will Benefit from This Book?

Developers new to XML can read the first chapters, along with their included guidelines and sample code, to familiarize themselves with the technology. This book attempts to minimize the impact of learning a new technology by offering guidelines and explanations to both the new developer and the team. Although parts of this book cover very complex topics, the complexity of each chapter is kept to a minimum wherever possible. The material is covered in small portions so as not to overwhelm most users and includes numerous code examples.

For project managers who have to manage a team of developers and produce solid applications, this book provides an overall view of XML coding with SQL Server 2000, its limitations, and its capabilities. This book can be used as a training document for individual developers or the project team.

Each chapter provides numerous examples, starting with easier instances to illustrate the basics and then becoming progressively more difficult.

Who Is This Book Not For?

This book is not a tutorial or a reference on the structured query language (SQL) or Microsoft's SQL Server 2000 other than its XML capabilities. There are many technical books and online references on both SQL and SQL Server 2000. This book addresses a need not found in those sources—the generation of valid and well-formed XML documents in a variety of ways. In an effort to stay focused on this goal, this book is meant to augment rather than replace any of these materials.

If you're looking for a book that addresses XML document generation from any platform other than Microsoft's SQL Server 2000, then this book is not for you. Although the first two chapters address the general topics of XML, XML Stylesheet Transformations, XML schemas, and DTDs, which are applicable to all development platforms, this book specifically addresses the Microsoft SQL Server 2000 Enterprise Database platform. This book assumes the use of Microsoft's Internet Explorer as the browser of choice.

The Organization of This Book

This book is organized into eight chapters.

Chapter 1, "XML," discusses the Extensible Markup Language (XML). Included in this chapter is a comprehensive discussion of Document Type Definitions (DTDs) and the new specification of XML schema. A discussion of Microsoft's Extended Data Reduced (XDR) Schema is held until Chapter 5, "Creating XML Views with XDR Schemas," where it is more appropriate.

Chapter 2, "XSLT Stylesheets," discusses the Extensible Stylesheet Language Transformation (XSLT). This language specifies how XML documents can be altered to HTML documents or other XML documents by the application of stylesheets.

Chapter 3, "IIS and Virtual Directories," is a do-it-yourself chapter in which the reader performs the setup procedure that enables SQL Server 2000 to process XML URL requests and template files. The chapter is a preparation for the detailed discussions in the succeeding chapters.

Chapter 4, "Accessing SQL 2000 via HTTP," provides a general discussion of several common client/server architectures. It discusses the following capabilities of SQL Server:

- Accepting SQL queries via an URL and then generating XML documents as the query results

- Processing SQL template files to produce the documents

- Utilizing stored procedures to accomplish the same result as processing template files

Chapters 5, "Creating XML Views with XDR Schemas," covers Microsoft's Extended Data Reduced (XDR) schemas in detail. It then introduces Microsoft's BizTalk Framework and provides examples. In closing, the chapter discusses XDR Schema Annotations and schema data types to complete Microsoft's differences with the W3C standard.

Chapter 6, "Using XPath Queries," presents an in-depth canvass of the XPath navigation language and its relation to providing results in XML format. A relatively large portion of this chapter is dedicated to implicit and explicit data type conversions. It also presents the data type differences between the XPath language and Microsoft's XDR schemas along with conversion processes between the two.

Chapter 7, "FOR XML," discusses the new extension to the SQL SELECT statement, FOR XML, which allows complete control of the hierarchy of elements in the generated XML document. A thorough canvass of its three modes—RAW, AUTO, and EXPLICIT—demonstrates the varying degrees with which the developer can control XML document generation.

Chapter 8, "OPENXML," discusses the last SQL extension, OPENXML. The OPENXML keyword causes an XML document to be presented as a data source similar to a view or a table. This enables data from XML documents to be entered into SQL Server tables.

The appendixes provide a reference section covering various topics in the text:

- Appendix A, "Northwind Database Schema," presents a complete breakdown of all tables in the Northwind database, which is the sample database employed throughout the text.

- Appendix B, "XSLT Instructions with Reference to Text Usage," is an index to all the XSLT elements in the text.

- Appendix C, "XPath Functions and Examples," provides a description of the major XPath functions along with a sample usage of each.

- Appendix D, "Microsoft XML Data Types," provides a listing and explanation of all XML data types.

- Appendix E, "Resources," provides a thorough resource listing of reference Web sites for further research.

- Appendix F, "IBM's XSL Editor," is an introduction to IBM's *XSL Editor*, the XSLT learning tool utilized in the text.

- Appendix G, "Microsoft's SQL Server XML View Mapper," is an introduction to Microsoft's XML View Mapper, a visual tool to create mapping schemas.

1

XML

THIS INTRODUCTORY CHAPTER COVERS THE EXTENSIBLE Markup Language (XML), and the following chapter covers the Extensible Stylesheet Language Transformations (XSLT). These chapters are for people who are quite knowledgeable about Microsoft's SQL Server 2000 but have little or no knowledge of XML and how to manipulate it. Because these two chapters are introductory in nature, if you are familiar with XML and XSLT, you can skip them and start with Chapter 3, "Internet Information Server and Virtual Directories."

This chapter will cover the following topics:

- The origin and promise of XML
- The components of XML documents
- How to write basic DTDs
- The problems with DTDs
- The W3C schema specification that is to replace DTDs
- The components of schema documents
- How to write a basic schema declaration document

This chapter is not intended to be an exhaustive discussion of XML, Document Type Definitions (DTDs), or XML schema. It will cover the basics of XML documents, DTDs, problems with DTDs, and the proposed XML schema solution to these problems.

Before we get to the details of these topics, however, let's talk about the history that has lead up to the present state of things.

The Origin of XML

XML, just like HTML, is a derivative of the Standard Generalized Markup Language (SGML), which first made its appearance in the mid-1980s. SGML has revolutionized the publishing industry. If you want to read more about how SGML accomplished this and what it does for the publishing industry, there is an outstanding white paper on the Web at the following address:

```
http://www.arbortext.com/data/getting_started_with_SGML/getting_started_
with_sgml.html
```

SGML is an international standard for the definition of device-independent, system-independent methods of representing text in electronic form, otherwise known as *ISO 8879: Information Processing—Text and Office Systems—Standard Generalized Markup Language,* ([Geneva]: ISO, 1986). More exactly, SGML is a *metalanguage,* a means of formally describing a language (in this case, a markup language). Before going any further, I will define these terms.

Markup, or (synonymously) *encoding,* is defined as any means of making explicit an interpretation of a text. All printed texts are encoded in this sense: Punctuation marks, use of capitalization, disposition of letters around the page, and even the spaces between words might be regarded as a kind of markup.

By a markup language, I mean a set of conventions used for encoding texts. A markup language must specify the following:

- What markup is allowed
- What markup is required
- How markup is distinguished from text
- What the markup means

There are four characteristics of SGML that distinguish it from other markup languages:

- Emphasis on descriptive rather than procedural markup, which just categorizes parts of a document
- A document-type concept to describe document structure
- Independence of any one system for representing the script in which a text is written to allow data transfer from one system to another with no loss of information
- Complexity and difficulty of learning

The first three bullets are official concepts concerning SGML. The fourth is mine. The complexity of SGML led to the use of subsets of the SGML language—HTML and XML.

We are all in one way or another familiar with HTML. If you listen to the hype surrounding it, XML has taken the place of the programming language Java, object technology, and probably several other technologies today as the global communication solution. It is touted as the duct tape that will allow all the disparate communications and data technologies, new or legacy, to communicate as if they were one homogenous business solution (see Figure 1.1).

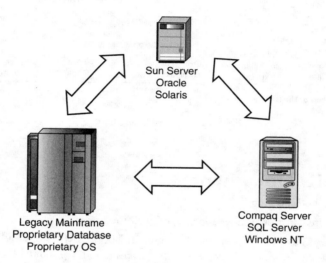

Figure 1.1   The XML promise.

Do you ever find yourself thinking (and you will if you haven't already), "Boy, there sure is a lot of hype surrounding XML. I wonder if it'll really go anywhere?" Stop and think about where Java itself was three years ago. That same soul searching was going on everywhere then. The hype surrounding Java has passed, and it is now providing enterprise solutions.

The Gartner Group has developed what has become known as the *Hype Chart*. This chart (see Figure 1.2) shows a plot of various technologies in relation to their visibility and maturity. Looking at the placement of XML on this chart, you can see that it also is poised to become an enterprise tool very soon.

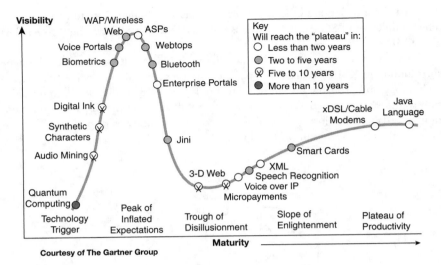

Figure 1.2   The Hype Chart.

The XML Document

XML is all of the following:

- License free, platform independent, and well supported.
- A World Wide Web Consortium Recommendation (XML 1.0, W3C Recommendation, February 1998). This makes it a global standard.

These are the stages that a document goes through within the W3C:

1. **Working Draft.** A *Working Draft* generally represents work in progress and a commitment by W3C to pursue work in a particular area. The label "Working Draft" does not imply consensus within W3C about the document.

2. **Candidate Recommendation.** A *Candidate Recommendation* is a stable Working Draft that the Director has proposed to the community for implementation experience and feedback.

3. **Proposed Recommendation.** A *Proposed Recommendation* is a Candidate Recommendation that has benefitted from implementation experience and that has been sent to the Advisory Committee for review.

4. **Recommendation.** A *Recommendation* reflects consensus within W3C, as represented by the Director's approval. W3C considers that the technology or ideas specified by a Recommendation are appropriate for widespread deployment and the W3C promotes its adoption.

A graphical representation of this process is given in Figure 1.3. A definitive explanation of the steps is given by the W3C in its process document located at http://www.w3.org/Consortium/Process-20010208/tr.html.

- An easier solution for transferring legacy or other business-to-business (B2B) information. Proprietary platforms, data formats, schema, business rules, and so on can now be linked through a common universal thread and consistently processed by the receiver.

- Used to describe the structure of information as well as the information itself. Think of it as a data description language.

- A family or suite of technologies, as listed in Table 1.1.

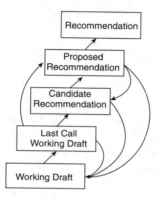

Figure 1.3   The XML process.

Table 1.1   **The W3C XML Technologies**

Name/URL	Status (Nov 2000)	Description
Extensible Markup Language 1.0 `http://www.w3c.org/TR/REC-xml`	Recommendation	The base syntax of XML.
XML Information Set `http://www.w3c.org/TR/xml-infoset`	Working draft	Describes an abstract data set that contains the useful information available from an XML document.
Namespaces in XML `http://www.w3c.org/TR/ REC-xml-names`	Recommendation	An addendum to XML 1.0, which provides a simple method for qualifying element and attribute names used in Extensible Markup Language documents by associating them with namespaces identified by URI references.

continues

Table 1.1 **Continued**

Name/URL	Status (Nov 2000)	Description
XML Base (XBase) `http://www.w3c.org/TR/xmlbase`	Candidate Recommendation	Another addendum similar to that of HTML BASE, for defining base URIs for parts of XML documents.
XML Inclusions (XInclude) `http://www.w3c.org/TR/xinclude`	Working draft	Specifies a processing model and syntax for merging a number of XML Infosets into a single composite Infoset.
Document Object Model (DOM) Level 2 `http://www.w3c.org/TR/DOM-level-2`	Recommendation	Programmatic interfaces that allow manipulation and creation of XML documents.
XML Schema Part 1:Structures `http://www.w3c.org/TR/xmlschema-1`	Candidate Recommendation	An XML-based language for describing XML elements and attributes as hierarchical types.
XML Schema Part 2:Datatypes `http://www.w3c.org/TR/xmlschema-2`	Candidate Recommendation	An XML-based language and set of textual data types for describing user-generated data types.
XML Path Language 1.0 (XPath) `http://www.w3c.org/TR/xpath`	Recommendation	A language for address-ing parts of an XML document, designed to be used by both XSLT and XPointer.
XML Pointer Language (XPointer) `http://www.w3c.org/TR/xptr`	Candidate Recommendation	A language utilizing XPath expressions to identify URI fragments.
XML Linking Language (XLink) `http://www.w3c.org/TR/xlink`	Candidate Recommendation	Allows elements to be inserted into XML doc-uments to create and describe links between resources.
Extensible Stylesheet Language Transformations 1.0 (XSLT) `http://www.w3c.org/TR/xslt`	Recommendation	A language that provides ways to transform one XML document to another or to a different form.

The XML Process

Let's take a look at how the different components of the XML system listed in Table 1.1 fit together. I call this the *XML process*. Figure 1.4 shows all the parts of the process from Table 1.1 that we'll be concerned with and their relationship to one another.

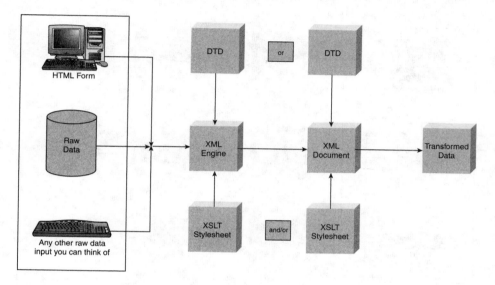

Figure 1.4　The XML process.

Here is the flow of data in the process:

1. Data from a data source is delivered to an XML engine. This can be accomplished via a recordset, cursor, or plain text file.

2. A DTD document can be applied at this point to verify the correct structure of the document created.

3. An XSLT document can be applied to modify the structure of the document to produce another, different XML document. This is usually done to produce documents for business-to-business data transfers with different data requirements. Also, HTML pages can be generated for end-user data viewing. A side benefit of this is that format and content are separated.

4. The generated XML document can have a DTD applied at this point if one was not already applied.

5. An XSLT document can be applied at this point to modify the structure of the document. This can take place regardless of whether or not one was applied earlier.

6. After these last two steps, the transformed document reaches its final form.

We'll return to this diagram several times to illustrate where we are in the process.

Components of an XML Document

Figure 1.5 shows where we currently are in the XML process.

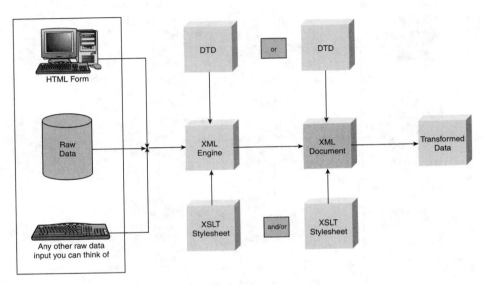

Figure 1.5   The document in the XML process.

Listing 1.1 is a sample XML document that I will use to illustrate and explain its various components.

Listing 1.1   **Sample XML Document**

```
<?xml version="1.0" standalone="no"?>
<!-- ******* Resumes for Potential Hires ******* -->
<RESUMES xmlns='http://www.myorg.net/tags'>
  <PERSON PERSONID="p1">
    <NAME>
      <LAST>Shelton</LAST>
      <FIRST>Rick</FIRST>
    </NAME>
    <ADDRESS>
      <STREET>911 Intranet Ave.</STREET>
      <CITY>Canberra</CITY>
      <COUNTRY>Australia</COUNTRY>
      <PC>A34G-90</PC>
    </ADDRESS>
```

```
            <TEL>(+612) 111-2345</TEL>
            <EMAIL>shelton@somewhere.com</EMAIL>
        </PERSON>

        <PERSON PERSONID="p2">
          <NAME>
            <LAST>Tenney</LAST>
            <FIRST>Corey</FIRST>
          </NAME>
          <ADDRESS>
            <STREET>211 Yardwork Circle</STREET>
            <CITY>Roy, UT</CITY>
            <COUNTRY>USA</COUNTRY>
            <ZIP>64067</ZIP>
          </ADDRESS>
          <TEL/>
          <EMAIL>tenney@yardwork.com</EMAIL>
        </PERSON>
    </RESUMES>
```

XML Declaration

Although it isn't required, XML documents can begin with the statement `<?xm...?>`. This is the XML declaration that specifies that the following data is an XML document. It also has additional attributes of `version`, `encoding`, and `standalone`. `version` is a required attribute, and the others are optional. Why are these important? If the version of XML ever changes (changes never happen, right?), there must be a mechanism in place for developers to determine what version they are working with. XSLT 1.0 just became 1.1, for example. The `encoding` and `standalone attributes` are important from a Unicode and DTD perspective, respectively. In the sample document, the following declaration

```
    <?xml version="1.0" standalone="no"?>
```

gives us the additional information that this XML document conforms to version 1.0 of the XML standard and that there is an external DTD associated with it. (*This document cannot stand alone.*) Of course, if this document had a DTD defined within it, then the `standalone` attribute would be `"yes"`.

After all this discussion about DTDs, you might think that DTDs are required; they're not. Later in this chapter, in the "Document Type Definition" and "The DOC-TYPE Declaration" sections, we'll go into much more detail on DTDs.

By the way, any statement in the form `<?...?>` is known as a *processing instruction*. Processing instructions tell an XML parser to perform tasks other than just interpreting the document data. For those of you who are familiar with C and C++, these are similar to preprocessor instructions. You can even create your own processing instructions as long as the external parser will understand them.

Markup Delimiters

An XML document is composed of one or more *elements* that are, in turn, composed of two (sometimes one) *tags*. The opening tag places the element name between a less than symbol (<) and a greater than (>) symbol. The closing tag is identical to the opening tag except that a forward slash (/) is placed before the element name. Our sample document shows that

```
<LAST>Shelton</LAST>
```

is one of its elements. The document has several more elements, one of which has the opening tag <STREET> and the closing tag </STREET>.

Element Names

The following are guidelines for choosing element names:

- Element names start with a letter or an underscore character (_).
- Name length is virtually unlimited but use common sense.
- Names are case sensitive. For example, <ADDRESS> is a different name than <Address>.
- Names cannot start with xml in any form.
- A name can contain any number of the following:
  - Letters
  - Numbers
  - Underscores
  - Periods
  - Hyphens

root Element

The root element delineates the starting and ending points of the document data. It is the outermost element of the document. In our example, <RESUMES>...</RESUMES> is the root element.

Empty Elements

There are cases in which an element will have no associated data with it. An example would be a null field in a database transferred to an XML document. The field exists whether or not it contains data, so we need an *empty* element for it. This is represented by a single tag having the forward slash (/) after the name. Remember that in the markup delimiters discussion, I said that sometimes an element consists of only one tag. In our example, there is no telephone number for the second person, so we place an empty element <TEL/>.

Attributes

XML element attributes are similar in appearance and function to attributes contained in HTML tags. They modify or further define the tag with which they are associated. They are contained inside the tag and consist of an attribute name and an accompanying value. The PERSON tag in our resumes document has an attribute, as shown in the following example:

```
<PERSON PERSONID="p1">
```

The attribute name is PERSONID, and its value in this instance is p1. The attribute value must be expressed in quotes.

Comments

XML comments are identical in form and function to HTML comments. They begin with <!-- and end with -->. The second line of our document

```
<!-- ******* Resumes for Potential Hires ******* -->
```

is an XML comment.

Entity References

Five characters are not allowed between tags in an XML document. These characters are shown in Table 1.2.

Table 1.2   **Entity Substitutions**

Character	Entity
& (ampersand)	Use &
' (apostrophe)	Use '
< (less than)	Use <
> (greater than)	Use >
" (quote)	Use "

A closer look will point out why using any of these entities would interfere with parsing. The ampersand delimits special characters like those in the Entity column of Table 1.2. The remaining entities delimit the tags themselves and attribute data.

CDATA

When you have a section of an XML document that you want to remain untouched or unprocessed by an XML parser, place it in a CDATA section. These sections are treated as plain text. They would be excellent for sections of code in which you don't want the parser to interpret any special characters such as the entity references mentioned previously. CDATA sections are delimited with <![CDATA[and]]>.

CDATA → PLAIN text

Watch the location and order of the brackets. This is the only declaration with a bracket between the ! and the keyword.

In the following example, the parser will treat the entities as plain text, and no interpretation will occur:

```
<![CDATA[Here is a section on CDATA & its syntax with <element> tags]]>
```

Namespaces

Namespaces are a recent addition to XML. They are not mandatory but are advisable to use. Their main purpose is to ensure element uniqueness. Think about the following situation. I could define a tag `<NETSTORAGE>` in a document about types of disk storage. It is likely that another XML author might have a different document defining the same tag. If these documents were ever combined (quite likely), then these elements would collide.

Here's an example. You have an XHTML document with standard XHTML tags. You want to add some elements of your own design to the document, but some of your tags have been defined with the same name as some of the XHTML tags. This would really mess up an HTML interpreter and would definitely give undesired results. Namespace assignments help avoid this situation by assigning a scope to tags. If this seems farfetched, remember that you can define two elements with the same name having two different meanings and have each one in a different document. The odds of you (or the company you work for) ever combining these documents can be pretty high.

Namespace definitions are usually specified as an attribute of a tag. These definitions can be assigned a name (scope) in the document by appending a colon and the desired name to the `xmlns` declaration.

In this example, I assigned the name `res` to the namespace `'http://www.myorg.net/restags'`:

```
<RESUMES xmlns:res='http://www.myorg.net/restags'>
```

In the following example, with this declaration, I prefix all tags with this name:

```
<RES:PERSON PERSONID="p1">
  <RES:NAME>
    <RES:LAST>Shelton</LAST>
    <RES:FIRST>Rick</FIRST>
```

Again, look at the XML document and the `root` element declaration. This example illustrates the default namespace for this document:

```
<RESUMES xmlns='http://www.myorg.net/tags'>
```

All tags in this document that do not have a namespace prefix are assumed to belong to this document's namespace. In the following example, the prefix isn't necessary:

```
<PERSON PERSONID="p1">
  <:NAME>
    <LAST>Shelton</LAST>
    <FIRST>Rick</FIRST>
```

This might seem like overkill right now, but in Chapter 3 when we talk about stylesheet transformations, you will see that this construct is used more often than not.

It is also possible to have more than one namespace declaration in the same XML document:

```
<RESUMES xmlns='http://www.myorg.net'>
        xmlns:phonenumbers='http://www.phones.net'
```

With this declaration, look at the document fragment in Listing 1.2.

Listing 1.2   **Resumes XML Document Fragment**

```
<ADDRESS>
  <STREET>911 Intranet Ave.</STREET>
  <CITY>Canberra</CITY>
  <COUNTRY>Australia</COUNTRY>
</ADDRESS>
<phonenumbers:TEL>(+612) 111-2345</TEL>
<EMAIL>shelton@somewhere.com</EMAIL>
```

Because the first namespace declaration had no name appended to it, it is the default namespace, and no prefix is necessary for the document tags except in the case of the <TEL> tag. A second namespace was defined for the document that applied to the <TEL> tag. This is not a trick. The fact that the <TEL> tag was associated with a different namespace than the other tags in the document was known by the document writer beforehand.

Well-Formed Documents

For an XML parser to properly process an XML document, it must be at a minimum what is known as *well-formed*. To meet this requirement, the document must conform to the following minimum criteria:

- The document must have an associated DTD or have an XML declaration with the standalone attribute set to no. Examine the XML declaration in our sample document, as shown in Listing 1.1.

- Attributes must be enclosed in quotes. It doesn't matter if these are single or double quotes. Look at the first <PERSON> element in the sample document.

- All elements must have both an opening and closing tag unless it is an empty tag.

- Empty tags must have a closing /. An example is the empty `<TEL/>` for the second person in our document.
- Tags must be properly nested. The following tag order is not allowed: `<font><strong>...</font></strong>`
- Markup tags cannot be used as part of element text.

Document Type Definition (DTD)

Now that we've discussed XML documents, we will move on to discuss the entity that describes the structure of XML documents. This document is the *Document Type Definition (DTD)*.

Let's review where we are in the XML process now (see Figure 1.6).

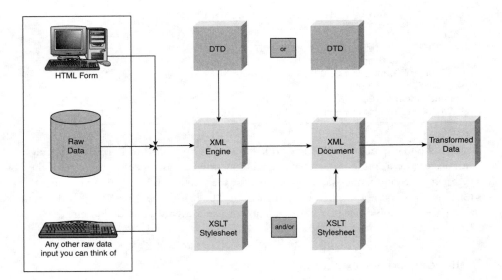

Figure 1.6   DTDs in the XML process.

I've heard DTDs called everything from a dead-end road to a waste of time to learn. This stems from the fact that the W3C is going to replace DTDs with the new method of describing XML document structures, XML schemas. (We'll talk about schemas later in this chapter.) The reasons for replacing DTDs are valid (see the topic "XML Schemas" in this chapter).

What I think some people are overlooking is that DTDs have been around a long time, and there are a lot of them out there. These DTDs will, first, need to be understood and, second, need to be converted to schema documents. It could be considered a little difficult to convert something to another form that you don't understand in the first place.

When do you use a DTD? DTDs are essential for large document-management projects. A serious problem with managing large volumes of documents of similar type is enforcing coherence to a standard. Documents are typically written or generated by more than one author over a period of time. Unfortunately, it's a fact of life that when left on their own, authors tend to adopt different styles. The resulting documents might turn out to have little or no resemblance to each other even though they are supposed to be identical! The solution to this is to adopt a style guide of some kind. Take this one step further and—voila!—you have DTDs. They force authors to conform to a standard document layout.

DTD = Rules

When do you not use a DTD? A DTD is a waste of time for small documents. Writing a DTD is not an easy task, just as writing information systems procedures is not easy.

Take this example: DTDs are overkill for letters, memos, faxes, and documents of this type. Usually, enforcing strict guidelines for these is not essential. You wouldn't want a DTD in which people are limited to the use of stationery. In contrast to these examples, though, you have to realize that there are environments in which a DTD would make sense for letters (for example, when there is a legal obligation to record correspondence).

DTDs can be defined internally to an XML document or referenced internally and accessed externally. Moreover, a DTD is not a required element of an XML document but an optional entity. A validating XML parser does need a DTD to ensure that a document conforms to a certain structure, but a nonvalidating parser can still interpret the document's data.

From here, we'll start looking at the components of DTDs and how they define an XML document's structure.

The *DOCTYPE* Declaration

The DOCTYPE declaration is really not a DTD declaration. It is an XML instruction with its own syntax, and it defines the root element of the XML document. Look at the following example:

```
<!DOCTYPE RESUMES [the rest of the declarations for this XML document]>
```

Here, the exclamation point (!) precedes the keyword DOCTYPE. This is followed by the root element of the document and then all of the declaration for the XML document enclosed in brackets [and].

Public Versus Private

The DOCTYPE declaration has two additional attributes that specify whether or not the DTD is *private* or *public*.

A public DTD is declared with the keyword PUBLIC. It has been publicized for widespread use and assigned a one-of-a-kind name, ensuring that the same DTD is used in every instance. It also gives the location of the DTD. An example of this is the DTD that defines the structure of HTML. The naming convention is known as the *formal public identifier*, and coverage is beyond the scope of this book. I refer those interested to the XML specification.

A private DTD utilizes the keyword SYSTEM. It specifies a DTD that is applied to all elements declared inside of the root element. This type of DTD is generally created for limited usage, such as an XML document regularly used by your company but not by the general public or other companies. Here's an example that expounds on the previous example. It shows both forms of the declaration.

```
<!DOCTYPE RESUMES SYSTEM "location of DTD">
<!DOCTYPE RESUMES PUBLIC "name" "location of DTD" >
```

I want to emphasize one point here: PUBLIC and SYSTEM apply only to external DTDs. If these keywords are left out and a DTD is required, then the DTD must be defined internally to the document.

> Remember the XML declaration statement we talked about earlier (<?xml...?>) and its standalone attribute? A standalone value of no requires a DTD with the document. Internal or external, it doesn't matter. A standalone value of yes means that no external DTD exists.

Comments

DTD comments are identical in form and function to HTML and XML comments. They begin with <!-- and end with -->. The following example is a DTD comment:

```
<!-- ******* Here are the element descriptions ******* -->
```

Declaring Elements

Each and every element of an XML document must be declared in the appropriate DTD. These declarations must be contained inside the brackets of the DOCTYPE declaration, as the following example shows:

```
<!DOCTYPE RESUMES [all element declarations here]>
```

To declare an element, use the following syntax:

```
<!ELEMENT elementname rule >
```

The *elementname* is the name between the tag delimiters. The rules that govern these names follow.

ANY

This is the simplest of the element rules. It specifies that between the opening tag and the closing tag, other tags and character data (PCDATA) can appear. It is written as follows:

```
<!ELEMENT RESUMES ANY>
```

When this rule is used, you will most commonly see it in the declaration of the root element.

Think about that for a minute. With this rule, you're actually saying *any* other tags and data. You are telling the parser to accept anything between the document root element and its closing tag. In effect, you are turning off validation checking of your document. You'll think you're the best DTD writer in the world because the parser will never report errors. I thought I was. Hey, this DTD writing can't be *that* bad— until your documents start to deviate from standards and you can't figure out why. Be careful where you use this.

#PCDATA

There are situations in which you might want only character data to appear. In this case, you would use the #PCDATA rule, which is stated like this:

```
<!ELEMENT ADDRESS (#PCDATA)>
```

PCDATA stands for *parsed character data*. In the previous example, notice that the declaration is enclosed in parentheses. Also, be aware that PCDATA means that other elements are not allowed between the opening and closing tags of the declared element, just character data. Table 1.3 lists PCDATA examples.

Table 1.3 **PCDATA Examples**

Example	Validity
`<STREET></STREET>`	Valid.
`<STREET>911 Intranet Ave.</STREET>`	Valid.
`<STREET>911 <b>Intranet Ave.</b></STREET>`	This is invalid because only PCDATA can appear between the `<STREET>` tags.

In contrast to the situations listed in Table 1.3, there will be situations in which you want to declare an element as mandatory within another element. Take a look at this example:

```
<!ELEMENT ADDRESS (STREET)>
<!ELEMENT STREET (#PCDATA)>
```

These declarations specify that the ADDRESS element must contain another element called STREET. This STREET element can contain only character data and can appear only once. Table 1.4 shows required element examples.

Table 1.4 **Required Element Examples**

Example	Validity
`<ADDRESS>` `<STREET>211 Yardwork Circle</STREET>`	Valid
`<ADDRESS>` `<CITY>Canberra</CITY>`	Not valid because a STREET element is required

Sequences

How can we specify more than one element in a required order (sequence) inside of another element? Declare the required elements within parentheses in the order they are to appear in a comma-separated list, similar to this example:

```
<!ELEMENT ADDRESS (STREET, CITY, COUNTRY)>
<!ELEMENT STREET (#PCDATA)>
<!ELEMENT CITY (#PCDATA)>
<!ELEMENT COUNTRY (#PCDATA)>
```

The declaration specifies that the ADDRESS element must contain three other elements: STREET, CITY, and COUNTRY in that order. The three other elements must consist of only PCDATA, such as the following:

```
<ADDRESS>
  <STREET>911 Intranet Ave.</STREET>
  <CITY>Canberra</CITY>
  <COUNTRY>Australia</COUNTRY>
</ADDRESS>
```

Choices

How would you declare that *either* a specific element appears within a given element *or* another different element appears (the either-or selection)? Easy, use the pipe (|) symbol between the elements from which you can select. Listing 1.3 shows an example of this.

Listing 1.3   **Specifying a Choice Between Elements**

```
<!ELEMENT ADDRESS (STREET, CITY, COUNTRY, (ZIP¦PC))>
<!ELEMENT STREET (#PCDATA)>
<!ELEMENT CITY (#PCDATA)>
<!ELEMENT COUNTRY (#PCDATA)>
<!ELEMENT ZIP (#PCDATA)>
<!ELEMENT PC (#PCDATA)>
```

Here, in addition to what we've already talked about with the STREET, CITY, and COUNTRY elements, we declare a mandatory fifth element, which can be *either* a zip code (ZIP) or a postal code (PC). If you look back at our sample XML document in the section "Components of an XML Document," you'll see that the first job candidate's address has a postal code whereas the second has a zip code.

Children

Generally speaking, *children* or *child elements* are elements that are contained within other elements. When we talk about XPath queries in Chapter 6, "Using XPath Queries," we'll give a more formal definition, but this definition is all that's necessary for a DTD discussion.

Now for the three things that I get confused about every time I have to use one of them. Those of you who are familiar with regular expressions will have no problems here.

It's possible that elements and grouping of elements in parentheses, although declared, might not appear in a specific instance of an element. Also, it's possible that an element might occur more than once within another element (multiple occurrences). There are other possibilities, and we're going to talk about these possibilities here.

One thing, though: Remember that we have already discussed the single occurrence of an element in the PCDATA examples section.

Here are the other possibilities:

- **One or more.** When an element or element group must appear once but could appear multiple times, append the plus sign (+) like this:

  ```
  <!ELEMENT PERSON (TEL)+>
  ```

  This example states that the PERSON element must contain a telephone number but could contain more than one.

- **Zero or more.** When an element or element group could appear as many times as necessary but might not appear at all, append an asterisk (*) like this:

  ```
  <!ELEMENT PERSON (TEL)*>
  ```

Here we declare that the PERSON element can contain a single telephone number element or more, or it might not contain a telephone number at all.

- **Zero or one.** When an element or element group must appear once or not at all, append a question mark (?) like this:

```
<!ELEMENT PERSON (TEL)?>
```

This declares that the PERSON element must contain a single telephone number element or none at all.

- **Parentheses.** Use parentheses as liberally as you feel necessary to convey the relationship between elements. It's important to remember, though, that an apparent minor move of parentheses can drastically affect a DTD definition. Here is our base declaration:

```
<!ELEMENT ADDRESS (STREET, CITY, COUNTRY, (ZIP|PC))>
```

In the preceding declaration, ADDRESS contains the elements STREET, CITY, COUNTRY, and *either* ZIP or PC.

In the following code, ADDRESS contains the elements STREET, CITY, and PC *or* STREET, CITY, COUNTRY, and ZIP.

```
<!ELEMENT ADDRESS (STREET, CITY, (COUNTRY, ZIP)|PC)>
```

Be careful! Parentheses in combination with the children (+, *, ?) provide additional flexibility in declaring elements. Look at the following:

```
<!ELEMENT PERSON (NAME, ADDRESS, (TEL | FAX)+, (ZIP | PC)>
```

The element PERSON must contain the elements NAME, ADDRESS, any number of TEL or FAX in any combination, and finally, either the ZIP or the PC element.

Empty Element

This is another simple declaration. Any element that is an empty element is declared with the keyword EMPTY in the declaration.

```
<!ELEMENT TEL EMPTY>
```

A valid TEL element with this declaration would be either <TEL/> or <TEL></TEL>.

Entities

In a DTD, an entity declaration functions very similarly to the way a macro functions in an application. In essence, a group of characters is substituted for another group of characters. I know this definition sounds redundant, but we'll get to an example.

An entity is declared as follows:

```
<!ENTITY name "substitute characters">
```

The quotation marks are required. After this declaration is made, the substitute characters will replace the name wherever the name occurs. Let's look at that example I promised you:

```
<!ENTITY trademark "&#x174">
```

After this declaration, you can make use of it with a statement such as the following:

```
<drive>
    Our GadgetDrive&trademark is revolutionary
</drive>
```

The &trademark will be replaced with the ™ symbol.

It's important to note here that we have been talking about a *general entity reference*, which only works inside of an XML document. There are several others types, but they are outside this book's scope.

Declaring Attributes

Attributes consist of a name and a value pair. They appear inside a starting tag and provide additional data or information concerning that tag or the data contained within that tag pair. Here's an example in which HAIRCOLOR is an attribute of the tag <STEPCHILD>.

```
<STEPCHILD HAIRCOLOR="red">John</STEPCHILD>
```

Now let's look at how various attribute situations are handled in DTDs.

Single Attribute

Attributes, which appear within XML elements, must be declared in the accompanying DTD. You specify these attributes by using the following declaration:

```
<!ATTLIST element attribute type default>
```

The first word after ATTLIST is the name of the element containing the attribute. Then comes the name of the attribute followed by the attribute's data type and then the default value.

Multiple Attributes

Most HTML tags have more than one possible attribute. An example is the <table> tag. It can have attributes of WIDTH, CELLSPACING, BORDER, and more. XML elements are no different. They, too, can have multiple attributes. There are two ways to declare multiple attributes in a DTD. The first is to have each attribute listed on its own line, referencing the same element like this:

```
<!ATTLIST TRIANGLE BASE CDATA "1">
<!ATTLIST TRIANGLE HEIGHT CDATA "1">
```

The second method relies on proper whitespace layout to make the declaration clear to the user. This is written as follows:

```
<!ATTLIST TRIANGLE BASE CDATA "1"
                   HEIGHT CDATA "1">
```

You can do it the way you prefer. The second method does rely on proper layout, and I'm sure you'll come across DTDs written this way, but you have to decide on the way you want to write it.

Default Values

It isn't always necessary to specify a default value. The DTD specification contains three keywords that allow some leeway with default values. These keywords are as follows:

- #REQUIRED. Suppose that, in our XML document, an element had an attribute that we wanted to force authors to populate with data (such as an author's email address so that author could be contacted). Write it as follows.

  ```
  <!ELEMENT AUTHOR EMPTY>
  <!ATTLIST AUTHOR EMAIL CDATA #REQUIRED>
  ```

  This would require the author to supply his email address.

- #IMPLIED. The IMPLIED keyword specifies that if the attribute doesn't show up in the element, it's okay; ignore it. It is necessary, however, for the XML parser interpreting this document to inform the application that called it that no value is available here. The application is then responsible to do whatever it feels necessary. Think of a SQL application that is told that no value is available for this attribute. If the attribute maps to a column in a SQL database, then the application can supply the null value for the column. Here's how to write it:

  ```
  <!ELEMENT AUTHOR EMPTY>
  <!ATTLIST AUTHOR TEL CDATA #IMPLIED>
  ```

  If the AUTHOR element's TEL attribute is missing, then ignore it.

- #FIXED. FIXED declares that the default value provided by the author cannot be changed. The following example shows that the default value of the author's LASTNAME attribute is set to Griffin and cannot be changed.

  ```
  <!ELEMENT AUTHOR EMPTY>
  <!ATTLIST AUTHOR LASTNAME CDATA #FIXED "Griffin">
  ```

  In effect, this is a read-only value.

Data Types

There are 10 different data types for attribute values. They are listed in Table 1.5.

Table 1.5   **Attribute Data Types**

Data Type	Description
CDATA	Character data
Enumerated	A series of values, only one of which can be chosen
ENTITY	An entity declared in the DTD
ENTITIES	Multiple whitespace-separated entities declared in the DTD
ID	A unique element identifier
IDREF	The value of a unique ID type attribute
IDREFS	Multiple whitespace-separated IDREFs of elements
NMTOKEN	Declares a legal XML name
NMTOKEMS	Multiple whitespace-separated XML name tokens
NOTATION	A notation declared in the DTD

Ninety percent of DTD attribute data types consist of either CDATA or enumerated. These types are covered in detail next. Coverage of the other eight data types is outside the scope of this book.

We will talk about two of them.

- **CDATA**. This is the most general type of attribute. An attribute of this type can be any string value as long as it doesn't contain the less-than tag (<) or the quotation mark ("). If the attribute value *must* include these characters, then just use the standard entity references (< and "). If the attribute value contains only a quote, then you can delimit the value with single quotes and avoid using the entity. This example assigns the value of 7 inches (") to the BASE attribute.

```
<!ATTLIST TRIANGLE BASE CDATA '7"'
```

If the attribute value contains both single and double quotes, then the one that does not delimit the value must be changed to the entity value.

- **Enumerated**. Earlier we talked about declaring elements, and you learned that a declaration could be made that stated that either one element or the other would show up in the document. Remember the following example:

```
<!ELEMENT ADDRESS (STREET, CITY, COUNTRY, (ZIP|PC))>
```

This states that the fourth element can be either a zip code or a postal code. Well, the same thing is possible with attribute value declarations. Look at this:

```
<!ATTLIST EMPLOYEE JOBDESC (PEON|GOPHER|NOBODY|LOSER) "PEON"
```

Here we have a JOBDESC attribute that may or may not have a value. This value can assume one of four possible values. If the attribute doesn't have a value assigned to it, then it assumes the value PEON.

Namespaces and DTDs

There is no direct support for namespaces in DTD. This is not surprising when you remember that namespaces came along *way* after SGML appeared on the scene. There is a way around this limitation, however. As far as a DTD is concerned, a namespace declaration is nothing more than an attribute of an element. Knowing this, then, it is possible to define a namespace declaration in a DTD. Here's a namespace declaration:

```
<VENDORS xmlns='http://www.myorg.com/tags'>
```

In the DTD, you would declare the following:

```
<!ATTLIST VENDORS xmlns CDATA #FIXED 'http://www.myorg.com/tags'>
```

Here we declare the xmlns declaration as an attribute of the VENDORS tag and use CDATA to prevent any interpretation of the attribute's value. We also protect the value by making it read-only (#FIXED).

Here are some examples for you. See if you can figure out the attribute declarations for each line. I'll put the answers at the end of the chapter.

```
<!ATTLIST PERSON PERSONID CDATA>

<!ATTLIST EMPLOYEE MALE (true|false) "true">

<!ATTLIST EMPLOYEE STATUS (single|double|divorced|widowed) #REQUIRED>
```

Valid Versus Well-Formed

Now that we've covered quite a bit of the properties of DTDs, I'd like to have a short discussion on what is a confusing topic to some.

Earlier we talked about a well-formed XML document and what that meant. You can refer to the section "Well-Formed Documents" earlier in this chapter to refresh yourself on the requirements of a well-formed XML document.

Now we have another term to become familiar with—*valid*. In essence, an XML document is *valid* when it has an associated DTD and it conforms to it.

Example of Writing a DTD for a Given XML Document

Now, let's do something different. Let's take an XML document and some verbiage that describes some things about the document that are not readily apparent and then generate a DTD for that document. Sound like fun? We'll use a portion of the SUPPLIERS table from the Northwind database of SQL Server 2000 (see Figure 1.7).

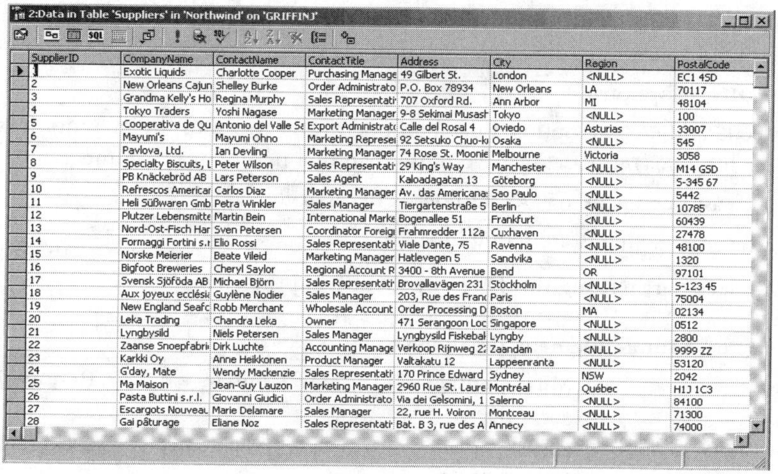
2:Data in Table 'Suppliers' in 'Northwind' on 'GRIFFINJ'

SupplierID	CompanyName	ContactName	ContactTitle	Address	City	Region	PostalCode
1	Exotic Liquids	Charlotte Cooper	Purchasing Manage	49 Gilbert St.	London	<NULL>	EC1 4SD
2	New Orleans Cajun	Shelley Burke	Order Administrato	P.O. Box 78934	New Orleans	LA	70117
3	Grandma Kelly's Ho	Regina Murphy	Sales Representati	707 Oxford Rd.	Ann Arbor	MI	48104
4	Tokyo Traders	Yoshi Nagase	Marketing Manager	9-8 Sekimai Musash	Tokyo	<NULL>	100
5	Cooperativa de Qu	Antonio del Valle Sa	Export Administrat	Calle del Rosal 4	Oviedo	Asturias	33007
6	Mayumi's	Mayumi Ohno	Marketing Represei	92 Setsuko Chuo-ku	Osaka	<NULL>	545
7	Pavlova, Ltd.	Ian Devling	Marketing Manager	74 Rose St. Moonie	Melbourne	Victoria	3058
8	Specialty Biscuits, L	Peter Wilson	Sales Representati	29 King's Way	Manchester	<NULL>	M14 GSD
9	PB Knäckebröd AB	Lars Peterson	Sales Agent	Kaloadagatan 13	Göteborg	<NULL>	S-345 67
10	Refrescos Americar	Carlos Diaz	Marketing Manager	Av. das Americana:	Sao Paulo	<NULL>	5442
11	Heli Süßwaren Gmb	Petra Winkler	Sales Manager	Tiergartenstraße 5	Berlin	<NULL>	10785
12	Plutzer Lebensmitte	Martin Bein	International Marke	Bogenallee 51	Frankfurt	<NULL>	60439
13	Nord-Ost-Fisch Har	Sven Petersen	Coordinator Foreigi	Frahmredder 112a	Cuxhaven	<NULL>	27478
14	Formaggi Fortini s.r	Elio Rossi	Sales Representati	Viale Dante, 75	Ravenna	<NULL>	48100
15	Norske Meierier	Beate Vileid	Marketing Manager	Hatlevegen 5	Sandvika	<NULL>	1320
16	Bigfoot Breweries	Cheryl Saylor	Regional Account R	3400 - 8th Avenue	Bend	OR	97101
17	Svensk Sjöföda AB	Michael Björn	Sales Representati	Brovallavägen 231	Stockholm	<NULL>	S-123 45
18	Aux joyeux ecclésia	Guylène Nodier	Sales Manager	203, Rue des Franc	Paris	<NULL>	75004
19	New England Seafc	Robb Merchant	Wholesale Account	Order Processing D	Boston	MA	02134
20	Leka Trading	Chandra Leka	Owner	471 Serangoon Loc	Singapore	<NULL>	0512
21	Lyngbysild	Niels Petersen	Sales Manager	Lyngbysild Fiskebal	Lyngby	<NULL>	2800
22	Zaanse Snoepfabrie	Dirk Luchte	Accounting Manage	Verkoop Rijnweg 22	Zaandam	<NULL>	9999 ZZ
23	Karkki Oy	Anne Heikkonen	Product Manager	Valtakatu 12	Lappeenranta	<NULL>	53120
24	G'day, Mate	Wendy Mackenzie	Sales Representati	170 Prince Edward	Sydney	NSW	2042
25	Ma Maison	Jean-Guy Lauzon	Marketing Manager	2960 Rue St. Laure	Montréal	Québec	H1J 1C3
26	Pasta Buttini s.r.l.	Giovanni Giudici	Order Administrato	Via dei Gelsomini, 1	Salerno	<NULL>	84100
27	Escargots Nouveau	Marie Delamare	Sales Manager	22, rue H. Voiron	Montceau	<NULL>	71300
28	Gai pâturage	Eliane Noz	Sales Representati	Bat. B 3, rue des A	Annecy	<NULL>	74000

Figure 1.7 Part of the SUPPLIERS table in SQL Server 2000.

Listing 1.4 shows the base document.

Listing 1.4 **Sample XML Document**

```
<SUPPLIERS>
   <SUPPLIER>
      <SUPPLIERID>1</SUPPLIERID>
      <COMPANYNAME>Exotic Liquids</COMPANYNAME>
      <CONTACTNAME>Charlotte Cooper</CONTACTNAME>
      <ADDRESS>49 Gilbert St.</ADDRESS>
      <CITY>London</CITY>
      <PC>EC1 4SD</PC>
      <COUNTRY>UK</COUNTRY>
      <PHONE>(171) 555-2222</PHONE>
</SUPPLIER>
   <SUPPLIER>
      <SUPPLIERID>2</SUPPLIERID>
      <COMPANYNAME>New Orleans Cajun Delights</COMPANYNAME>
      <CONTACTNAME>Shelley Burke</CONTACTNAME>
      <ADDRESS>P.O. Box 78934</ADDRESS>
      <CITY>New Orleans</CITY>
      <REGION>LA</REGION>
      <PC>70117</PC>
      <COUNTRY>USA</COUNTRY>
      <PHONE>(100) 555-4822</PHONE>
   </SUPPLIER>
<SUPPLIERS>
```

Here are a few points concerning this document that describe information you can't deduce by just examining it.

- REGION is optional.
- PHONE and FAX are optional (though one of the two must be present). It is possible for a CONTACTNAME to have more than one phone or fax number.
- At least one PHONE or FAX number is necessary.
- All other elements are required.

All right, let's start writing this DTD by identifying the elements.

Table 1.6   **Sample Element Breakdown**

Element	Must Contain	May Contain	Required In
SUPPLIERS	SUPPLIER		
SUPPLIER	SUPPLIERID, COMPANYNAME, CONTACTNAME, ADDRESS, CITY, PC, COUNTRY	REGION, PHONE, FAX	SUPPLIERS
SUPPLIERID	PCDATA		SUPPLIER
COMPANYNAME	PCDATA		SUPPLIER
CONTACTNAME	PCDATA		SUPPLIER
ADDRESS	PCDATA		SUPPLIER
CITY	PCDATA		SUPPLIER
REGION	PCDATA		
PC	PCDATA		SUPPLIER
COUNTRY	PCDATA		SUPPLIER
PHONE	PCDATA		
FAX	PCDATA		

First we must identify the root element. This is the SUPPLIERS element. We use the DOCTYPE declaration for this, as shown in the following example:

```
<!DOCTYPE SUPPLIERS[......]>
```

Remember that this declaration specifies only the root element; it does nothing for structure specification. So next we declare SUPPLIERS in an element declaration.

```
<!ELEMENT SUPPLIERS (SUPPLIER)+>
```

This states that SUPPLIERS must have at least one element contained within it named SUPPLIER and that there can be more than one of them.

Here's what we have so far:

```
<!DOCTYPE SUPPLIERS[
    <!ELEMENT SUPPLIERS (SUPPLIER)+>
]>
```

Within SUPPLIERS, there must be the element SUPPLIER specified like this:

```
<!DOCTYPE SUPPLIERS[
    <!ELEMENT SUPPLIERS (SUPPLIER)+>
    <!ELEMENT SUPPLIER...>
]>
```

As enumerated in Table 1.6, several elements required within the element SUPPLIER: SUPPLIERID, COMPANYNAME, CONTACTNAME, ADDRESS, CITY, PC, and COUNTRY. Here are those additions:

```
<!DOCTYPE SUPPLIERS[
    <!ELEMENT SUPPLIERS (SUPPLIER)+>
    <!ELEMENT SUPPLIER (SUPPLIERID, COMPANYNAME, CONTACTNAME, ADDRESS,
                        CITY, PC, COUNTRY)>
]>
```

As my daughters, Stephanie and Katie, used to say, "ARE WE THERE YET?" (Don't you just hate that?) No, not quite but we're close.

We still have to consider REGION, PHONE, and FAX. REGION is optional so use the ? like this:

```
<!DOCTYPE SUPPLIERS[
    <!ELEMENT SUPPLIERS (SUPPLIER)+>
    <!ELEMENT SUPPLIER (SUPPLIERID, COMPANYNAME, CONTACTNAME, ADDRESS,
                        CITY, (REGION)?, PC, COUNTRY)>
]>
```

The question mark after REGION says that it may appear 0 or 1 time.

For PHONE and FAX, at least one is required, but more than one can appear in any combination. So use the | symbol in combination with + like this:

```
<!DOCTYPE SUPPLIERS[
    <!ELEMENT SUPPLIERS (SUPPLIER)+>
    <!ELEMENT SUPPLIER (SUPPLIERID, COMPANYNAME, CONTACTNAME, ADDRESS,
                        CITY, (REGION)?, PC, COUNTRY, (PHONE | FAX)+)>
]>
```

Of course, it is mandatory to include the ELEMENT definitions of each of the declared elements with PCDATA, so here it is in Listing 1.5.

Listing 1.5   **Completed DTD**

```
<!DOCTYPE SUPPLIERS[
    <!ELEMENT SUPPLIERS (SUPPLIER)+>
    <!ELEMENT SUPPLIER (SUPPLIERID, COMPANYNAME, CONTACTNAME, ADDRESS,
                        CITY, (REGION)?, PC, COUNTRY, (PHONE | FAX)+)>
    <!ELEMENT SUPPLIERID (#PCDATA)>
    <!ELEMENT COMPANYNAME (#PCDATA)>
    <!ELEMENT CONTACTNAME (#PCDATA)>
    <!ELEMENT ADDRESS (#PCDATA)>
    <!ELEMENT CITY (#PCDATA)>
    <!ELEMENT REGION (#PCDATA)>
    <!ELEMENT PC (#PCDATA)>
    <!ELEMENT COUNTRY (#PCDATA)>
    <!ELEMENT PHONE (#PCDATA)>
    <!ELEMENT FAX (#PCDATA)>

]>
```

This is the DTD in all its glory. A simplistic one, yes, but think about what you've accomplished up to this point.

Example of an Invalid XML Document

Let's take a step back now and look at the entire picture of what we've talked about in this chapter, an XML document from start to finish.

Listing 1.6 shows a sample XML document that would never make it through any XML parser. See if you can find the problems. Again, I'll put the answers at the end of the chapter.

Listing 1.6   **A DTD That Needs Corrections**

```
<?xml version="1.0 standalone="no"?
xmlns:vend='http://www.myorg.com/companytags'
>
<!DOCTYPE VENDORS [
<!ELEMENT VENDORS (VENDOR)?>
<!ELEMENT (NAME, LOCATION, BUSINESS, DIVISION+)>
<!ATTLIST DIVISION
    NAME    CDATA #REQUIRED
    BUDGET CDATA #IMPLIED
>
<!ELEMENT NAME (#PCDATA)>
<!ELEMENT LOCATION (#PCDATA)>
<!ELEMENT BUSINESS (#PCDATA)>
<!ELEMENT DIVISION (#PCDATA)>
<!ELEMENT LOCATION (STREET, CITY, STATE, ZIP)>
<!ATTLIST ZIP CDATA #REQUIRED>
<!ELEMENT STREET (#PCDATA)>
<!ELEMENT CITY (#PCDATA)>
```

```
<!ELEMENT STATE (#PCDATA)>
<!ELEMENT ZIP (#PCDATA)>
]
<VENDORS>
  <VENDOR>
      <NAME>Iomega</NAME>
      <LOCATION>
          <STREET>1821 W.Iomega</STREET>
          <comment -- this is a test file-->
          <CITY>Roy</CITY>
          <STATE>UT</STATE>
          <ZIP SUB="8441">84067
      </LOCATION>
      <BUSINESS>Manufacturing</BUSINESS>
      <DIVISION NAME="Sales" BUDGET="350000">
      </DIVISION>
      <DIVISION NAME="IT" BUDGET="650000">
      </DIVISION>
      <DIVISION NAME="HR" BUDGET="650000">
      </DIVISION>
  </VENDOR>
   <VENDOR>
      <NAME>Dell</NAME>
      <LOCATION>
          <STREET>1000 W. Addison</STREET>
          <CITY>Dallas</CITY>
          <STATE>TX</STATE>
          <ZIP SUB="3456">40078
      </LOCATION>
      <BUSINESS>Computer Manufacturing</BUSINESS>
      <DIVISION NAME="Sales" BUDGET="650000">
      </DIVISION>
      <DIVISION NAME="IT" BUDGET="750000">
      </DIVISION>
      <DIVISION NAME="HR" BUDGET="1650000">
      </DIVISION>
  </VENDOR>
</VENDORS>
```

XML Schemas

The World Wide Web Consortium is currently working on a replacement for DTDs. Why would the Consortium want to do this? DTDs seem to do a decent job at what they were designed to do. Is it just old technology? No, the problem is that they are far from the perfect solution. DTDs are not without their problems, and we're going to discuss these problems here.

- They are written in a different (non-XML) syntax. Remember that DTDs come directly from SGML.

- DTDs have no direct support for namespaces. We've seen that there is a workaround for this though.

As a reminder, here is what namespaces accomplish: Namespaces prevent a tag used by one author from clashing with a tag of the same name but with a different meaning that was developed by another author.

- DTDs only offer extremely limited data typing. They can only express the data type of attributes in terms of explicit enumerations and a few coarse string formats. There's no facility for describing numbers, dates, currency values, and so forth. Furthermore, DTDs have no capability to express the data type of character data in elements.
- Many people think that DTDs are just too difficult to understand and implement.

An example of one of these problems that occurs often is the ability to put any type of data, even garbled text, in a field that is supposed to contain a date. This is allowed because there is no type checking.

The Schema Specification

With this myriad of problems present, the W3C put together a goals list for the DTD replacement. At a minimum, the replacement would be all the following:

- More expressive than XML DTDs
- Expressed in XML
- Self-describing
- Usable by a wide variety of applications that employ XML
- Directly usable on the Internet
- Optimized for interoperability
- Simple enough to implement with modest design and runtime resources
- Coordinated with relevant W3C specs (XML Information Set, links, namespaces, pointers, style and syntax, as well as DOM, HTML, and RDF schema)

The result, so far, is a specification consisting of three documents:

- **Part 0: Primer**. This document provides an easily readable description of the XML schema facilities and is oriented toward quickly understanding how to create schemas using the XML schema language. It is located at `http://www.w3.org/TR/xmlschema-0/`.
- **Part 1: Structures**. This document describes the structure and constrains the contents of XML documents, provides XML namespace support, and substantially reconstructs and considerably extends DTDs. It is located at `http://www.w3.org/TR/xmlschema-1/`.

- **Part 2: Datatypes.** This document defines facilities for defining data types. The data type language, which is itself represented in XML, provides a superset of the capabilities found in DTDs for specifying data types on elements and attributes. It is located at `http://www.w3.org/TR/xmlschema-2/`.

This is personal opinion, but the one thing that the W3C missed the boat on was the one thing that drove the development of an alternative system to DTDs, *simplicity*. If you think DTDs are difficult to understand and write, just wait until we get to the point where we can talk about schemas with a little working knowledge. I believe this will hurt XML schema adoption. In November 2000, Elliott Rusty Harold, who is in the forefront of XML discussions and who wrote *The XML Bible*, after briefly noting the dangers of predictions, said he felt there would be only a partial success for the XML schema language. Knowing that XML developers need schemas desperately, he also said he felt that these were too complex. Also, he felt that once it was determined what was useful and what was not, schemas would be replaced. This is at least 10 years in the future, though.

Adding a little more fog to the equation is Microsoft. Rather than wait for XML schemas to become a standard, Microsoft went and developed its own schema mechanism based on the original XML–Data note (`http://www.w3.org/TR/1998/NOTE-XML-data-0105/`) and the Document Content Description note (`http://www.w3.org/TR/NOTE-dcd`). These references are very outdated. If you want more information, you can go to `http://msdn.microsoft.com/xml/reference/schema/start.asp`. This is Microsoft's schema reference. Because of this, I will be covering the W3C recommendation here and will discuss the Microsoft differences later in the book when necessary.

The Basics of Schemas

For a change, let's look at schemas in a kind of tutorial mode. We'll take an XML document and its schema document and analyze how a schema document is pieced together.

First let's look at the XML document in Listing 1.7. This is also known as an *instance* document of a schema because it has a schema associated with it, as given in Listing 1.8.

Listing 1.7 **The Starting XML Document**

```
<?xml version="1.0"?>
<resumes applicationDate="2000-12-20">
  <applicant>
    <name>Troy Miller</name>
    <street>MBA Way</street>
    <city>Roy</city>
    <state>UT</state>
    <zip>84067</zip>
```

continues

Listing 1.7 **Continued**

```xml
  </applicant>
  <applicant>
    <name>Mark Hilliard</name>
    <street>1821 W. 2400 S.</street>
    <city>Roy</city>
    <state>UT</state>
    <zip>84067</zip>
  </applicant>
  <comment>Can we hire one of these people, please?</comment>
  <jobsAvailable>
    <job num="1176A0">
      <title>Programmer</title>
      <positions>Emp 4</positions>
      <salary>45000</salary>
      <comment>What programming language?</comment>
    </job>
    <job num="A5-113-2">
      <title>Claim Adjuster</title>
      <position>Emp 6</position>
      <salary >32000</salary>
      <hiredate>2000-12-21</hiredate>
    </ job >
  </jobsAvailable >
</resumes>
```

Notice, first of all, that this is a well-formed XML document. It has a root element `<resumes>` that contains other elements (`<department>`, `<applicant>`), which in turn contain subelements until you come to either numbers or test values.

Even though it is not shown in the resumes document, there are ways to declare the location of the associated schema file for this instance document via a namespace mechanism. We'll cover that a little later in this chapter.

Now let's look at the schema document shown in Listing 1.8.

Listing 1.8 **Schema Document Associated with the XML Document in Listing 1.7**

```xml
<xsd:schema xmlns:xsd="http://www.w3.org/2000/08/XMLSchema">

  <xsd:annotation>
    <xsd:documentation>
      Resumes schema for resumes.xml.
    </xsd:documentation>
  </xsd:annotation>

  <xsd:element name="resumes" type="resumesType"/>

  <xsd:element name="comment" type="xsd:string"/>
```

```
    <xsd:complexType name="resumesType">
      <xsd:sequence>
        <xsd:element name="applicant" type="address"/>
        <xsd:element name="jobsAvailable" type="jobListType"/>
        <xsd:element ref="comment" minOccurs="0"/>
      </xsd:sequence>
      <xsd:attribute name="applicationDate" type="xsd:date"/>
    </xsd:complexType>

    <xsd:complexType name="address">
      <xsd:element name="name"   type="xsd:string"/>
      <xsd:element name="street" type="xsd:string"/>
      <xsd:element name="city"   type="xsd:string"/>
      <xsd:element name="state"  type="xsd:string"/>
      <xsd:element name="zip"    type="xsd:decimal"/>
    </xsd:complexType>

    <xsd:complexType name="jobListType">
      <xsd:sequence>
        <xsd:ComplexType name="job" type="jobDesc"
          <xsd:attribute name="num" type="xsd:string"/>
        </xsd:complexType>
      </xsd:sequence>
    </xsd:complexType>

    <xsd:complexType name="jobDesc">
      <xsd:element name="title"    type="xsd:string"/>
      <xsd:element name="position" type="xsd:string"/>
      <xsd:element name="salary">
        <xsd:simpleType>
          <xsd:restriction base="xsd:positiveInteger">
            <xsd:maxExclusive value="55000"/>
          </xsd:restriction>
        </xsd:simpleType>
      </xsd:element>
    </xsd:complexType>

</xsd:schema>
```

Notice again, just like the XML document with which it is associated, this schema document is a well-formed XML document.

We'll be going through this document for much of the rest of this chapter. Looking at this document now, you can see several new element names throughout the listing, with <complexType> and <simpleType> the more important among them. In brief, elements that contain subelements or that carry attributes are said to be *complex types*, whereas elements that contain numbers (and strings, and dates, and so on) but do not contain any subelements are said to be *simple types*. Some elements have attributes; attributes always have simple types.

This distinction between the two different types of elements is critical to schemas. The XML schema specification comes with many different simple types already defined, which we will see in the next table, while we declare complex types ourselves. It is also possible to declare new simple types. We'll see that also.

The important thing to remember about how to go about writing a schema is that, conceptually, you do it just like you write a DTD. Start with the `root` element. If it has subelements, define it as a `complexType`. Now define each subelement. If the subelements do not have subelements themselves, define them as either an element (in which case you're done with it) or a `simpleType` if you want to embellish its description. Repeat these last steps as many times as necessary until all elements are defined.

If you are familiar with the C or C++ programming languages, you might think of a complex type as a named `struct` with the simple types as the `struct` components.

Until we get around to discussing schema namespaces, please bear with the prefix `xsd:` and accept it as is. It won't affect the discussion for now.

Simple Types

As I said earlier, the XML schema specification has a set of predefined simple types. These are listed in Table 1.7.

Table 1.7   **Predefined Simple Data Types**

Type	Definition
binary	Holds binary data like 101110
boolean	Holds items such as true, false, 0 or 1
byte	Holds an integer value with maximum value of 255
century	Holds a century value such as 19 or 20
date	Holds a date in YYYY-MM-DD format
decimal	Holds negative and positive real numbers such as −5.2, 3.14159
double	Holds a double-precision, 64-bit, floating-point number
ENTITIES	Represents the XML ENTITIES attribute type
ENTITY	Represents the XML ENTITY attribute type
float	Holds a single-precision, 32-bit, floating-point number
ID	Represents the XML ID attribute type
IDREF	Represents the XML IDREF attribute type
IDREFS	Represents the XML IDREFS attribute type
int	Holds an integer value such as 3202
integer	Represents an integer
language	Holds the XML 1.0 defined language identifier such as *en* or *fr*
long	Holds a long integer value such as 987654321
month	Holds a month value such as 2000-12

Name	Holds the XML 1.0 Name type
NCName	Holds an XML name without the namespace prefix and colon
negativeInteger	Holds a negative integer such as −5
NMTOKEN	Represents the XML NMTOKEN attribute type
NMTOKENS	Represents the XML NMTOKENS attribute type
nonNegativeInteger	Holds a positive integer value
nonPositiveInteger	Holds a negative integer value
NOTATION	Represents the XML NOTATION attribute type
positiveInteger	Holds a positive integer value
QName	Holds a value of type *Namespace Qualified Name*
recurringDate	Holds a recurring date such as …12-25, or every December 25th
recurringDay	Holds a recurring day such as …25, or every 25th
recurringDuration	Holds a recurring duration such as …12-25T06:00:00, or every December 25th at 6 AM
short	Holds a short integer value such as 54321
String	Holds a string of text
time	Holds a time value such as 06:00:00.000
timeDuration	Holds a time duration such as P2Y3M6DT12H45M1.2S, OR 2 years, 3 months, 6 days, 12 hours, 45 minutes, and 1.2 seconds
timeInstant	Holds a time value such as 2000-12-25T06:00:00-04:00 (time zone adjustment)
timePeriod	Holds a time period such as 2000-12-25T06:00
unsignedByte	Holds an unsigned byte value
unsignedInt	Holds an unsigned integer value
unsignedLong	Holds an unsigned long value
unsignedShort	Holds an unsigned short value
uriReference	Holds an URL value such as http://www.myorg.com
year	Holds a year value such as 2000

These built-in simple data types are used in two cases, one of which is when defining the type of an `<element>`, as in the following example:

```
<xsd:element name="title" type="xsd:string"/>
```

The other case is when you are deriving a new `simpleType`, which we'll talk about in the next section.

An important concept concerning `simpleTypes` is what I call *declaration scope*. If an element or attribute declaration appears as a child of the `<xsd:schema>` declaration and is external to any `complexType` declaration, then it is considered a *global* declaration.

This allows it to be referenced with the *ref* attribute, making it unnecessary to redeclare the element.

```
<xsd:element name="comment" type="xsd:string"/>
    .
    .
    <xsd:element name="jobsAvailable" type="jobListType"/>
    <xsd:element ref="comment" minOccurs="0"/>
</xsd:sequence>
```

Here, the fact that the comment element meets the two necessary criteria allows us to declare a reference to the comment element. This keeps us from having to repeatedly redefine the same type of elements.

Again, by definition, simple types contain no subelement or attributes. Both built-in simple types and their derivations can be used in all element and attribute declarations.

New simple types are defined by deriving them from existing simple types, both those already built-in and simple types that have been previously derived. In particular, we can derive new simple types by a process known as *restriction*. We do this by making the legal range of values for the new type a subset of the existing type's range of values. We need two elements to accomplish this: first, the `<simpleType>` element to define and name the new simple type, and second, the `<restriction>` element to indicate the base type of the element and to identify the facets that constrain the range of values. Don't let this new term throw you. There's nothing magical about it. Think of facets as a synonym for properties, and you should have no problem. A complete list of facets is provided in Tables 1.8, 1.9, and 1.10. These tables list the built-in simple types and which facets apply to them.

Table 1.8 **Simple Data Types and Associated Facets**

Data Type	Facet					
	LENGTH	MIN LENGTH	MAX LENGTH	PATTERN	ENUMERATION	WHITE-SPACE
binary	✓	✓	✓		✓	
boolean				✓		
byte				✓	✓	
CDATA	✓	✓	✓	✓	✓	✓
century				✓		
date				✓	✓	
decimal				✓	✓	
double				✓	✓	
ENTITIES	✓	✓	✓		✓	
ENTITY	✓	✓	✓	✓	✓	
float				✓	✓	
ID	✓	✓	✓	✓	✓	

	LENGTH	MIN LENGTH	MAX LENGTH	PATTERN	ENUMERATION	WHITE-SPACE
IDREF	✓	✓	✓	✓	✓	
IDREFS	✓	✓	✓		✓	
int				✓	✓	
integer				✓	✓	
language	✓	✓	✓	✓	✓	
long				✓	✓	
month				✓	✓	
Name	✓	✓	✓	✓	✓	
NCName	✓	✓	✓	✓	✓	
negativeInteger				✓	✓	
NMTOKEN	✓	✓	✓	✓	✓	
NMTOKENS	✓	✓	✓		✓	
nonNegativeInteger				✓	✓	
nonPositiveInteger				✓	✓	
NOTATION	✓	✓	✓	✓	✓	
positiveInteger				✓	✓	
QName	✓	✓	✓	✓	✓	
recurringDate				✓	✓	
recurringDay				✓	✓	
recurringDuration				✓	✓	
short				✓	✓	
string	✓	✓	✓	✓	✓	✓
time				✓	✓	
timeDuration				✓	✓	
timeInstant				✓	✓	
timePeriod				✓	✓	
token	✓	✓	✓	✓	✓	✓
unsignedByte				✓	✓	
unsignedInt				✓	✓	
unsignedLong				✓	✓	
unsignedShort				✓	✓	
uriReference	✓	✓	✓	✓	✓	
year				✓	✓	

Table 1.9 **Ordered Simple Data Types and Associated Facets**

Data Type	Facet						
	MAX INCLUSIVE	MAX EXCLUSIVE	MIN INCLUSIVE	MIN EXCLUSIVE	PRECISION	SCALE	ENCODING
binary							✓
byte	✓	✓	✓	✓	✓	✓	
century	✓	✓	✓	✓			
date	✓	✓	✓	✓			
decimal	✓	✓	✓	✓	✓	✓	
double	✓	✓	✓	✓			
float	✓	✓	✓	✓			
int	✓	✓	✓	✓	✓	✓	
integer	✓	✓	✓	✓	✓	✓	
long	✓	✓	✓	✓	✓	✓	
month	✓	✓	✓	✓			
negativeInteger	✓	✓	✓	✓	✓	✓	
nonNegativeInteger	✓	✓	✓	✓	✓	✓	
nonPositiveInteger	✓	✓	✓	✓	✓	✓	
positiveInteger	✓	✓	✓	✓	✓	✓	
recurringDate	✓	✓	✓	✓			
recurringDay	✓	✓	✓	✓			
recurringDuration	✓	✓	✓	✓			
short	✓	✓	✓	✓	✓	✓	
time	✓	✓	✓	✓			
timeDuration	✓	✓	✓	✓			
timeInstant	✓	✓	✓	✓			
timePeriod	✓	✓	✓	✓			
unsignedByte	✓	✓	✓	✓	✓	✓	
unsignedInt	✓	✓	✓	✓	✓	✓	
unsignedLong	✓	✓	✓	✓	✓	✓	
unsignedShort	✓	✓	✓	✓	✓	✓	
year	✓	✓	✓	✓			

Table 1.10   **Time and Date Ordered Simple Data Types and Associated Facets**

Data Type	Facet	
	PERIOD	DURATION
century	✓	✓
date	✓	✓
month	✓	✓
recurringDate	✓	✓
recurringDay	✓	✓
recurringDuration	✓	✓
time	✓	✓
timeDuration		
timeInstant	✓	✓
timePeriod	✓	✓
year	✓	✓

Just about all of the facets defined in Tables 1.8, 1.9, and 1.10 are straightforward. One of most interesting, however, is *enumeration*, which is a facet in Table 1.8. Enumeration limits a simple type to a set of distinct values. For example, we could define an element militaryMonth derived from a string whose value must be one of the standard military abbreviations for months of the year.

Suppose we want to create a new type of integer called salary whose range of values is between 25000 and 75000 (inclusive). We know this is of type integer, so we base it on the integer type. Our base type integer consists of values less than 25000 and greater than 75000. So we restrict the range of the salary element by employing two facets, minInclusive and maxInclusive (see Listings 1.9 and 1.10).

Listing 1.9   **Schema Fragment Detailing *minInclusive* and *maxInclusive***

```
<xsd:element name="salary">
  <xsd:simpleType>
    <xsd:restriction base="xsd:positiveInteger">
      <xsd:minExclusive value="25000"/>
      <xsd:maxExclusive value="75000"/>
    </xsd:restriction>
  </xsd:simpleType>
</xsd:element>
```

Listing 1.10   **Enumeration Facet Example**

```
<xsd:simpleType name="militaryMonth" base="xsd:String">
  <xsd:enumeration value = "JAN">
  <xsd:enumeration value = "FEB">
  <xsd:enumeration value = "MAR">
  <xsd:enumeration value = "APR">
  <xsd:enumeration value = "MAY">
  <xsd:enumeration value = "JUN">
  <xsd:enumeration value = "JUL">
  <xsd:enumeration value = "AUG">
  <xsd:enumeration value = "SEP">
  <xsd:enumeration value = "OCT">
  <xsd:enumeration value = "NOV">
  <xsd:enumeration value = "DEC">
</xsd:simpleType>
```

Enumeration values specified for a particular type must be unique.

Complex Types

We define new complex types with the `<complexType>` element. These definitions usually contain other element declarations, element references, and attribute declarations.
The declarations are not themselves types; rather, they declare a relationship between a
name and constraints, which dictates how that name appears in documents governed
by the associated schema. Listing 1.11 shows our `complexType` *address* definition:

Listing 1.11   *complexType address*

```
<xsd:complexType name="address">
  <xsd:element name="name"   type="xsd:string"/>
  <xsd:element name="street" type="xsd:string"/>
  <xsd:element name="city"   type="xsd:string"/>
  <xsd:element name="state"  type="xsd:string"/>
  <xsd:element name="zip"    type="xsd:decimal"/>
</xsd:complexType>
```

This definition declares that any element appearing in an instance document whose
type is declared to be *address* must consist of five elements. These elements must be
called `name`, `street`, `city`, `state`, and `zip`, as specified by the values of the declarations'
name attributes, and the elements must appear in the same order in which they are
declared. The first four of these elements will each contain a string, and the fifth will
contain a decimal number.

Default and Fixed Content

The `<xsd:element>` element has two unique attributes that we have not discussed, `fixed` and `default`. Only one of these attributes can be used in the same element at a time. `fixed` specifies the value of an element and also declares that the value cannot be changed.

In the following example, the `width` element is declared to always have a value of 10.

```
<xsd:element name="width" type="xsd:integer" fixed="10"/>
```

`default` assigns a value to an element, but this value can change as needed or stay the same. It's never a good idea to declare a variable in an algebraic equation as empty or 0 in case the variable is ever divided into another number. Division by 0 is a very bad thing. So you can assign a default value other than 0 to the element that defines the variable and solves the problem.

```
<xsd:element name="width" type="xsd:integer" default="10"/>
```

Here the `width` element is declared to have a value of 10, and this value can be changed as deemed necessary.

Attribute Declarations

Attributes are declared with the `<attribute>` element. This element has a type attribute that specifies the simple type of the attribute. Remember that attributes can only be of simple type. Attributes can appear once or not at all (the default), so attribute occurrence syntax is different than element syntax. Specifically, a `use` attribute is placed in an attribute declaration to indicate whether the attribute is required or optional and, if optional, whether the attribute's value is fixed or there is a default. This is an identical usage to the way elements are declared to have a fixed or default value (see Table 1.11).

Table 1.11   **The Possible Values of *use***

use Attribute	Definition
required	The attribute is required and can contain any value.
optional	The attribute is optional and can contain any value.
fixed	The attribute value is fixed, and the value attribute contains its value.
default	If the attribute is absent, the value attribute specifies its value; if it does appear, its value is assigned by the document.
prohibited	The attribute must not be present.

A second attribute, `value`, provides any value that is called for.

Let's look at an example:

```
<xsd:attribute name="age" type="xsd:int" use="default" value="32">
```

This declaration means that the appearance of an age attribute is optional, although its value must be 32 if it does appear. If it does not appear, a schema processor will create an age attribute with this value.

Gathering the facets and attributes that affect the number of times an element or attribute can appear (minOccurs, maxOccurs, fixed, default, use, and value), we can summarize their effect as shown in Table 1.12.

Table 1.12   **Attribute/Element Occurrence Constraints**

minOccurs	maxOccurs	fixed	default	use	value	Notes
1	1	-	-	required	-	Element/attribute must appear once; it may have any value.
1	1	22	-	required	22	Element/attribute must appear once; its value must be 22.
2	unbounded	22	-	n/a	22	Element must appear twice or more; its value must be 22. In general, minOccurs and maxOccurs values may be positive integers, and maxOccurs value may alsobe "unbounded."
0	1	-	-	optional	optional	Element/attribute may appear once; it may have any value.
0	1	22	-	fixed	22	Element/attribute may appear once. If it does appear, its value must be 22.
0	1	-	22	default	22	Element/attribute may appear once. If it does not appear, its value is 22; otherwise, its value is that given.
0	2	-	22	n/a	22	Element may appear once, twice, or not at all. If it does not appear, its value is 22; otherwise, its value is that given. In general, minOccurs and maxOccurs values may be positive integers, and maxOccurs value may also be "unbounded."
0	0	-	-		prohibited	Element/attribute must not appear.

Element Content

What, exactly, can an element contain? After all, we've talked about everything else except that. The XML schema specification makes provisions for two types of content: empty content and mixed content.

Empty Content

Just as in a DTD, there can be empty elements in the schema. They contain no data, but they can have attributes. Declaring a complexType and assigning the value empty to the type attribute of the element specifies empty elements. Let's say we have the following XML element:

```
<RECTANGLE WIDTH='12' HEIGHT='8'>
```

This element has no content, only attributes, so we call this an empty element. Listing 1.12 shows the associated schema declaration for this element.

Listing 1.12   Schema Declaration for the RECTANGLE Element

```
<xsd:element name="rectangle"
  <xsd:complexType content="empty">
    <xsd:attribute name="width" type="xsd:int" use="default" value"1"/>
    <xsd:attribute name="height" type="xsd:int" use="default" value"1"/>
  </xsd:complexType>
</xsd:element>
```

Notice that there is no content, only attribute declarations.

Mixed Content

Our resume schema can be characterized as elements containing subelements, and the deepest subelements contain character data. There are also provisions for the construction of schemas where character data can appear alongside subelements, and this character data is not necessarily confined to the deepest subelements. To accomplish this construction, we use the mixed value of the content attribute.

Listing 1.13 shows an XML snippet from a letter in reply to a resume sent for review.

Listing 1.13   **XML Snippet of a Letter**

```
<?xml version="1.0"?
  <letter>
    <salutation>Dear Mr. <name>Troy Miller</name>.</salutation>
      Your resume dated <resumeDate>12 December 2000</resumeDate>
        was received on
          <resumereceivedDate>
            1999-05-21
          </resumereceivedDate>.
  </letter>
```

Notice the text appearing between elements and their child elements. Specifically, text appears between the elements <salutation>, <name>, <resumeDate>, and <receivedDate>, which are all children of <letter>, and text appears around the element name, which is the child of a child of <letter>. Listing 1.14 shows a schema snippet declaring <letter>.

Listing 1.14 **Schema for the Resume Letter**

```xml
<xsd:element name="letter">
  <xsd:complexType content="mixed">
      <xsd:element name="salutation">
          <xsd:complexType content="mixed">
              <xsd:element name="name" type="xsd:string"/>
          </xsd:complexType>
      </xsd:element>
      <xsd:element name="resumeDate" type="xsd:string"/>
      <xsd:element name="receivedDate" type="xsd:date" minOccurs="0"/>
      <!-- etc -->
  </xsd:complexType>
</xsd:element>
```

If you take a close look at this schema definition and the original XML document declaration, you might say, "Well, this schema covers the occurrence of text inside the `<salutation>` element (Dear Mr.), but what about the other text `'Your resume dated'` and `'was received on'`?" These occurrences were taken care of by declaring the main element, `<letter>`, as being of *mixed* content. Think of it as, "Any text outside of child elements of their parent element is covered by declaring the parent element as being of mixed content." How's that for a quote?

Schema Annotations

There must be a way to provide comments in schemas, right? DTDs use XML comments, so what's the parallel with schemas? If you were thinking that comment methods in schemas might be more complicated than in DTDs, you would be right. There is an upside to this complexity, however.

Schemas provide three elements for the addition of annotations:

- `<xsd:annotation>`
- `<xsd:documentation>`
- `<xsd:appInfo>`

An interesting twist to annotations in schemas is that the W3C took into account the fact that annotations are not just for the human reader in human-readable form but also for the machine that likes to read them in machine-readable form. You'll understand in a minute.

Both of the elements `<documentation>` and `<appInfo>` appear as subelements of the `<annotation>` element. The `<annotation>` element can appear at the beginning of schema constructs. Look at Listing 1.15, which appeared at the beginning of the resumes XML document.

Listing 1.15   **The** *<xsd:documentation>* **Element**

```
<xsd:schema xmlns:xsd="http://www.w3.org/2000/08/XMLSchema">

  <xsd:annotation>
    <xsd:documentation>
      Resumes schema for resumes.xml.
    </xsd:documentation>
  </xsd:annotation>
```

Here we've provided what is basically nothing more than a comment. This is the human-readable text we talked about. Annotations can also appear at the beginning of other schema constructs such as simpleType and attribute.

The appInfo element, which wasn't in our resumes example, can be used to provide information for program tools, stylesheets, and any other applications written to take advantage of it. This is the machine-readable form that complements the human-readable form. Listing 1.16 enumerates what facets, properties, and restrictions the float and double types have in a way that could be machine readable. It is from the W3C XML Schema Part 2: Datatypes specification.

Listing 1.16   **Facets and Properties of the Float and Double Data Types**

```
<simpleType name="float" id="float">
  <annotation>
    <appinfo>
      <hfp:hasFacet name="pattern"/>
      <hfp:hasFacet name="enumeration"/>
      <hfp:hasFacet name="whiteSpace"/>
      <hfp:hasFacet name="maxInclusive"/>
      <hfp:hasFacet name="maxExclusive"/>
      <hfp:hasFacet name="minInclusive"/>
      <hfp:hasFacet name="minExclusive"/>
      <hfp:hasProperty name="ordered" value="true"/>
      <hfp:hasProperty name="bounded" value="true"/>
      <hfp:hasProperty name="cardinality" value="finite"/>
      <hfp:hasProperty name="numeric" value="true"/>
    </appinfo>
    <documentation xml:lang="en"
      source="http://www.w3.org/TR/xmlschema-2/#float"/>
  </annotation>
  <restriction base="anySimpleType">
    <whiteSpace value="collapse"/>
  </restriction>
</simpleType>

<simpleType name="double" id="double">
  <annotation>
    <appinfo>
      <hfp:hasFacet name="pattern"/>
```

continues

Listing 1.16 **Continued**

```
                <hfp:hasFacet name="enumeration"/>
                <hfp:hasFacet name="whiteSpace"/>
                <hfp:hasFacet name="maxInclusive"/>
                <hfp:hasFacet name="maxExclusive"/>
                <hfp:hasFacet name="minInclusive"/>
                <hfp:hasFacet name="minExclusive"/>
                <hfp:hasProperty name="ordered" value="true"/>
                <hfp:hasProperty name="bounded" value="true"/>
                <hfp:hasProperty name="cardinality" value="finite"/>
                <hfp:hasProperty name="numeric" value="true"/>
            </appinfo>
            <documentation xml:lang="en"
             source="http://www.w3.org/TR/xmlschema-2/#double"/>
        </annotation>
        <restriction base="anySimpleType">
            <whiteSpace value="collapse"/>
        </restriction>
    </simpleType>
```

Advanced Topics

To close out this chapter, we're going to discuss some topics that I consider to be a little more advanced than what we've covered so far. These topics are namespaces, qualified and unqualified locals, and finally, schema file location.

Namespaces and Qualifications

Toward the beginning of this chapter, when we were working with the code in Listing 1.8, I told you that I would explain the usage of the element prefix xsd: later in this chapter. Well, that's what we're going to cover now.

Just as a DTD has a namespace called a target namespace to which its elements belong, so do schemas. We now have a new attribute for the <schema> element, the targetNamespace attribute. The targetNamespace enables distinction between definitions and declarations from different schema. For example, target namespaces would distinguish between the element in the XML schema language and a declaration for an element in a listing of the periodic table. The first element is part of the http://www.w3.org/1999/XMLSchema target namespace; the other is not.

To check that an instance document conforms to one or more schemas, we need to identify which element and attribute declarations and type definitions in the schemas should be used to check the corresponding elements and attributes in the instance document. That's what the target namespace is for.

Those of us who are writing or will be writing schema documents have several options that affect how the identities of elements and attributes are represented in instance documents. We have to decide whether or not locally declared elements and attributes in an instance document must be qualified when used in a namespace.

> Earlier I defined what I called *declaration scope*. If an element or attribute declaration appears as an immediate child of the <xsd:schema> declaration and is external to any complexType declaration, then it is considered a *global* declaration.

Schemas allow us to determine whether or not local declarations need to be qualified either by using an explicit prefix or implicitly by default. These decisions we make have a number of consequences concerning the structure of schemas and instance documents.

To specify whether elements and attributes are qualified or unqualified, there are two new attributes for the <schema> element. The attribute attributeFormDefault specifies whether or not attributes are to be qualified or unqualified, and elementFormDefault specifies whether or not elements are to be qualified or unqualified.

We'll look at qualified local declarations first.

Qualified Locals

Here's the beginning of our resumes schema as we originally declared it:

```
<schema xmlns="http://www.w3.org/2000/08/XMLSchema">
...
    <annotation>
      <documentation>
```

Now let's add some additional attributes to this declaration (see Listing 1.17).

Listing 1.17 **Expanded Schema Declaration**

```
<schema xmlns=http://www.w3.org/2000/08/XMLSchema
    xmlns:res="http://www.myorg.com/namespace"
    targetNameSpace=" http://www.myorg.com/namespace"
    elementFormDefault="qualified"
    attributeFormDefault="unqualified"
>
<element name="resumes" type="res:resumesType"/>

<element name="comment" type="xsd:string"/>

< complexType name="resumesType">
  <sequence>
    <element name="applicant" type="res:address"/>
    <element name="jobsAvailable" type="res:jobListType"/>
    <element ref="comment" minOccurs="0"/>
  </sequence>
```

continues

Listing 1.17   **Continued**

```
    <attribute name="applicationDate" type="date"/>
</complexType>

</schema>
```

The first `xmlns` attribute specifies the W3C default schema namespace. All elements without a namespace prefix are assumed to belong to it. The second `xmlns` attribute specifies a local namespace that implements the prefix `res` and points to the same namespace as the target namespace. All locally declared elements, *if required*, must be qualified with this namespace prefix; otherwise, a schema processor will not know in which namespace to look for the element definition.

The next two attributes specify the qualifications. The attribute `elementFormDefault` says that all locally declared elements must be prefixed with the appropriate namespace prefix, in this case `res`. The `attributeFormDefault` states that attributes remain unqualified. Another point I'd like to mention here is that `qualified` is the default value for these two attributes, so it isn't really necessary to declare them. I recommend that you do, however, in the interest of good readability. There's no sense in making something harder than it already is.

An instance document that follows this schema declaration would look like what is shown in Listing 1.18.

Listing 1.18   **XML Document that Adheres to the Expanded Schema**

```
<?xml version="1.0"?>
<res:resumes applicationDate="2000-12-20"
xmlns:res="http://www.myorg.com/namespace">
  <res:applicant>
    <res:name>Troy Miller</name>
    <res:street>MBA Way</street>
    <res:city>Roy</city>
    <res:state>UT</state>
    <res:zip>84067</zip>
  </res:applicant>
  <res:applicant>
    <res:name>Mark Hilliard</name>
    <res:street>1821 W. 2400 S.</street>
    <res:city>Roy</city>
    <res:state>UT</state>
    <res:zip>84067</zip>
  </res:applicant>
  <res:comment>Can we hire one of these people, please?</comment>
  <res:jobsAvailable>
    <res:job num="1176A0">
      <res:title>Programmer</title>
      <res:positions>Emp 4</positions>
      <res:salary>45000</salary>
      <res:comment>What programming language?</comment>
```

```
    </res:job>
    <res:job num="A5-113-2">
      <res:title>Claim Adjuster</title>
      <res:position>Emp 6</position>
      <res:salary >32000</salary>
      <res:hiredate>2000-12-21</hiredate>
    </res:job >
  </res:jobsAvailable >
</res:resumes>
```

Notice that the xmlns declaration matches the declaration in the schema declaration, as it should.

Here's the explanation for the use of the xsd prefix that we've used up to this point. If you look back at when this prefix was first used (in the "The Basics of Schema" section of this chapter), you'll see that the default namespace declared in this schema was assigned the prefix xsd. Here's the line that did this:

```
<xsd:schema xmlns:xsd="http://www.w3.org/2000/08/XMLSchema">
```

So, it was necessary to prefix all elements of the schema with that namespace identifier. Although it isn't dictated anywhere, if you do assign a prefix to W3C elements through the use of the xmlns attribute, the generally accepted standard is to use xsd.

Unqualified Locals

Listing 1.19 shows the resumes schema again. We'll keep the same attributes as the previous qualified examples, but we'll change the elementFormDefault to unqualified.

Listing 1.19   **The Resumes Schema with *unqualified* Specifically Stated**

```
<schema xmlns=http://www.w3.org/2000/08/XMLSchema
    xmlns:res="http://www.myorg.com/namespace"
    targetNameSpace=" http://www.myorg.com/namespace"
    elementFormDefault="unqualified"
    attributeFormDefault="unqualified"
>
<element name="resumes" type="res:resumesType"/>

<element name="comment" type="xsd:string"/>

< complexType name="resumesType">
  <sequence>
    <element name="applicant" type="res:address"/>
    <element name="jobsAvailable" type="res:jobListType"/>
    <element ref="comment" minOccurs="0"/>
  </sequence>
  <attribute name="applicationDate" type="date"/>
</complexType>

</schema>
```

The only thing different here is that the `elementFormDefault` attribute was changed to `unqualified`.

Listing 1.20 shows what the instance document looks like for this schema.

Listing 1.20   **XML Document Conforming to Listing 1.19**

```
<?xml version="1.0"?>
<res:resumes applicationDate="2000-12-20"
xmlns:res="http://www.myorg.com/namespace">
  <applicant>
    <name>Troy Miller</name>
    <street>MBA Way</street>
    <city>Roy</city>
    <state>UT</state>
    <zip>84067</zip>
  </applicant>
  <applicant>
    <name>Mark Hilliard</name>
    <street>1821 W. 2400 S.</street>
    <city>Roy</city>
    <state>UT</state>
    <zip>84067</zip>
  </applicant>
  <res:comment>Can we hire one of these people, please?</comment>
  <jobsAvailable>
    <job num="1176A0">
      <title>Programmer</title>
      <positions>Emp 4</positions>
      <salary>45000</salary>
      <comment>What programming language?</comment>
    </job>
    <job num="A5-113-2">
      <title>Claim Adjuster</title>
      <position>Emp 6</position>
      <salary >32000</salary>
      <hiredate>2000-12-21</hiredate>
    </job >
  </jobsAvailable >
</res:resumes>
```

As expected, all locally declared elements are unqualified. The globally declared elements, though, are still prefixed with the namespace prefix.

Schema File Location

There's one last topic concerning XML schema that I'd like to cover before moving on: how to specify the location and name of schema files in an instance document. This specification requires the introduction of one more namespace definition.

We know that the default namespace for XML schema is `http://www.w3.org/1999/XMLSchema`. This is used to qualify all constructs that appear in schema documents. To qualify any XML schema attributes that might appear in instance documents, we declare the namespace `http://www.w3.org/1999/XMLSchema-instance`. Makes sense, doesn't it? Keep the names consistent and everything is much easier to read. The generally accepted default prefix for this namespace, if required, is `xsi:`. You'll see its implementation next.

The schema specification defines the attribute `schemaLocation` to provide the functionality of specifying a schema's location. The `schemaLocation` attribute contains a whitespace-delimited list of whitespace-delimited namespace-location pairs. Listing 1.21 shows an XML document fragment.

Listing 1.21 **Declaring a Schema Location**

```
<?xml version="1.0"?>
<resumes xmlns:res="http://www.myorg.com/namespace"
         xmlns:xsi="http://www.w3.org/1999/XMLSchema-instance"
         xsi:schemaLocation="http://www.myorg.com
                            "http://www.myorg.com/resumes.xsd"
>
  <res:applicant>
    <res:name>Tracy Lance</name>
    <res:street>Intranet Avenue</street>
….
```

Here we declare the `instance` namespace first to define the `xsi:` prefix. Next we declare the location and name of the schema document that applies to this XML document. The `xsi:schemaLocation` specifies that the schema that applies to this document is located at `http://www.myorg.com` and the filename associated with this schema is `resumes.xsd`.

We've covered a lot in this chapter. You now have the capability to write basic DTDs and schema documents. Although you probably feel a little overwhelmed, it will all come in time. If you have further questions about any topic in this chapter, I refer you to any of the excellent texts out there that cover this topic. Also, you should obtain a copy of the W3C specification and keep it close.

It's time to take a break from XML and move on to other topics. In the following chapter, we'll discuss the Extensible Stylesheet Language Transformations. It is a language that enables you to take an XML document and transform it into just about any other format you can think of: HTML, another XML document, and so on. So let's get going.

Answers to the Two Exercises in the Chapter

Here are the answers to the two exercises I gave you in this chapter.

Attribute List

The first exercise was to write an element line given an attribute declaration.
Attribute declaration:

```
<!ATTLIST PERSON PERSONID CDATA>
```

Element line:

```
<PERSON PERSONID="176">
```

The value of the attribute can be any type of character data.
Attribute declaration:

```
<!ATTLIST EMPLOYEE MALE (true|false) "true">
```

Element line:

```
<EMPLOYEE MALE="false">
```

The MALE attribute can be either true or false. If it isn't explicitly declared, it defaults
to true.
Attribute declaration:

```
<!ATTLIST EMPLOYEE STATUS (single|married|divorced|widowed) #REQUIRED>
```

Element line:

```
<EMPLOYEE STATUS="divorced">
```

The STATUS attribute can be one of four possible values, as specified in the attribute
list. The attribute must be present and specified.

Invalid XML Document

The second exercise was to identify the problems with the XML document shown in
Listing 1.22.

Listing 1.22   **Incorrect XML Document**

```
<?xml version="1.0 standalone="no"?>
<!DOCTYPE VENDORS [
<!ELEMENT VENDORS (VENDOR)?>
<!ELEMENT (NAME, LOCATION, BUSINESS, DIVISION+)>
<!ATTLIST DIVISION
    NAME    CDATA #REQUIRED
    BUDGET  CDATA #IMPLIED
>
<!ELEMENT NAME (#PCDATA)>
<!ELEMENT LOCATION (#PCDATA)>
```

```
<!ELEMENT BUSINESS (#PCDATA)>
<!ELEMENT DIVISION (#PCDATA)>
<!ELEMENT LOCATION (STREET, CITY, STATE, ZIP)>
<!ATTLIST ZIP CDATA #REQUIRED>
<!ELEMENT STREET (#PCDATA)>
<!ELEMENT CITY (#PCDATA)>
<!ELEMENT STATE (#PCDATA)>
<!ELEMENT ZIP (#PCDATA)>
]
<VENDORS xmlns:vend='http://www.myorg.com/companytags'>
  <VENDOR>
      <NAME>Iomega</NAME>
      <LOCATION>
         <STREET>1821 W.Iomega</STREET>
         <comment -- this is a test file-->
         <CITY>Roy</CITY>
         <STATE>UT</STATE>
         <ZIP SUB="8441">84067
      </LOCATION>
      <BUSINESS>Manufacturing</BUSINESS>
      <DIVISION NAME="Sales" BUDGET="350000">
      </DIVISION>
      <DIVISION NAME="IT" BUDGET="650000">
      </DIVISION>
      <DIVISION NAME="HR" BUDGET="650000">
      </DIVISION>
  </VENDOR>
   <VENDOR>
      <NAME>Dell</NAME>
      <LOCATION>
         <STREET>1000 W. Addison</STREET>
         <CITY>Dallas</CITY>
         <STATE>TX</STATE>
         <ZIP SUB="3456">40078
      </LOCATION>
      <BUSINESS>Computer Manufacturing</BUSINESS>
      <DIVISION NAME="Sales" BUDGET="650000">
      </DIVISION>
      <DIVISION NAME="IT" BUDGET="750000">
      </DIVISION>
      <DIVISION NAME="HR" BUDGET="1650000">
      </DIVISION>
  </VENDOR>
</VENDORS>
```

Here is the list of corrections needed to make this a valid, well-formed XML document and schema.

- The document defines an `xml` namespace.

```
xmlns:vend='http://www.myorg.com/companytags'
```

  The entire document isn't using the prefix `vend` to define the tags. The document should be a continuation of the following:

```
<vend:VENDOR>
    <vendNAME>Iomega</NAME>
```

- The question mark (`?`, 0 or 1 elements present) helping to define the `VENDORS` element should be a plus sign (`+`, 1 or more elements present).

```
<!ELEMENT VENDORS (VENDOR)?>
```

- The `ZIP` element's attribute list is missing the name of the attribute.

```
<!ATTLIST ZIP CDATA #REQUIRED>
```

  It should instead be as follows:

```
<!ATTLIST ZIP SUB CDATA #REQUIRED>
```

- There is no comment element defined in the DTD, so the line

```
<comment -- this is a test file-->
```

  must be an actual comment, in which case it is written incorrectly. It should be as follows:

```
<!-- comment -- this is a test file-->
```

- The `ZIP` element is missing its closing tag in both cases.
- Bonus points: Did you remember that there is no attribute declared for the `VENDOR` element that defines the `xmlns` attribute?

Recap of What Was Discussed in This Chapter

- XML is a descendant of the Standardized General Markup Language (SGML) and, as such, is a cousin to HTML.
- XML documents consist of several components. Not only are there tags that delimit data components, there are also constructs that define the structure of the document.
- Document Type Definitions (DTDs) are constructs that are used to confirm the validity of the XML document. They accomplish this by ensuring that the document's structure confirms to the DTD definitions.

- DTDs have several problems, not the least of which are complexity and very limited type-checking capabilities.
- The W3C committee has proposed a replacement for DTDs, the XML Schema Definition Language.
- XML schema is, in essence, a language of its own that not only describes the structure of an XML document but also defines the type of each element contained in the document. The two basic types, `complexType` and `simpleType`, are used to define 99 percent of the elements of a schema document.
- Although many of the problems presented by DTDs are solved by schema, they definitely do not solve the problem of complexity. Writing a schema document can be a daunting process, but if you break it down into individual components and proceed in a step-by-step approach, the process will be eased.

2

XSLT Stylesheets

WELL, WE'VE DISCUSSED XML, DTDs, SCHEMA, VALIDITY, well-formedness, and more in Chapter 1. Now we'll talk about XSLT. Where does XSLT fit into the picture? Let me answer that by relating another question posed to me by a couple of my co-workers who are just starting to work with XML. That question was roughly, "John, what exactly can these tags and delimiters that surround the extracted database data do for us? The XML spec doesn't cover much. What if we need this data in a different format than what the database or parser provides to us?"

This chapter will attempt to answer these questions by covering the following topics:

- The Extensible Stylesheet Language Transformations (XSLT) and why it is needed
- The difference between cascading stylesheets (CSS) and XSLT
- Document tree navigation through an ancestry style of naming elements and structure
- The many elements that make up XSLT
- How to create and modify elements and attributes
- Output formatting, conditional processing, and looping
- The different types of output possible with XSLT
- Some heavyweight examples

Extensible Stylesheet Language Transformations (XSLT)

Just because you are given XML data in a specific layout doesn't mean that is the final format in which the data is required. For one thing, the tag layout might have to be completely rearranged. Maybe, instead of individual departmental budget data, a total budget dollar amount is all that is needed. Enter XSLT. With this new XML–related language (that's right, it is considered to be a complete language, as you'll find out in this chapter), it is possible to take a raw XML document and *transform* it into whatever format is required. An XML document can be completely rearranged into another XML document, or it can be changed to an HTML document for display on the World Wide Web. You can generate or modify just about any format you can think of by utilizing XSLT.

The Whole Is Greater than the Sum of Its Parts

I'd like to take this discussion just a little bit further and use an analogy to illustrate an important point about XML. Those of you who are familiar with the Transmission Control Protocol/Internet Protocol (TCP/IP) know that it is composed of many individual, different protocols, each with its own specific job to carry out. We call it a suite of protocols. Those of you who are not familiar with TCP/IP might recognize some of these other acronyms. Do you send or receive email? Simple Mail Transfer Protocol (SMTP) is a separate TCP/IP protocol that probably everyone who reads this book uses at least once a day. It is what transfers your email for you. Do you download or upload files on the World Wide Web? The TCP/IP protocol that makes this happen is the File Transfer Protocol (FTP).

Why am I all of a sudden talking about TCP/IP in an XML and SQL Server book? I want you to understand the old saying, *"The whole is greater than the sum of its parts."* The XML specification doesn't accomplish as much by itself as it does when it is combined with the other "X" specifications: XSLT, XPath, XBase, and XLink just to name a few. When the parts are combined as needed, much more can be accomplished than with what appears on the surface. We will accomplish quite a bit with the skills learned in this book.

Let's get back to XSLT for the time being. XSLT is a subset of the Extensible Stylesheet Language (XSL). XSL, as of this writing, is not an official standard just yet, but it will be one by the time this book is published. The other part of XSL that deals with the XML vocabulary for specifying formatting semantics is XSL Formatting Objects (XSLFO). We will not be discussing XSLFO in this book.

XSLT itself became a W3C Recommendation on November 16, 2000, and is located at `http://www.w3.org/TR/1999/REC-xslt-19991116`. To show how quickly things are moving forward with XSLT, on December 12, 2000, the W3C released the "XSLT 1.0 Errata" documentation; on December 13, 2000, the first draft of XSLT 1.1

was published. This should clearly demonstrate that a lot of attention is being focused on XSLT and its improvement, and the next couple years of its growth from child to teen should be very interesting.

XSL Editor

Before we get started on the details of XSLT stylesheets, I want to recommend a tool that will help you learn these stylesheets with a minimum of pain on your part. IBM has written a Java-based program called XSL Editor, and it is available at `http://www.alphaworks.ibm.com/tech/xsleditor`. How this program functions is covered in Appendix F, "IBM's XSL Editor." This is a very simple piece of software, so the learning curve is absolutely minimal. The only disadvantage to this software is that it must run on an older version of Java, 1.x. It will not work on the newer versions. Perhaps IBM will have this fixed by the time this book is published.

Because it is a Java-based program, you will need to get the Java runtime environment that is downloadable from `http://java.sun.com`. Now, all you non-Java programmers don't worry about it! All you have to do is install the run-time environment; there's not a whole lot to it. Then you install XSL Editor. It will find the Java environment itself; you don't have to tell it anything. Look at the length of Appendix F. That should show you it couldn't be that big of a problem to learn.

What Are Stylesheets?

Let's look at Figure 2.1 to see where we are in our XML process.

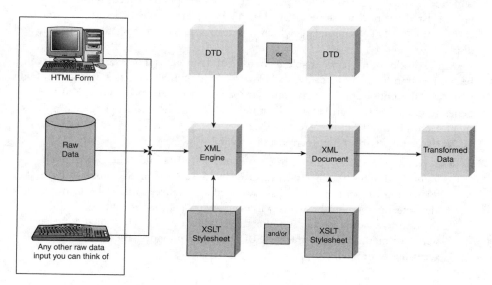

Figure 2.1   Stylesheets in the XML process.

Stylesheets describe how documents are presented to the viewer. Stylesheets attached to structured documents on the Web (for example, HTML) enable authors to change the presentation of documents without sacrificing device independence or adding new HTML tags.

Currently, there are two different types of stylesheets. One is the Extensible Stylesheet Language, which is what this chapter is about, and the other actually consists of two W3C Recommendations, Cascading Stylesheets Level 1 and Cascading Stylesheets Level 2 (CSS1 and CSS2).

Why have two types of stylesheets? Let's look at Table 2.1 for a comparison.

Table 2.1 **Stylesheet Functional Comparison**

	CSS	**XSL**
Used with HTML?	Yes	No
Used with XML?	Yes	Yes
Transformations?	No	Yes
Syntax	CSS	XML

The table shows the answer to the question of why there are two separate kinds of stylesheets. Each type was designed to accomplish a different job.

CSS generally is used to style HTML documents. CSS, however, is only a formatting language: It attaches style properties to the elements of a source document. It was not designed to take data and analyze or modify it in any way other than the way in which it is visually presented. It expects an external program to accomplish this process. Isn't that how it's done today? Information from a server database is extracted and put into an HTML template, which is sent to a client's browser for formatting and display.

XSLT, on the other hand, is able to transform documents. For example, XSLT can be used to transform XML data into HTML/CSS documents on the Web server. Did you catch the importance of that statement? One can generate the other; XSLT can generate CSS as part of an HTML document. This way, the two languages complement each other and can be used together.

XSLT can be used to transform data in several ways:

- Server-side XSLT is utilized to transform XML data into other XML documents with CSS stylesheets. In this case, because XML itself comes with no formatting conventions, it will always need a stylesheet to describe its display characteristics. Client browsers will need additional functionality with this method to accomplish the stylesheet interpretation. One additional concern with this method is that unless XSLT sheets are provided, there might be accessibility problems.

- Server-side XSLT is utilized to transform XML data into HTML documents with CSS stylesheets. Presently, this is the most common combination of XSLT and CSS. Because HTML is so widespread and well known, this method has the side benefit of being one of the best ways to ensure that information in lesser-known formats is accessible. Client browsers will need no new additional functionality with this method.

- Client-side generation of HTML/CSS utilizes XSLT and XML on the client. The content is passed through HTML/CSS to take advantage of current implementations. Client browsers will need additional functionality with this method.

- Last, utilize a standalone program external to both the server and the client. This program will utilize an XSLT stylesheet to perform the transformations and to generate the required document. A disadvantage of this method is that it really can't and shouldn't be used to provide real-time data transformations and updates. It's just not practical. A benefit of this method, just like the previous point, is that client browsers will need no new additional functionality with this method. A common example is business-to-business e-commerce document interchange in which an XML document needs to be rearranged into another different XML document.

The first and second points are methods employed by Microsoft's SQL Server 2000 to accomplish transformations.

The W3C has a note on the Internet that makes for interesting reading. "Using XSL and CSS Together" is available at `http://www.w3.org/TR/1998/NOTE-XSL-and-CSS-19980911`.

HTML Stylesheet

Listing 2.1 is an example of a CSS for an HTML document.

Listing 2.1   **CSS for an HTML Document**

```
<style type="text/css">
  body {
    font-family: geneva,arial,sans-serif;
    color: #333333;
    margin-top: 0px;
    margin-left: 0px;
    }
  A {
    color: #006666;
    }
  hr {
    color: #999999;
    height: 1px
    }
  <!-- for disks/catalog listings - tightens leading -->
```

continues

Listing 2.1   **Continued**

```
tr.small {
  line-height: 1;
  }
.bodycopy {
  font-family: geneva,arial,sans-serif;
  font-size: 12px;
  color: #333333;
  }
.bodycopysmall {
  font-family: geneva,arial,sans-serif;
  font-size: 11px;
  color: #333333;
  }
.productname {
  font-family: geneva,arial,sans-serif;
  font-size: 12px;
  color: #333333;
  }
</style>
```

The stylesheet is delimited with <STYLE>…</STYLE> and is given the attribute
type="text/css", letting the client's browser know to interpret the following statements as a CSS stylesheet. Inside the stylesheet, there are a variety of element definitions. For example, the HTML tag elements <A> (anchor), <HR> (horizontal rule), and
<TR> (table row) are defined with the characteristics they will use throughout the doc-
ument unless overridden. In addition, there are some definitions that are not HTML
tags themselves but that define properties to be used with any HTML tags to which
the definitions are attached. This is usually done with the CLASS attribute of HTML
tags, like this:

```
<FONT CLASS="productname">Iomega Zip Drive</FONT>
```

Not all browsers support CSS. Netscape and Internet Explorer do support CSS, but each has its own level
of support. The moral of the story? It will be a while before there is uniform support for CSS.

Simple XSLT Stylesheet

Listing 2.2 is an example of an XSLT stylesheet.

Listing 2.2   **Sample XSLT Stylesheet**

```
<?xml version="1.0"?>
<xsl:stylesheet xmlns:xsl="http://www.w3.org/TR/WD-xsl">
<xsl:template match="/">
  <HTML>
  <BODY>
```

```
    <TABLE BORDER="2">
      <TR>
        <TD>Name</TD>
        <TD>Address</TD>
        <TD>Tel</TD>
        <TD>Fax</TD>
        <TD>Email</TD>
      </TR>
  <xsl:for-each select="PEOPLE/PERSON">
      <TR>
        <TD>
  <xsl:value-of select="NAME" />
        </TD>
        <TD>
  <xsl:value-of select="ADDRESS" />
        </TD>
        <TD>
  <xsl:value-of select="TEL" />
        </TD>
        <TD>
  <xsl:value-of select="FAX" />
        </TD>
        <TD>
  <xsl:value-of select="EMAIL" />
        </TD>
      </TR>
  </xsl:for-each>
      </TABLE>
    </BODY>
    </HTML>
</xsl:template>
</xsl:stylesheet
```

This stylesheet will generate an HTML page that is a listing of addresses obtained from an XML document.

Looking at this example, we see a lot of things that we've seen before and some that we haven't. The following are some of the things we've seen before:

- First, the XML declaration `<?xml version="1.0"?>`. After all, an XSLT stylesheet is an XML document.

- Second, a namespace declaration declaring the tag prefix of XSL, `xmlns:xsl="http://www.w3.org/TR/WD-xsl"`. This is the generally accepted default for XSLT stylesheets.

- Third, a lot of HTML tags. These tags will be inserted in the output document at the appropriate place dictated by the stylesheet.

Some of the things we haven't seen before are, first, the stylesheet delimiters `<xsl:stylesheet>…</xsl:stylesheet>`. These perform the same function as the CSS `<STYLE>` tag. Second, we haven't seen three new declarations that belong to the domain of the stylesheet:

- `xsl:template match=`
- `xsl:for-each select=`
- `xsl:value-of select=`

We'll cover these new instructions in depth in this chapter. Right now, I just want you to see that, as different as CSS and XSLT stylesheets are in appearance, they are also different in function.

Nodes and Trees, Not Documents

To understand the operation of XSLT stylesheets on XML data, we are going to have to learn to think a little bit differently than we have up to this point.

XSLT defines itself as a series of operations on a *tree*, which is a representation of an XML document. This tree is an intangible entity that has no defined application programming interface (API); it only describes the objects in the tree, their relationships, and their associated properties. Let's look at a more detailed portion of our XML process diagram and see what this new concept does for us.

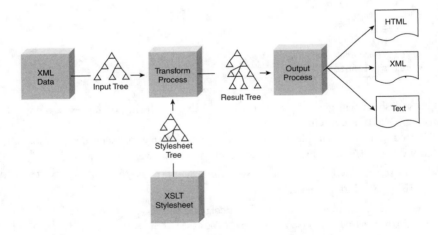

Figure 2.2   Modifying the tree via XSLT.

So the tree representation of data is combined in the transform process with the tree of the stylesheet to produce a new tree structure. The new tree can then be output in any of three formats: HTML, text, or XML. This isn't to say that other output formats cannot be generated, but these are the three outlined in the specification.

Now that we have the process diagrammed via the tree concept, let's look at an XML document itself in a tree-style format. Conceptually, there's nothing magical about thinking of an XML document as a tree. Listing 2.3 is a portion of our sample XML document.

Listing 2.3   **A Sample XML Document**

```
<PERSON PERSONID="p2">
  <NAME>
    <LAST>Tenney</LAST
    <FIRST>Corey</FIRST>
  </NAME>
  <ADDRESS>
    <STREET>211 Home Improvement Circle</STREET>
    <CITY>Roy, UT</CITY>
    <COUNTRY>USA</COUNTRY>
    <ZIP>64067</ZIP>
  </ADDRESS>
  <TEL/>
  <EMAIL>tenney@yardwork.com</EMAIL>
</PERSON>
```

Now let's look at this document as a tree representation.

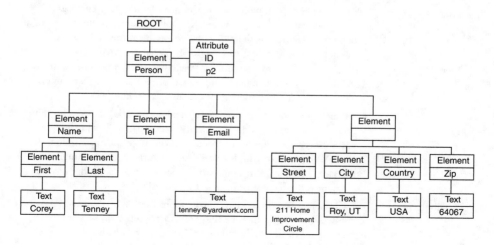

Figure 2.3   An XML document tree.

The ROOT element can be thought of as a representation of the document as a whole. It is the starting point for document processors.

The concept of a ROOT element comes from the WC3 XPath specification, which became a Recommendation on November 17, 1999. The specification is available at `http://www.w3.org/TR/1999/REC-xpath-19991116`. The primary purpose of XPath is to address *parts* of an XML document. To help accomplish this, it also provides basic methods for manipulation of strings, numbers, and Boolean values. It is important to know that XSLT relies very heavily on XPath.

Nodes

The entire concept of a document tree comes from XPath's model of an XML document as a tree of nodes. What is a node? In its simplest form, a *node* is defined as an object in a document tree. Another new object is a context node. This is defined as the node at which you are currently located in the tree during processing. Every time a process is carried out and you move to another node to process it, the context node changes to follow you. Processes are carried out, and relationships between nodes are stated as being in relation to the context node. If this is a little difficult to understand, I'll be showing an example in the next section, "Location Paths."

Table 2.2 shows the seven type of nodes contained in a document tree.

Table 2.2 **XML Document Nodes Types**

Node Type	Description
Root node	There is one and only one root node for every XML document. An important point here is that the root node is not the same thing as the document element, which is the singular element that encloses all other elements in a well-formed XML document. An illustration of a document element is the <RESUMES> element in the well-formed sample XML document of Chapter 1, "Database XML."
Element node	There is an element node for every element in the document. It is delineated by a starting and ending tag or, in the case of an empty element, just an empty element tag such as </TEL>.
	An element node may have a unique identifier (ID). This is the value of the attribute that is declared in the accompanying DTD as type <ID>. No two elements in a document can have the same unique ID. If an XML processor finds two elements in the same document with the same unique ID (meaning the document is invalid), the second element is treated as not having a unique ID.
Attribute node	Each element node can have an associated set of attribute nodes, which are declared within the opening tag of a tag set within an empty tag. Namespace declarations, although they appear to be attributes of the <STYLESHEET> tag by virtue of the *xmlns* designation, are not considered to be attribute nodes. They have their own node type, which is discussed later.

Node Type	Description
Text node	Character data is grouped into text nodes and never have an immediately following or preceding text node. These nodes are usually defined within a CDATA section of the accompanying DTD. A text node always has at least one character of data.
Comment node	There is a comment node for every comment in a document. These comments are delimited just as you would expect by the `<! — ... —>` entities. This definition does not apply to comments that occur within the document type declaration.
Processing instruction node	There is a processing instruction node for every processing instruction delimited by the usual `<?...?>`. The definition does not apply to any processing instruction that occurs within the document type declaration. Also, although the XML declaration `<?xml version = "1.0"?>` looks like a processing instruction, it is not considered to be one and never has a node in a document tree.
Namespace node	Each element has an associated set of namespace nodes, one for each distinct namespace prefix that is in scope for the element (including the XML prefix, which is implicitly declared by the XML Namespaces Recommendation) and one for the default namespace if one is in scope for the element.

Armed with these definitions, now I think we can revisit Figure 2.3 and make a lot more sense out of it.

Location Paths

There is one more set of definitions to learn before we dive into the actual structure of stylesheets. XPath introduces, along with other concepts that will be covered at various points in this chapter, the model of self, children, descendents, siblings, and ancestors. XPath uses these terms to describe the concept of *location paths*, or to put it succinctly, a means of navigation around an XML tree. Table 2.3 defines the location path entities.

Table 2.3   **XPath Location Path Entities**

Entity Name	Direction	Description
self	n/a	Identifies the context node.
child	Forward	Identifies the children of the context node.
parent	Reverse	Identifies the context node's parent if one exists.
descendent	Forward	Identifies the descendents of the context node, which are a child, a child of a child, and so on. Attribute nodes and namespace nodes are never considered descendents.

continues

Table 2.3 **Continued**

Entity Name	Direction	Description
ancestor	Reverse	Identifies the ancestors of the context node, which are a parent, a parent of a parent, and so on. The root node is always an ancestor unless it is the context node itself.
sibling	n/a	Identifies all nodes that are at the same depth as the context node in document order.
preceding-sibling	Reverse	Identifies all siblings in the same document as the context node that precede the context node in document order. This does not include ancestors, attribute nodes, or namespace nodes.
following-sibling	Forward	Identifies all siblings in the same document as the context node that follow the context node in document order. This does not include descendents, attribute nodes, or namespace nodes.

Remember the context node concept that I brought up in the earlier section "Nodes"? Well, these new terms like "children" and so on are defined in terms of a context node. Examples and syntax for these location paths will be discussed in the section "Patterns (Abbreviated Syntax)" later in this chapter. For now, though, I want you to see the interrelationships of these entities, and we'll do this utilizing our XML document tree in Figure 2.3 in concert with our sample document in Listing 2.3. Let's look at Table 2.4 and the element relationships expressed there, using keywords from XPath.

Table 2.4 **XPath Location Path Entity Relationships**

Entity	Nodes
self	Address (This is the context node.)
child	Street, city, country, zip
parent	Person
descendent	Street, city, country, zip, 211 Home Improvement Circle, Roy, UT, USA, 64067
ancestor	Person
sibling	Name, tel, email
preceding	Name, last, first, Tenney, Corey
preceding-sibling	Name
following	Tel, email, tenney@yardwork.com
following-sibling	Tel, email

Did the entities "preceding" and "following," along with their sibling counterparts, throw you?

Remember the definitions in Table 2.3. They are defined in terms of document order. If the tree diagram is not drawn exactly according to the document order, it can lead you to incorrect results. Be sure the diagram is correct before you use it to navigate a document.

Stylesheet Structure

How is a stylesheet laid out? Are there restrictions on element placement? Do they even contain elements? We'll answer these questions here.

A stylesheet contains a set of template rules. A template rule has two parts: a pattern, which is matched against nodes in the source tree, and a template, which details a portion of the result tree and how it is constructed (transformed). This enables a stylesheet to be applied to a wide document set that has similar source tree structures.

Associating Stylesheets with XML Documents

One note of importance here is that the XSLT specification does not designate how an XSLT stylesheet is associated with an XML document. The W3C does recommend, however, that XSL processors follow the method described in the W3C document "Associating Stylesheets with XML Documents Version 1.0" located at `http://www.w3.org/1999/06/REC-xml-stylesheet-19990629`. This document was made a W3C recommendation on June 29, 1999.

In essence, this document states that stylesheets should be associated with an XML document by using a processing instruction whose target is `xml-stylesheet`. This is similar to the behavior of the HTML 4.0 tag `<LINK REL="stylesheet">`. Here's an example:

```
<?xml-stylesheet href="mystyle.css" type="text/css"?>
```

Table 2.5 defines the following attributes for the `xml-stylesheet` statement.

Table 2.5   *xml-stylesheet* **Statement Attributes**

Attribute	Required	Default	Description
href	Yes	n/a	Specifies the URL of the stylesheet document. Example: `href="mystylesheet.xsl"`.
type	Yes	n/a	Specifies that this is a stylesheet document. Example: `type="text/css"`.
title	No	n/a	Specifies a title for this stylesheet.

continues

Table 2.5 **Continued**

Attribute	Required	Default	Description
media	No	n/a	Specifies that this stylesheet be designed for use with the specified media. For example, graphical displays, television screens, handheld devices, speech-based browsers, braille-based tactile devices, and so on. The currently defined media are as follows:

screen	Intended for nonpaged computer screens.
tty	Intended for media using a fixed-pitch character grid, such as teletypes, terminals, or portable devices with limited display capabilities.
tv	Intended for television-type devices (low resolution, color, limited scrollability).
projection	Intended for projectors.
handheld	Intended for handheld devices (small screen, monochrome, bitmapped graphics, limited bandwidth).
print	Intended for paged, opaque material and for documents viewed onscreen in print preview mode.
braille	Intended for braille tactile feed-back devices.
aural	Intended for speech synthesizers.
all	Suitable for all devices.

Attribute	Required	Default	Description
charset	No	n/a	The charset parameter identifies a character encoding, which is a method of converting a sequence of bytes into a sequence of characters. For one byte per character, this is straightforward. No conversion is necessary. For two (Unicode) or three (Universal Naming Convention) bytes per character, this becomes important.
alternate	No	"no"	Designates substitute versions for the document in which the link occurs, in case a specified stylesheet is unavailable.

To me, the `media` descriptor is the most interesting. It's rarely used today, but I think you can see there is a lot of potential for the various categories listed. For example, an XSL stylesheet could be utilized to transform an XML document into a Wireless Application Protocol (WAP) document.

Those of you who are HTML gurus might have noticed that the linguistics of the attributes are exactly as with `<LINK REL="stylesheet">` in HTML 4.0, with the exception of the `alternate` pseudo attribute. If `alternate="yes"` is specified, then the processing instruction has the linguistics of `<LINK REL="alternate stylesheet">` instead of `<LINK REL="stylesheet">`.

Let's look at some of the tags and their place in a stylesheet and then move on to a detailed discussion of these things called templates.

<xsl:stylesheet>

This is the base tag for an XSL stylesheet. It encompasses the entire document. Here is its definition with attributes:

```
<xsl:stylesheet>
    version = number>
    <!-- Content: (xsl:import, other top-level-elements) -->
</xsl:stylesheet>
```

An `<xsl:stylesheet>` element *must* have a version attribute, indicating the version of XSLT that the stylesheet requires. As of this writing, the version of XSLT should be 1.0. I think this value will change very soon to 1.1. This requirement will allow compatibility with future versions of XSLT. Stylesheets can check for the version number and process accordingly. As you know, in any programming language, as versions change so does the language.

`<xsl:transform>` is allowed as a synonym for `<xsl:stylesheet>`, and it has the identical attributes and definitions as `<xsl:stylesheet>`.

Layout and Order of Elements

The `<xsl:stylesheet>` element can contain the following types of elements:

- `xsl:import`
- `xsl:include`
- `xsl:strip-space`
- `xsl:preserve-space`
- `xsl:output`
- `xsl:key`
- `xsl:decimal-format`
- `xsl:namespace-alias`

- `xsl:attribute-set`
- `xsl:variable`
- `xsl:param`
- `xsl:template`

We'll be covering most of these in the rest of this chapter.

An element occurring as an immediate child of the `<xsl:stylesheet>` element is called a *top-level* element. The order in which these children occur isn't important except for `xsl:import` elements. If an `xsl:import` element occurs in a stylesheet, it must be the immediate child of the `<xsl:stylesheet>` element. The other elements can be ordered in any way you want, and as a result, it isn't necessary for stylesheet creation tools to provide control over the order in which the elements occur. (This should serve to explain the `comment` tag that's in the example in the preceding section.)

Example of Stylesheet Structure

Listing 2.4 is an example of the structure of a stylesheet. I've left this as a bare-bones example to illustrate element layout. Ellipses (...) indicate where I've left out attribute values or content. Although this example shows one of each type of allowed element, stylesheets do not have to have all these elements, and there can be more than one of each of them.

Listing 2.4 **Sample Stylesheet Structure**

```
<xsl:stylesheet version="1.0"
                xmlns:xsl="http://www.w3.org/1999/XSL/Transform">
  <xsl:import href="..."/>

  <xsl:include href="..."/>

  <xsl:strip-space elements="..."/>

  <xsl:preserve-space elements="..."/>

  <xsl:output method="..."/>

  <xsl:key name="..." match="..." use="..."/>

  <xsl:decimal-format name="..."/>

  <xsl:namespace-alias stylesheet-prefix="..." result-prefix="..."/>

  <xsl:attribute-set name="...">

  </xsl:attribute-set>

  <xsl:variable name="...">...</xsl:variable>
```

```
<xsl:param name="...">...</xsl:param>

<xsl:template match="...">

</xsl:template>

<xsl:template name="...">

</xsl:template>
</xsl:stylesheet>
```

Again, we'll be discussing most of these elements shortly.

Templates

Templates consist of a pattern match to the source tree, a set of rules to apply to generate the result tree, and possibly data to transfer to the result tree.

A template is employed by a source element to create part of the result tree. Construction of the result tree starts by finding the template rule for the root node and employing its template. A template also can contain elements from the XSLT namespace that are instructions for creating result tree fragments or parts of the result tree. When a template is employed, each instruction in the template is executed and replaced by the result tree fragment it creates.

A template can contain elements that specify literal result element structure. A *literal result element* is literal text within a template that is transferred to the output tree as is (literally). An example of this that you'll see many times in this book is a template that has the literal text element <HTML>, which is the starting tag for an HTML document. When a source tree node match is found for the template that contains this literal element, the <HTML> tag will be transferred to the result tree, and an HTML document will be started. We'll see examples very shortly.

Let's begin with the first part of a template, a discussion of patterns and how we match them. It's impossible to generate a result tree that means anything if we incorrectly identify the element we want to modify.

Patterns (Abbreviated Syntax)

This section is called "Abbreviated Syntax" for a reason. Remember that the XPath specification, among other important things, defines how we navigate around an XML document using location paths. Well, Microsoft does not support the entire XPath specification, and rather than waste your time giving you the entire specification, I'll explain what is called the *abbreviated syntax*. When we get to the point where the supported syntax will be necessary to understand what we're doing, I'll explain in detail what Microsoft supports and what it doesn't.

As shown in the example I gave previously, `xsl:template` uses the `"match="` attribute to determine whether it should apply its rules to the current context node. A pattern specifies a set of conditions on a node. A node that satisfies the conditions matches the pattern; a node that does not satisfy the conditions does not match the pattern.

The abbreviated form of pattern matching is, as I am sure you'll notice, uncannily similar to the method UNIX and DOS use to navigate their directory structure. Hopefully, this will make it simpler for you to learn the syntax.

Table 2.6 contains the symbols used for pattern matching and describes how they are employed. Extensive examples will be given in the next section.

Table 2.6 **Symbols Used for Pattern Matching**

Symbol	Description
/	This is the basic match pattern used to match an element ancestry. It separates ancestor from parent from child.
//	Allows any number of elements to appear between the element searched for and an ancestor.
.	Represents the context node.
..	Represents the parent of the context node.
@	Specifies an attribute.
*	This is the wildcard match. It matches any element.
| (pipe)	This is the OR function. It will match on one element OR the other
[]	Performs a test. Used in concert with other symbols. It matches provided that the test in parentheses is valid.
not()	Used with the test brackets to reverse the conditions of the test.
pi()	Matches a processing instruction node.
comment()	Matches a comment node.
text()	Matches a text node.

Pattern Examples

So, armed with the definitions listed in Table 2.6, we should be able to identify just about any node of an XML document. Let's take our original XML document from Chapter 1, given again in Listing 2.5, and look at some examples to make sure we know how these work. The examples are given in Table 2.7.

Listing 2.5 **Sample XML Document**

```
<!-- ******* Resumes for Potential Hires ******* -->
<RESUMES xmlns='http://www.myorg.net/tags'>
  <PERSON PERSONID="p1">
    <NAME>
      <LAST>Shelton</LAST>
      <FIRST>Rick</FIRST>
    </NAME>
    <ADDRESS>
      <STREET>911 Intranet Ave.</STREET>
      <CITY>Canberra</CITY>
      <COUNTRY>Australia</COUNTRY>
      <PC>A34G-90</PC
    </ADDRESS>
    <TEL>(+612) 111-2345</TEL>
    <EMAIL>shelton@somewhere.com</EMAIL>
  </PERSON>

  <PERSON PERSONID="p2">
    <NAME>
      <LAST>Tenney</LAST
      <FIRST>Corey</FIRST>
    </NAME>
    <ADDRESS>
      <STREET>211 Yardwork Circle</STREET>
      <CITY>Roy, UT</CITY>
      <COUNTRY>USA</COUNTRY>
      <ZIP>64067</ZIP>
    </ADDRESS>
    <TEL/>
    <EMAIL>tenney@yardwork.com</EMAIL>
  </PERSON>
</RESUMES>
```

Table 2.7 **XPath Pattern Examples**

Pattern	Description
`<xsl:template match="address/zip">`	Matches a zip code element with an address parent.
	This will not match this document fragment because address is not the parent of `<zip>`.
	`<person>`
	`<zip>`

continues

Table 2.7   **Continued**

Pattern	Description
	It also will not match this document fragment because the `address` element is not the *direct* parent of `<zip>`.
	`<address>`
	`<home>`
	`<zip>`
`<xsl:template match="address//zip">`	Matches a `<zip>` element with an `address` ancestor and any combination of ancestors (including 0) in between. Now `address//zip` matches the fragment.
	`<address>`
	`<home>`
	`<zip>`
	You can really get specific here. Now `resumes//address/zip` matches a `zip` element with an immediate parent of `address` and an ancestor of `resumes`.
`<xsl:template match="ancestor (person)/name">`	Matches the `name` element of the first person ancestor of the context node. The person element does not have to be the immediate parent of the context node.
`<xsl:template match="./street">`	Matches the `street` element, which is the direct child of the context node.
	If the context node were `city`, then `street` would not match. A context node of `address` would match.
`<xsl:template match="../street">`	Matches the `street` element that is a sibling of the context node.
	If the context node were `city`, then `street` would match. A context node of `address` would not match.
`<xsl:template match="*/city">`	Matches all occurrences of the `city` element where it is the direct child of any element.
	If the `city` element is the root element, this doesn't work.
	Reversing our template to `city/*` matches any element that has the `city` element as its immediate parent.
`<xsl:template match="city|state">`	Matches either the `city` element or the `state` element.

Pattern	Description
`<xsl:template match= "address[pc]/street">`	Matches `street` elements that have an immediate parent of `address`. The `address` element must have a `pc` direct child (`pc` and `street` are siblings).
`<xsl:template match= "person[@personid]">`	Matches `person` elements that have a `personid` attribute. The @ symbol and the brackets work in concert. You can be very specific here also. `person[@personid='p1']` matches any `person` element that has a `personid` attribute equal to p1.
`<xsl:template match= "person[not(@personid='p1')]">`	Matches all `person` elements that do not have a `personid` attribute of p1.
`<xsl:template match= "person/comment()">`	Matches any `comment` node that is a child of a `person` element.
`<xsl:template match= "person/pi(word)">`	Matches any processing instruction node that is a child of a `person` element and uses the `word` application. `<person>   <?word version="6.0" document="mydoc.ndx" ?> </person>`

Template Rules

Listing 2.6 gives the template tag definition.

Listing 2.6 **Template Tag Syntax**

```
<!-- Category: top-level-element -->
<xsl:template
    match = pattern
    name = name
    priority = number
    mode = name>
    <!-- Content: (instructions, data) -->
</xsl:template>
```

When a stylesheet is applied to an XML source document for processing, the first thing the processor does is convert these documents into a stylesheet tree and a source tree, respectively, in memory. After this is accomplished, the transformation process can begin.

Root Node "/"

The first order of business for the transformation process is to find the root node of the source document, like this:

```
<xsl:template match="/">
...
</xsl:template>
```

There should be a template like the previous one that locates this root node. If there is more than one template that could be a candidate for processing the root, there is an established order of precedence so that only one will perform the processing.

- Templates with greater importance are chosen over those of lesser importance. Stylesheet templates imported inside another stylesheet are of lesser importance than the stylesheet that imported them.

- After the previous test, the template with the highest priority is chosen as specified by the priority attribute of the template.

Applying Template Rules

Let's look a little deeper into what exactly is contained within this template. Take a look at the comment node in the template definition given in Listing 2.6. It states that there are instructions and data and that's all. We've seen this in a previous discussion in this chapter. The instructions in the template are carried out one by one, and the data is transferred to the result tree as it is encountered in the processing. The data contained in the template is referred to as literal result elements, as shown by Listing 2.7.

Listing 2.7 **Literal Result Elements**

```
<xsl:template match="/">
    <xsl:comment>My first template</xsl:comment>
    <HTML>
...
    </HTML>
    This is just text
</xsl:template>
```

This template consists of an instruction (`xsl:comment`), some literal result elements (the two HTML elements), and text. When this template is employed, the instructions will be executed according to their rules, the literal result elements will be copied as element nodes, and the text will be copied as a text node.

Let's take our template example from Listing 2.7 a little further. Look at Listing 2.8.

Listing 2.8 **Apply Templates with Literal Result Elements**

```
<xsl:template match="/">
    <xsl:comment>My first template</xsl:comment>
    <HTML>
<BODY>            <xsl:apply-templates/>
        </BODY>
    </HTML>
    This is just text
</xsl:template>
```

In addition to the instruction and literal result elements we just discussed, we now have two additional literal result elements (the two BODY tags), but we also have something new here: an XSL instruction! This instruction is of critical importance when written as it is here. This instruction says, *"Select all child nodes of the current element and employ the matching template rule for each of them if any exist."*

What does all this mean? Let's say our XML document is well formed and therefore has a single document element <resumes>. Sound familiar? Our processor will begin to search our stylesheet and try to find a template that matches <resumes>, like this one:

```
<xsl:template match="resumes"
```

Listing 2.9 gives the <xsl:apply-templates> definition. If and when it finds a matching template, it will carry out the same procedures that our previous template did. It will check for multiple template matches and use the precedence rules to determine the correct one to use. If no template is found, the appropriate built-in template will be called. The matching template is processed. By the way, if the node being processed has no child nodes, <xsl:apply-templates/> doesn't do anything.

Listing 2.9 *<xsl:apply-templates>* **Definition**

```
<!-- Category: instruction -->
<xsl:apply-templates
    select = node-set-expression
    mode = qname>
    <!-- Content: (xsl:sort | xsl:with-param)* -->
</xsl:apply-templates>
```

The select attribute is used to process nodes, specifically selected nodes instead of processing every child node. The value of the select attribute is an XPath expression, which must evaluate to a set of nodes. The selected set of nodes is processed in document order unless you've specified a sort order. We'll talk about sorting shortly.

The following example processes all of the zip code or postal code children of the address node:

```
<xsl:template match="address">
    <xsl:apply-templates select="pc|zip">
</xsl:template>
```

The following example processes all of the `first` elements of the `name` elements that are children of `person`:

```
<xsl:template match="person">
  <fo:inline-sequence>
    <xsl:apply-templates select="name/first"/>
  </fo:inline-sequence>
</xsl:template>
```

This example processes all of the `street` descendant elements of the `resumes` element.

```
<xsl:template match="resumes">
    <xsl:apply-templates select=".//street"/>
</xsl:template>
```

Hopefully, by now you've made the connection between these template matches and how you move the context node around.

<xsl:value-of>

The `<xsl:value-of>` element creates a text node in the result tree. The `select` attribute, which is mandatory, is an XPath expression identical to the expressions used in the `"select="` attribute of `apply-templates`. This XPath expression is evaluated, and the resulting object is converted to a string, which specifies the string value of the created text node. If the string is empty, no text node will be created. Examine the following code:

```
<!-- Category: instruction -->
<xsl:value-of
   select = string-expression
   disable-output-escaping = "yes" | "no"
/>
```

For example, Listing 2.10 creates an HTML paragraph from a `last` child of a `name` element. The paragraph will contain the test "`Last name is: `" followed by the value of the `last` element, which is the current node.

Listing 2.10 **Demonstrating the *value-of* Clause**

```
<xsl:template match="name/last">
  <p>
   <xsl:text>Last name is : </xsl:text>
   <xsl:value-of select="last"/>
  </p>
</xsl:template>
```

We'll be talking about `xsl:text` later in this chapter. For now, just know that whatever is between the opening and closing `xsl:text` element will transfer to the result tree.

Listing 2.11 accomplishes the exact same thing. Notice the different `select` expression.

Listing 2.11   **Specifying the "." to Select the Current Element**

```
<xsl:template match="name/last">
  <p>
   <xsl:text>Last name is : </xsl:text>
   <xsl:value-of select="."/>
  </p>
</xsl:template>
```

In one last example here, Listing 2.12 creates an HTML paragraph from a `person` element with `first` and `last` children elements. The paragraph will contain the string value of the `first` child element of the current node followed by a space and the string value of the `last` child element of the current node.

Listing 2.12   **Adding Whitespace**

```
<xsl:template match="person">
  <p>
   <xsl:value-of select="given-name"/>
   <xsl:text> </xsl:text>
   <xsl:value-of select="family-name"/>
  </p>
</xsl:template>
```

Default Templates

If no matching template can be found for a `<xsl:apply-templates match= >` instruction, the built-in template rules are used.

Table 2.8 illustrates what the built-in template rules do for each type of node.

Table 2.8   **Default Rules for Template Matches**

Node	Built-In Rule
Root	Call `<xsl:apply-templates>` to process the root node's children, allowing processing to continue.
Element	Call `<xsl:apply-templates>` to process this node's children, allowing processing to continue.
Attribute	Copy the attribute value to the result tree as text, not as an attribute node.
Text	Copy the text to the result tree.
Comment	Do nothing.
Processing instruction	Do nothing.
Namespace	Do nothing.

There is no pattern that can match a namespace node, so the built-in template rule is the only template rule applied for namespace nodes.

Also, the built-in template rules have lower import precedence than any other template rule. Thus, they can be overridden by including an explicit template rule.

Named Templates

You can directly employ a template by name using the `xsl:call-template` element, which has a required `name` attribute that identifies the template to be employed. An `xsl:template` element that has a defined `name` attribute specifies a named template, as illustrated by the following example:

```
<!-- Category: instruction -->
<xsl:call-template
    name = qname>
    <!-- Content: xsl:with-param* -->
</xsl:call-template>
```

The value of the `name` attribute is a `QName`. A `QName` is an XML name that optionally has a namespace prefix attached. An example of a nonprefixed name is `resume` or `person`. An example of a prefixed name is `xsl:address` or `xsl:street`. If the `QName` has a prefix, it must match a namespace that is in scope at the location the name is used.

The `match`, `mode`, and `priority` attributes on an `xsl:template` element do not affect whether the template is invoked by an `xsl:call-template` element. Similarly, the `name` attribute on an `xsl:template` element does not affect whether the template is invoked by an `xsl:apply-templates` element.

Here are some important points to remember about `xsl:template`:

- Having a `name` attribute present does not stop the possibility of an `xsl:template` also having a match attribute.

- Unlike `xsl:apply-templates`, `xsl:call-template` does not change the context node.

- Stylesheets cannot contain more than one template with the same name and same import precedence.

Creating the Tree

Up to this point, we've taken what's in the source tree and the stylesheet tree and created a result tree that is basically a rigid copy of what's in the source tree. This doesn't do much for flexibility. What if we have to create brand-new elements in the result tree based on what we find in the source tree? How about taking an element in the source tree and converting it to an attribute of a result tree element or taking an attribute of the source tree and making it an element in the result tree? XSLT elements such as `xsl:element`, `xsl:attribute`, and `xsl:text`, when used in conjunction with attribute templates, can accomplish these conversions. In essence, with these new XSLT elements, we can create, delete, or modify XML elements and attributes on the fly. The following sections discuss these elements.

Attribute Templates

Let's say we want to change the `name` element in our original resumes document from having the children elements of `first` and `last` to having the attributes of `first` and `last`. We want to change

```
<NAME>
  <LAST>…</LAST>
  <FIRST>…</FIRST>
</NAME>
```

to

```
<NAME LAST="…" FIRST="…" />
```

How can we do this? One thing we definitely can't do is this:

```
<xsl:template match="NAME">
  <NAME LAST="<xsl:value-of select='LAST'/>"
        FIRST="<xsl:value-of select='FIRST'/>"
  />
```

Why not? The < character is not allowed inside attribute values.

So what do we do? We create an *attribute value template*. In an attribute value that is interpreted as an attribute value template, an XPath expression can be used by surrounding the XPath expression with curly braces ({}). The expression, together with its surrounding curly braces, will be replaced by the result of evaluating the expression and converting the resulting object to a string. Listing 2.13 gives the partial template employed to accomplish what we want.

Listing 2.13   **XSLT Template Utilizing Attribute Value Templates**

```
<xsl:template match="NAME">
  <NAME LAST="{LAST}'
        FIRST="{FIRST}"

  />
  />
```

The applicable fragment of the source tree originally was as follows:

```
<PERSON PERSONID="p1">
  <NAME>
    <LAST>Shelton</LAST>
    <FIRST>Rick</FIRST>
  </NAME>
```

After applying the template in Listing 2.13, the result tree fragment will be as follows:

```
<PERSON PERSONID="p1">
   <NAME LAST="Shelton" FIRST="Rick"
```

Creating New Elements

Now let's create new elements. The `xsl:element` element creates new elements in the result tree. The name of a new element to be created is specified by a required `name` attribute and an optional `namespace` attribute. The `name` attribute will be an attribute value template, which we learned about in the previous section. The `xsl:element` element's content is a template for the attributes and children of the element created in the result tree, as illustrated in Listing 2.14.

Listing 2.14 **Syntax for the *<xsl:element...>* Element**

```
<!-- Category: instruction -->
<xsl:element
  name = { qname }
  namespace = { uri-reference }
  <!-- Content: template -->
</xsl:element>
```

Again, the best way of teaching is by example, so first we take our resumes file and add an element to it. Suppose we have our last example, in which the `name` element has the two attributes of `first` and `last`. We want to change the two attributes to new elements named `FIRST` and `LAST`. These two new elements will be children of the `name` element. Here's our source tree:

```
<PERSON PERSONID="p1">
   <NAME LAST="{LAST}"
         FIRST="{FIRST}"
   />
```

Listing 2.15 shows the template used to create the new elements.

Listing 2.15 **The Template that Creates New Elements**

```
<xsl:template match="NAME">
  <NAME>
    <xsl:element name={@LAST}
      <xsl:value-of select="LAST">
    </xsl:element>
    <xsl:element name={@FIRST}
      <xsl:value-of select="FIRST">
    </xsl:element>
  </NAME>
  />
```

Here's our result tree:

```
<PERSON PERSONID="p1">
  <NAME>
    <LAST>Shelton</LAST>
    <FIRST>Rick</FIRST>
  </NAME>
```

Creating New Attributes

In the same way that we created new elements in the preceding section, we can create new attributes. The name of a new element to be created is specified by a required `name` attribute and an optional `namespace` attribute. The `name` attribute will be an attribute value template. An `xsl:attribute` element adds an attribute node to the element node in which it is contained. The content of the `xsl:attribute` element is a template for the value of the created attribute, as illustrated in Listing 2.16.

Listing 2.16   **Syntax for the** *<xsl:attribute...>* **Element**

```
<!-- Category: instruction -->
<xsl:attribute
  name = { qname }
  namespace = { uri-reference }>
  <!-- Content: template -->
</xsl:attribute>
```

Again, let's go to examples. We'll take the `name` element of our document and make the `email` element (depending on what's there) a new attribute. Listing 2.17 is our source tree fragment, and Listing 2.18 is our template.

Listing 2.17   **Source Tree Element Used in Listing 2.18**

```
<NAME>
  <LAST>Shelton</LAST>
  <FIRST>Rick</FIRST>
</NAME>
<ADDRESS>
  <STREET>911 Intranet Ave.</STREET>
  <CITY>Canberra</CITY>
  <COUNTRY>Australia</COUNTRY>
  <PC>A34G-90</PC>
</ADDRESS>
<TEL>(+612) 111-2345</TEL>
<EMAIL>shelton@somewhere.com</EMAIL>
```

Listing 2.18 **Template File that Makes the *email* Element an Attribute**

```
<xsl:template match="NAME">
  <NAME>
    <xsl:attribute name={EMAIL}
      <xsl:value-of select="EMAIL">
    </xsl:element>
  </NAME>
/>
```

Here's the result tree fragment:

```
<NAME EMAIL="shelton@somewhere.com">
  <LAST>Shelton</LAST>
  <FIRST>Rick</FIRST>
</NAME>
```

Copying Nodes

The `xsl:copy` element provides an easy way to copy the current node and its namespace nodes. The attributes and children of the node are not automatically copied, though. This is what gives `xsl:copy` its power. You can specify exactly what you want copied and what you don't want copied, as illustrated in the following example:

```
<!-- Category: instruction -->
<xsl:copy
  use-attribute-sets = qnames>
  <!-- Content: template -->
</xsl:copy>
```

The following example shows how I would generate a result tree that contained only the elements of the source tree. All comments, processing instructions, text, and attributes would be filtered out as shown.

```
<xsl:template match="*">
  <xsl:copy>
    <xsl:apply-templates select="*"/>
  </xsl:copy>
</xsl:template>
```

The result of this would be as in Listing 2.19.

Listing 2.19 **Filtering Out Everything but the Elements**

```
<RESUMES>
  <PERSON>
    <NAME>
      <LAST></LAST>
      <FIRST></FIRST>
    </NAME>
ETC.
```

I didn't tell the template to copy text nodes, so no element content was copied. If I wanted the content, the match and select expressions should be "`* | text()`".

Creating Text Nodes

A template also can contain text nodes. Each text will create a text node with the same string value in the result tree. This enables the stylesheet author to replace whole elements with text, for example, if need be. This is illustrated in the following example:

```
<!-- Category: instruction -->
<xsl:text
  disable-output-escaping = "yes" | "no">
  <!-- Content: #PCDATA -->
</xsl:text>
```

One reason to use `xsl:text` elements is to insert whitespace in the result tree. If we were to combine the person's first and last name into a single element, we could insert a space character between them, as in Listing 2.20.

Listing 2.20 **Inserting Whitespace**

```
<xsl:template match="NAME">
  <NAME>
    <xsl:value-of select="FIRST">
    <xsl:text> </xsl:text>          <!--pass a single space character -->
    <xsl:value-of select="LAST">
  </NAME>
/>
```

It is your responsibility as the stylesheet author to explicitly generate any spaces that are needed in the result.

Remember the entities that we talked about when we were discussing DTDs? I didn't think so. Here's a list of them in Table 2.9.

Table 2.9 **Entities**

Character	Entity
& (ampersand)	&amp;
' (apostrophe)	&apos;
< (less than)	&lt;
> (greater than)	&gt;
" (quote)	&quot;

The problem with these entities is that text is processed at the tree level, so putting markup of < in a template will be represented in the stylesheet tree by a text node that includes the character <. This will create a text node in the result tree that contains a < character, which will be represented by the markup < (or an equivalent character reference) when the result tree is output as an XML document. To prevent this from happening, set the `disable-output-escaping` of the `xsl:text` element to "yes", as shown:

```
<xsl:text disable-output-escaping="yes">
  &lt;NAME&lt;         <!--another way to create a NAME element -->
</xsl:text>
```

The output document will contain `<NAME>`.

<xsl:comment>

The `<xsl:comment>` element creates a comment node in the result tree. The content of the `<xsl:comment>` element is a template for the string value of the comment node. The following example illustrates the syntax:

```
<!-- Category: instruction -->
<xsl:comment>
  <!-- Content: template -->
</xsl:comment>
For example,
<xsl:comment>
  This file was generated via an XSL Transformation.
</xsl:comment>
```

This would create the following comment:

```
<!-- This file was generated via an XSL Transformation.-->
```

<xsl:processing-instruction>

The `<xsl:processing-instruction>` element creates a processing instruction node. The `<xsl:processing-instruction>` content is a template for the string value of the processing instruction node that is generated as shown:

```
<!-- Category: instruction -->
<xsl:processing-instruction
  name = { ncname }>
  <!-- Content: template -->
</xsl:processing-instruction>
```

The `<xsl:processing-instruction>` element has a required `name` attribute that specifies the name of the processing instruction node, as shown in the following example. The value of the `name` attribute is interpreted as an attribute value template. The following code generates the processing instruction:

```
<xsl:processing-instruction
    name="xml-stylesheet">
    href="resumes.css"
    type="text/css"
</xsl:processing-instruction>
```

Formatting Numbers for Output

Formatting numbers becomes especially important for HTML output. XSL Transformations provide several elements and functions that convert numeric formats to readable strings. In this section, we'll cover two of these methods to give you a taste of what's possible: `<xsl:decimal-format>` and the `format-number()` function.

<xsl:decimal-format>

The `<xsl:decimal-format>` function defines the characters and symbols used by the `format-number()` function when converting numbers to human readable strings, as shown by Listing 2.21.

Listing 2.21   **Syntax for the** *<xsl:decimal-format...>* **Element**

```
<!-- Category: top-level-element -->
<xsl:decimal-format
  name = qname
  decimal-separator = char
  grouping-separator = char
  infinity = string
  minus-sign = char
  NaN = string
  percent = char
  per-mille = char
  zero-digit = char
  digit = char
  pattern-separator = char />
```

All the attributes are optional and are defined in Table 2.10.

Table 2.10   **Decimal-Format Attribute Definitions**

Attribute	Value	Default	Description
name	QName	n/a	The name of the format that, if omitted, specifies the default decimal format.
decimal separator	Character	.	Separates the integral and decimal parts of a number.
grouping separator	Character	,	Separates groups of numbers.
infinity	String	Infinity	String that represents the value infinity.
minus sign	Character	-	Indicates negative numbers.
NaN	String	NaN	String that represents the value NaN (not a number).

continues

Table 2.10   **Continued**

Attribute	Value	Default	Description
percent	Character	%	Indicates percentages.
per-mille	Character	‰	Indicates per-mille (per thousand).
zero digit	Character	0	Indicates where a digit is required.
digit	Character	#	Indicates where a digit might appears unless it's a leading or trailing zero
pattern separator	Character	;	Indicates the separator for positive and negative format patterns.

format–number( ) Function

The `format-number` (*number*, *format*, name) function converts numbers into human readable strings. The `<xsl:decimal-format>` element utilizes this function to provide the format for the string. This function draws on the formatting specification defined in Java 1.1. For detailed information, that is the place to look.

The three arguments are defined as follows:

- number. This is the numeric input value.
- format. This is a format pattern string explained later in this chapter.
- name. This is the name (QName) string of a decimal format created by the `<xsl:decimal-format>` element. If no named format is present, a `default decimal-format` is used. A default format is provided by specifying a `<xsl:decimal-format>` element and not giving it a name.

Although you can use `<xsl:decimal-format>` to use any character you want for the following values, the default is given. The characters used in specifying the output format are given in Table 2.11. Examples of the usage of different formatting functions are given in Table 2.12.

Table 2.11   **Formatting Characters**

Character	Default	Description
Zero-digit	0	A digit always appears at this point.
Digit	#	A digit may appear at this point unless it's a leading or trailing zero.
Decimal point	.	Separates the integral and decimal parts of a number.
Grouping separator	,	Separates groups of numbers.

Character	Default	Description
Minus sign	-	Indicates negative numbers.
Percent sign	%	A number multiplied by 100 and shown as a percent.
Per-mille	%	A number multiplied by 1,000 and shown as per-mille.
Pattern separator	;	Separates the positive and negative format patterns. This enables you to specify separate patterns for each. See the examples.
Apostrophe	'	Escapes special characters in the output so that no translation takes place. To have an output of "★★94" use the format pattern '★★'00.
E	n/a	Separates mantissa and exponent in scientific notation.
⬚	n/a	The universal currency symbol (#xA4), which must be in single quotes (different Java versions handle this differently).

Table 2.12 **Formatting Examples**

Number	Format Pattern	Result
5678.9	#,#00.00	5,678.90
1000000	#,##0.0#	1,000,000.0
0567	#,##0.0#	567.0
.33	#00%	33%
−4.5	#0.0#;(#0.0#)	(4.5)

Conditional Processing

XSL Transformations have the capability to make decisions at run-time (that is, during processing of the source tree). They have the equivalent of the `if` statement and also the equivalent of the `switch` statement as used in other languages. Both of these elements perform a test on an expression and proceed accordingly.

These elements use XPath functions to perform their tests, which we have not covered and will not cover in detail. I'll explain what each of the functions does when it is used. A list of the XPath functions supported by Microsoft can be found in Appendix C.

The *<xsl:if>* Element

The `<xsl:if>` element performs a Boolean test, as illustrated in the following example, that does one of two possible actions.

```
<!-- Category: instruction -->
<xsl:if
  test = boolean-expression>
  <!-- Content: template -->
</xsl:if>
```

Here's an example that follows the syntax in the preceding example. The `position()` function and what this code accomplishes are explained in the sidebar.

```
<xsl:template match="NAME">
  <xsl:value-of select="FIRST"/>
  <xsl:value-of select="LAST"/>
  <xsl:if test="position() != last()">, </xsl:if>
</xsl:template>
```

The `position()` function returns the value of the position of the context element. During processing, each node is given a position value. The first element starts at 1. The `last()` function returns the number of the last node in the tree. In this example, these functions tell the processor when the last node is being processed so that a comma will not be added to the end of the list.

After each first and last name combination is output, a comma and space are added. The result is a comma-separated list of names like this:

Scott Fitchet, Stephanie Wall, Rubi Olis, John Griffin

The *<xsl:choose>* Element

The `<xsl:choose>` element, as illustrated in Listing 2.22, selects between multiple choices. If there are only two items from which to choose, it performs the equivalent of the *IF-THEN-ELSE* statement. If there are more than two alternatives, it performs the equivalent of the `switch` or `select` statement used in other languages.

Listing 2.22   **Syntax for the *<xsl:choose...>* Element**

```
<!-- Category: instruction -->
<xsl:choose>
  <!-- Content: (xsl:when+, xsl:otherwise?) -->
<xsl:when
  test = boolean-expression>
  <!-- Content: template -->
</xsl:when>
<xsl:otherwise>
  <!-- Content: template -->
</xsl:otherwise>
</xsl:choose>
```

The <xsl:choose> element also has two other elements associated with it that allow it to perform its function.

The *<xsl:when>* Element

Each <xsl:when> element has a single attribute, test, that is identical to the test attribute of the <xsl:if> element. The content of the <xsl:when> element is a template. When an <xsl:choose> element is processed, each of the <xsl:when> elements is tested in turn by converting the expression to a Boolean value. The content of the first, and only the first, <xsl:when> element whose test is true is used.

The *<xsl:otherwise>* Element

Each <xsl:choose> element has an optional <xsl:otherwise> element. If no <xsl:when> is true, the content of the <xsl:otherwise> element is used. If no <xsl:when> element is true and no <xsl:otherwise> element is present, no output is generated.

Looping

The <xsl:for-each> element processes a set of nodes selected by an XPath expression and performs the same processing on each of these nodes. The select attribute is required and contains the XPath expression, which selects the node set to process. The following example illustrates the syntax for the <xsl:for-each...> element

```
<!-- Category: instruction -->
<xsl:for-each>
  select = node-set-expression>
  <!-- Content: (template) -->
</xsl:for-each>
```

For example, take an XML document with the structure illustrated in Listing 2.23:

Listing 2.23   **XML Document Structure**

```
<resumes>
  <person>
    <name>
      <first>...</first>
      <last>...</last>
... </name>
  </person>
  <person>
    <name>
    <first>...</first>
    <last>...</last>
...</name>
  </person>
</resumes>
```

The example shown in Listing 2.24 would create an HTML document containing a
table with a row for each `person` element.

Listing 2.24 **Resulting HTML Document**

```
<xsl:template match="/">
  <html>
    <head>
      <title>Resumes</title>
    </head>
    <body>
      <table>
      <tbody>
      <xsl:for-each select="resumes/person">
        <tr>
          <th>
            <xsl:apply-templates select="name"/>
          </th>
          <td>
            <xsl:value-of select="last"/>
          </td>
          <td>
            <xsl:value-of select="first"/>
          </td>
        </tr>
      </xsl:for-each>
      </tbody>
      </table>
    </body>
  </html>
</xsl:template>
```

Controlling Output

An XSL stylesheet is abstractly processed in two stages. The first step creates a result
tree from a source tree, and the second step generates serialized output of this result
tree. The `<xsl:output>` element governs this second step. This process isn't required by
the specification; in fact, if a processor doesn't provide output in serial format, this element is ignored. Listing 2.25 shows an example.

Listing 2.25 **Syntax for the *<xsl:output...>* Element**

```
<!-- Category: top-level-element -->
<xsl:output
    method = "xml" | "html" | "text" | qname-but-not-ncname
    version = nmtoken
    encoding = string
    omit-xml-declaration = "yes" | "no"
```

```
   standalone = "yes" | "no"
   doctype-public = string
   doctype-system = string
   cdata-section-elements = qnames
   indent = "yes" | "no"
   media-type = string
 />
```

The following sections discuss the three output formats of the `<xsl:output>` element.

XML Output Method

Setting the `method` attribute to `XML` forces XML output. This is also the default output format and the one invoked if the `method` attribute is not present. Usually, the output form will be a well-formed XML document, but it is only required to be an XML fragment that can be incorporated into another XML document with an entity reference such as `"&legal_woes"`.

HTML Output Method

Setting the `method` attribute to `HTML` forces HTML output. Processing instructions (`<?...?>`, and so on will be filtered from the output, which is standard HTML 4.0. Entity references do not require escaping, meaning `"<"` will be output as `"<"` net `"&lt;"`.

Have you found yourself wondering how a stylesheet knows that the output tree it's generating is in HTML format without being told? There are three rules that must be followed:

- There must be at least one `child` element.
- The first element child of the root node must be `<HTML>` (dead giveaway, huh?). This is case insensitive.
- There can be no test nodes before the `<HTML>` element unless they consist solely of whitespace.

Text Output Method

Setting the `method` attribute to `text` forces text output. The `text` output method outputs the result tree by outputting the string value of every text node in the result tree in document order without any escaping. All other nodes are ignored.

A fourth output method is provided for vendor extensions and is invoked by providing a QName for the `method` attribute. This method is not defined in the specification.

The `<xsl:output>` element is a top-level element only.

xsl:output **Attributes**

The other attributes on `<xsl:output>` provide parameters for the output method. The following attributes are allowed:

- `version`. Specifies the value of the version attribute of the XML declaration that is output.
- `indent`. Specifies whether the XSLT processor can add additional whitespace when outputting the result tree to make for better readability. The value must be `yes` or `no`.
- `encoding`. Specifies the preferred character encoding that the XSLT processor should use to encode sequences of characters as sequences of bytes; the value of the attribute should be treated case insensitively and must contain only characters in the range #x21 to #x7E (that is, printable ASCII characters).
- `media-type`. Specifies the media type (MIME content type) of the data that results from outputting the result tree.
- `doctype-system`. Specifies the system identifier for an external DTD.
- `doctype-public`. Specifies the public identifier for an external DTD.
- `omit-xml-declaration`. Specifies whether the XSLT processor should output an XML declaration; the value must be `yes` or `no`. This is not applicable to HTML output.
- `standalone`. Specifies whether the XSLT processor should output a standalone document declaration; the value must be `yes` or `no`. This is not applicable to HTML output.
- `cdata-section-elements`. Specifies a list of the names of elements whose text node children should be output using CDATA sections. This is not applicable to HTML output.

Here are some examples of the `<xsl:output...>` element.

Generate an XML indented document with all `<SCRIPT>` elements translated to `"<![CDATA[]]>"` sections. We also need a SYSTEM DTD declaration with a standalone attribute of no. The result shown in Listing 2.26.

Listing 2.26 **Answer to the First Example**

```
<xsl:output
  method="xml"
  indent="yes"
  encoding="iso-8859-1"
  cdata-section-elements="script"
  doctype-system="resumes.dtd"
  standalone="no"
/>
```

For a second example, generate a text document in ASCII format. The result is as follows:

```
<xsl:output
  method="text"
  encoding="us-ascii"
/>
```

Modes

Modes allow a document to be processed multiple times; each time through the document, different output is provided to the result tree. Why would you want to do this? The next time you're on the Internet, take a look at one of the W3C documents on the W3C's Web site at www.w3c.org. An example would be the XML specification at http://www.w3.org/TR/2000/REC-xml-20001006. Notice how they all start with a complete document table of contents? This wasn't generated by hand, I can guarantee you. It was generated utilizing modes with an XSL stylesheet. Generation of tables of content and indices is a common use of this technique.

Here's how it's done. Both xsl:template and xsl:apply-templates have an optional mode attribute.

We'll use our resumes XML document and write a stylesheet to generate a table of contents that lists the name of each person in the XML document, and we'll make each of these names a hyperlink to each of their data. The list of names will be followed by the data applicable to each person. To do this, we'll write a stylesheet that has an <xsl:apply-templates select="..." mode="namelist"> to generate the name list that has a hyperlink to the name of each person in the file. We'll also have another <xsl:apply-templates select="..." mode="namedata"> to generate the body of the document.

A list of HTML hyperlinks is written like this:

```
<UL>
<LI><A HREF="#...">...</A></LI>
<LI><A HREF="#...">...</A></LI>
...
```

The anchor points in the HTML page to which these links point are written like this:

```
<A NAME="...">...</A><P>
data here
</P>
...
```

Listing 2.27 shows the stylesheet.

Listing 2.27   **XSLT Stylesheet That Generates a Table of Contents**

```xml
<?xml version="1."?>
<xsl:stylesheet
  xmlns:xsl=http://www.w3.org/XSL/Transform/1.0>
<xsl:template match="RESUMES">
    <HTML>
      <HEAD>
        <TITLE>Candidates</TITLE>
      </HEAD>
      <BODY>
        <H4>Candidate Resumes</H4>
        <UL>
          <xsl:apply-templates select="PERSON" mode="namelist">
        </UL>
<H4>Candidate Information</H4>
        <xsl:apply-templates select="PERSON" mode="namedata">
</BODY>
      </HTML>
  </xsl:template>
  <xsl:template match="PERSON" mode="namelist">
    <LI><A>
      <xsl:attribute name="HREF">#
        <xsl:value-of select="@PERSONID"
      </xsl:attribute>
      <xsl:value-of select="NAME/LAST"/>, <!--comma & space -->
      <xsl:value-of select="NAME/FIRST"/>
    </A></LI>
  </xsl:template>
<xsl:template match="PERSON" mode="namedata">
    <A>
      <xsl:attribute name="NAME">
        <xsl:value-of select="@PERSONID"
      </xsl:attribute>
      <xsl:value-of select="NAME/LAST"/>, <!--comma & space -->
      <xsl:value-of select="NAME/FIRST"/>
    </A><P>
    Address:
    <xsl:value-of select="STREET"/><BR>
    <xsl:value-of select="CITY"/><BR>
    ...
    </P>
  </xsl:template>
</xsl:stylesheet>
```

The first time through the stylesheet, the parser will notice that there are two different modes in the document. It now knows that it must make two passes through the data. During the first pass, the PERSON template is parsed because it was associated with the first mode. This results in all person names being listed as hyperlinks in "last name, first name" order. During the second pass through the data, the second mode (namelist) causes an anchor list to be generated consisting of the person's name, street, and city. These anchors are pointed to by the hyperlinks created during the first data pass-through.

Example—An Enterprise Quarterly Fiscal Report

As a last coding illustration in this chapter, I want to present a real-world example. This example was taken from a corporate intranet site, and it generates a quarterly fiscal report for the company in an HTML tabular format. The table we want to create is shown in Figure 2.4. The XML data file and stylesheet are available for download at `http://www.newriders.com`.

Listing 2.28 shows the XML data file `Channels.xml`.

Listing 2.28   *Channels.xml* **Document**

```
<CHANNELS>
  <CHANNEL TYPE="Aftermarket">
    <AREA LOCATION="Americas">
      <BOOKINGS>
          <DAY>1837183</DAY>
          <MTD>55839513</MTD>
      </BOOKINGS>
      <RETURNS>
          <DAY>-502987</DAY>
          <MTD>-4203783</MTD>
      </RETURNS>
      <BACKLOG>
          <GT_7DAYS>-4203783</GT_7DAYS>
          <LT_7DAYS>5622736</LT_7DAYS>
      </BACKLOG>
      <FUTURE_ORDERS>
          <CURRWK>2861866</CURRWK>
          <WK7-31-00>423176</WK7-31-00>
          <WK8-7-00>42549</WK8-7-00>
          <WK8-14-00>22950</WK8-14-00>
          <WK_GT_8-21-00>55515</WK_GT_8-21-00>
          <CURR_QTR>3406056</CURR_QTR>
      </FUTURE_ORDERS>
    </AREA>
    <AREA LOCATION="Asia/Pacific">
      <BOOKINGS>
          <DAY>246073</DAY>
          <MTD>7743758</MTD>
      </BOOKINGS>
      <RETURNS>
```

continues

Listing 2.28 **Continued**

```xml
        <DAY>-42723</DAY>
        <MTD>125894</MTD>
    </RETURNS>
    <BACKLOG>
        <GT_7DAYS>845567</GT_7DAYS>
        <LT_7DAYS>228438</LT_7DAYS>
    </BACKLOG>
    <FUTURE_ORDERS>
        <CURRWK>404541</CURRWK>
        <WK7-31-00>1394951</WK7-31-00>
        <WK8-7-00>1204360</WK8-7-00>
        <WK8-14-00>1096666</WK8-14-00>
        <WK_GT_8-21-00>2241186</WK_GT_8-21-00>
        <CURR_QTR>6336203</CURR_QTR>
    </FUTURE_ORDERS>
</AREA>
<AREA LOCATION="Europe">
    <BOOKINGS>
        <DAY>3068642</DAY>
        <MTD>19753369</MTD>
    </BOOKINGS>
    <RETURNS>
        <DAY>-25060</DAY>
        <MTD>-1671616</MTD>
    </RETURNS>
    <BACKLOG>
        <GT_7DAYS>343785</GT_7DAYS>
        <LT_7DAYS>2138534</LT_7DAYS>
    </BACKLOG>
    <FUTURE_ORDERS>
        <CURRWK>364145</CURRWK>
        <WK7-31-00>1014554</WK7-31-00>
        <WK8-7-00>563798</WK8-7-00>
        <WK8-14-00>1365700</WK8-14-00>
        <WK_GT_8-21-00>3464202</WK_GT_8-21-00>
        <CURR_QTR>6683236</CURR_QTR>
    </FUTURE_ORDERS>
</AREA>
<AREA LOCATION="World Wide">
    <BOOKINGS>
        <DAY>5151898</DAY>
        <MTD>83336640</MTD>
    </BOOKINGS>
    <RETURNS>
        <DAY>-570771</DAY>
        <MTD>-6001293</MTD>
    </RETURNS>
    <BACKLOG>
        <GT_7DAYS>8442583</GT_7DAYS>
        <LT_7DAYS>7989708</LT_7DAYS>
```

```
        </BACKLOG>
        <FUTURE_ORDERS>
            <CURRWK>3630552</CURRWK>
            <WK7-31-00>2832681</WK7-31-00>
            <WK8-7-00>1810706</WK8-7-00>
            <WK8-14-00>2485316</WK8-14-00>
            <WK_GT_8-21-00>5760903</WK_GT_8-21-00>
            <CURR_QTR>16425494</CURR_QTR>
        </FUTURE_ORDERS>
    </AREA>
</CHANNEL>
<CHANNEL TYPE="OEM">
    <AREA LOCATION="Americas">
        <BOOKINGS>
            <DAY>285052</DAY>
            <MTD>12129683</MTD>
        </BOOKINGS>
        <RETURNS>
            <DAY/>
            <MTD>-161641</MTD>
        </RETURNS>
        <BACKLOG>
            <GT_7DAYS>401291</GT_7DAYS>
            <LT_7DAYS>252617</LT_7DAYS>
        </BACKLOG>
        <FUTURE_ORDERS>
            <CURRWK>15400</CURRWK>
            <WK7-31-00>231960</WK7-31-00>
            <WK8-7-00>118668</WK8-7-00>
            <WK8-14-00/>
            <WK_GT_8-21-00>231960</WK_GT_8-21-00>
            <CURR_QTR>597988</CURR_QTR>
        </FUTURE_ORDERS>
    </AREA>
    <AREA LOCATION="Asia/Pacific">
        <BOOKINGS>
            <DAY>24769</DAY>
            <MTD>2156458</MTD>
        </BOOKINGS>
        <RETURNS>
            <DAY/>
            <MTD>-147435</MTD>
        </RETURNS>
        <BACKLOG>
            <GT_7DAYS>771100</GT_7DAYS>
            <LT_7DAYS>240155</LT_7DAYS>
        </BACKLOG>
        <FUTURE_ORDERS>
            <CURRWK>270800</CURRWK>
            <WK7-31-00>278991</WK7-31-00>
            <WK8-7-00>406481</WK8-7-00>
            <WK8-14-00>668844</WK8-14-00>
            <WK_GT_8-21-00>653683</WK_GT_8-21-00>
```

continues

Listing 2.28 **Continued**

```
                <CURR_QTR>2194810</CURR_QTR>
            </FUTURE_ORDERS>
        </AREA>
        <AREA LOCATION="Europe">
            <BOOKINGS>
                <DAY>243435</DAY>
                <MTD>2238751</MTD>
            </BOOKINGS>
            <RETURNS>
                <DAY>-4718</DAY>
                <MTD>-29353</MTD>
            </RETURNS>
            <BACKLOG>
                <GT_7DAYS/>
                <LT_7DAYS/>
            </BACKLOG>
            <FUTURE_ORDERS>
                <CURRWK>154300</CURRWK>
                <WK7-31-00>165354</WK7-31-00>
                <WK8-7-00>63620</WK8-7-00>
                <WK8-14-00>104620</WK8-14-00>
                <WK_GT_8-21-00>185220</WK_GT_8-21-00>
                <CURR_QTR>673114</CURR_QTR>
            </FUTURE_ORDERS>
        </AREA>
        <AREA LOCATION="World Wide">
            <BOOKINGS>
                <DAY>553256</DAY>
                <MTD>16524892</MTD>
            </BOOKINGS>
            <RETURNS>
                <DAY>-4718</DAY>
                <MTD>-338429</MTD>
            </RETURNS>
            <BACKLOG>
                <GT_7DAYS>1172391</GT_7DAYS>
                <LT_7DAYS>492772</LT_7DAYS>
            </BACKLOG>
            <FUTURE_ORDERS>
                <CURRWK>440500</CURRWK>
                <WK7-31-00>676305</WK7-31-00>
                <WK8-7-00>588769</WK8-7-00>
                <WK8-14-00>773464</WK8-14-00>
                <WK_GT_8-21-00>1070863</WK_GT_8-21-00>
                <CURR_QTR>3465912</CURR_QTR>
            </FUTURE_ORDERS>
        </AREA>
    </CHANNEL>
</CHANNELS>
```

Figure 2.4 shows the HTML table we want to end up with.

Bookings and Orders Report

Report as of - 2000-Jul-27

Channel	Region	Bookings		Returns		Backlog			Future Orders				Curr Qtr
		Day	MTD	Day	MTD	>7 Days	1-7 Days	Curr Wk	7/31/00	8/7/00	8/14/00	>08/21/00	
Aftermarket	Americas	1,837,183	55,839,513	(502,987)	(4,203,783)	(4,203,783)	5,622,736	2,861,866	423,176	42,549	22,950	55,515	3,406,056
	Asia/Pacific	246,073	7,743,758	(42,723)	125,894	845,567	228,438	404,541	404,541	1,204,360	1,096,666	2,241,186	6,336,203
	Europe	3,068,642	19,753,369	(25,060)	(1,671,616)	343,785	2,138,534	364,145	364,145	563,798	1,365,700	3,464,202	6,683,236
	Worldwide	5,151,898	83,336,640	(570,771)	(6,001,293)	8,442,583	7,989,708	3,630,552	3,630,552	1,810,706	2,485,316	5,760,903	16,425,494
OEM	Americas	285,052	12,129,683	10,345	(161,641)	401,291	252,617	15,400	231,960	118,668	6,754	231,960	597,988
	Asia/Pacific	24,769	2,156,458	4,589	(147,435)	771,100	240,155	270,800	270,800	406,481	668,844	653,683	2,194,810
	Europe	243,435	2,238,751	(4,718)	(29,353)	(910)	86	154,300	154,300	63,620	104,620	185,220	673,114
	Worldwide	553,256	16,524,892	10,216	(338,429)	1,171,481	492,858	440,500	440,500	588,769	780,218	1,070,863	3,465,912

Figure 2.4 Quarterly fiscal report in HTML format.

XSLT Stylesheet

Listing 2.29 shows the XSLT stylesheet used to generate the table. This is a very long example, but it is much more attune to the real world. I've attempted to use as many XSLT elements as possible to give you good examples of their use. And remember one thing: There is no one way to write a stylesheet! Some ways are more efficient than others, but first get the correct answer.

One thing in this stylesheet that I did not cover explicitly in the book is the use of variables. Just as I gave you some exercises in Chapter 1 to work out on your own, I purposely left variables out of the discussion to give you some practice in looking up definitions.

I again refer you to Figure 2.4 for the table that this stylesheet generates.

Listing 2.29 **The Stylesheet That Generates the HTML Corporate Financial Report**

```
<?xml version='1.0'?>
<xsl:stylesheet xmlns:xsl='http://www.w3.org/XSL/Transform/1.0'>

  <xsl:output method="html" indent="yes"/>
  <xsl:decimal-format/>    <!-- declares the default number format -->

  <xsl:template match="/">
    <HTML>
    <BODY>
      <TABLE border='0' cellPadding='0' cellSpacing='0' width='100%'>
      <TR>
        <TD colspan='14' align='middle' bgColor='#ffffff' height='20'><B>
            <FONT color='black' face='Arial' size='3'>Bookings and Orders
            Report</FONT></B></TD>
      </TR>
      <TR>
        <TD colspan='14' align='middle' bgColor='#ffffff'
          height='20'><I><B>
            <FONT color='black' face='Arial' size='2'>Report as of -
            2000-Jul-27</FONT></B></I></TD>
      </TR>
      </TABLE>
      <TABLE border='1' cellPadding='0' cellSpacing='0' width='100%'>
      <TR>
        <TD bgColor='#000000' height='18'>
          <xsl:text> </xsl:text>
        </TD>
        <TD bgColor='#000000'>
          <xsl:text> </xsl:text>
        </TD>
        <TD align='middle' bgColor='#000000' colSpan='2'><B>
            <FONT color='white' face='Arial' size='1'>Bookings</FONT>
            </B></TD>
```

```
            <TD align='middle' bgColor='#000000' colSpan='2'><B>
                <FONT color='white' face='Arial' size='1'>Returns</FONT>
                </B></TD>
            <TD align='middle' bgColor='#000000' colSpan='2'><B>
                <FONT color='white' face='Arial' size='1'>Backlog</FONT>
                </B></TD>
            <TD align='middle' bgColor='#000000' colSpan='6'><B>
                <FONT color='white' face='Arial' size='1'>Future
                Orders</FONT></B></TD>
        </TR>
      <TR>
        <TD align='right' bgColor='#000000' height='15'><B><FONT
        color='white' face='Arial' size='1'>
          Channel
        </FONT></B>
        </TD>
        <TD align='middle' bgColor='#d1d1d1'><B><FONT face='Arial' size='1'>
        Region</FONT></B></TD>
        <TD align='middle' bgColor='#d1d1d1'><B><FONT face='Arial' size='1'>
        Day</FONT></B></TD>
        <TD align='middle' bgColor='#d1d1d1'><B><FONT face='Arial' size='1'>
        MTD</FONT></B></TD>
        <TD align='middle' bgColor='#d1d1d1'><B><FONT face='Arial' size='1'>
        Day</FONT></B></TD>
        <TD align='middle' bgColor='#d1d1d1'><B><FONT face='Arial' size='1'>
        MTD</FONT></B></TD>
        <TD align='middle' bgColor='#d1d1d1'><B><FONT face='Arial' size='1'>
        &gt; 7 Days</FONT></B></TD>
        <TD align='middle' bgColor='#d1d1d1'><B><FONT face='Arial' size='1'>
        1-7 Days</FONT></B></TD>
        <TD align='middle' bgColor='#d1d1d1'><B><FONT face='Arial' size='1'>
        Curr Wk</FONT></B></TD>
        <TD align='middle' bgColor='#d1d1d1'><B><FONT face='Arial' size='1'>
        7/31/00</FONT></B></TD>
        <TD align='middle' bgColor='#d1d1d1'><B><FONT face='Arial' size='1'>
        8/7/00</FONT></B></TD>
        <TD align='middle' bgColor='#d1d1d1'><B><FONT face='Arial' size='1'>
        8/14/00</FONT></B></TD>
        <TD align='middle' bgColor='#d1d1d1'><B><FONT face='Arial' size='1'>
        &gt;08/21/00</FONT></B></TD>
        <TD align='middle' bgColor='#d1d1d1'><B><FONT face='Arial' size='1'>
        Curr Qtr</FONT></B></TD>
      </TR>

    <xsl:apply-templates/>

    </TABLE>
    </BODY>
    </HTML>
</xsl:template>
```

continues

Listing 2.29 **Continued**

```
<xsl:template match="CHANNEL">
  <TR>
    <TD align='right' bgColor='#000000' height='15'><B><FONT
     color='white' face='Arial' size='1'>
        <xsl:value-of select="@TYPE"/>
        </FONT></B>
    </TD>
        <xsl:apply-templates select="AREA"/>
  </TR>
</xsl:template>

<xsl:template match="AREA">
  <xsl:choose>
    <xsl:when test="'Americas'=@LOCATION">
      <TD align='right' bgColor='#ffffff'><B><FONT face='Arial' size='1'>
          Americas
          </FONT></B></TD>
      <TD align='right' bgColor='#ffffff'><B><FONT face='Arial' size='1'>
        <xsl:variable name="amount" select="BOOKINGS/DAY"/>
        <xsl:value-of select="format-number($amount, '#,#00;(#,#00)')"/>
        </FONT></B></TD>
      <TD align='right' bgColor='#ffffff'><B><FONT face='Arial' size='1'>
        <xsl:variable name="amount" select="BOOKINGS/MTD"/>
        <xsl:value-of select="format-number($amount, '#,#00;(#,#00)')"/>
        </FONT></B></TD>
      <TD align='right' bgColor='#ffffff'><B><FONT face='Arial' size='1'>
        <xsl:variable name="amount" select="RETURNS/DAY"/>
        <xsl:value-of select="format-number($amount, '#,#00;(#,#00)')"/>
        </FONT></B></TD>
      <TD align='right' bgColor='#ffffff'><B><FONT face='Arial' size='1'>
        <xsl:variable name="amount" select="RETURNS/MTD"/>
        <xsl:value-of select="format-number($amount, '#,#00;(#,#00)')"/>
        </FONT></B></TD>
      <TD align='right' bgColor='#ffffff'><B><FONT face='Arial' size='1'>
        <xsl:variable name="amount" select="BACKLOG/GT_7DAYS"/>
        <xsl:value-of select="format-number($amount, '#,#00;(#,#00)')"/>
        </FONT></B></TD>
      <TD align='right' bgColor='#ffffff'><B><FONT face='Arial' size='1'>
        <xsl:variable name="amount" select="BACKLOG/LT_7DAYS"/>
        <xsl:value-of select="format-number($amount, '#,#00;(#,#00)')"/>
        </FONT></B></TD>
      <TD align='right' bgColor='#ffffff'><B><FONT face='Arial' size='1'>
        <xsl:variable name="amount" select="FUTURE_ORDERS/CURRWK"/>
        <xsl:value-of select="format-number($amount, '#,#00;(#,#00)')"/>
        </FONT></B></TD>
      <TD align='right' bgColor='#ffffff'><B><FONT face='Arial' size='1'>
        <xsl:variable name="amount" select="FUTURE_ORDERS/WK7-31-00"/>
        <xsl:value-of select="format-number($amount, '#,#00;(#,#00)')"/>
        </FONT></B></TD>
```

```
    <TD align='right' bgColor='#ffffff'><B><FONT face='Arial' size='1'>
      <xsl:variable name="amount" select="FUTURE_ORDERS/WK8-7-00"/>
      <xsl:value-of select="format-number($amount, '#,#00;(#,#00)')"/>
      </FONT></B></TD>
    <TD align='right' bgColor='#ffffff'><B><FONT face='Arial' size='1'>
      <xsl:variable name="amount" select="FUTURE_ORDERS/WK8-14-00"/>
      <xsl:value-of select="format-number($amount, '#,#00;(#,#00)')"/>
      </FONT></B></TD>
    <TD align='right' bgColor='#ffffff'><B><FONT face='Arial' size='1'>
      <xsl:variable name="amount" select="FUTURE_ORDERS/WK_GT_8-21-00"/>
      <xsl:value-of select="format-number($amount, '#,#00;(#,#00)')"/>
      </FONT></B></TD>
    <TD align='right' bgColor='#ffffff'><B><FONT face='Arial' size='1'>
      <xsl:variable name="amount" select="FUTURE_ORDERS/CURR_QTR"/>
      <xsl:value-of select="format-number($amount, '#,#00;(#,#00)')"/>
      </FONT></B></TD>
</xsl:when>

<xsl:otherwise>
  <TR>
  <TD bgColor='#000000'></TD>
  <TD align='right' bgColor='#ffffff'><B><FONT face='Arial' size='1'>
    <xsl:variable name="location" select="@LOCATION"/>
    <xsl:value-of select="@LOCATION"/>
    </FONT></B></TD>
  <TD align='right' bgColor='#ffffff'>
    <B><FONT face='Arial' size='1'>
    <xsl:variable name="amount" select="BOOKINGS/DAY"/>
    <xsl:value-of select="format-number($amount, '#,#00;(#,#00)')"/>
    </FONT></B></TD>
  <TD align='right' bgColor='#ffffff'><B><FONT face='Arial' size='1'>
    <xsl:variable name="amount" select="BOOKINGS/MTD"/>
    <xsl:value-of select="format-number($amount, '#,#00;(#,#00)')"/>
    </FONT></B></TD>
  <TD align='right' bgColor='#ffffff'><B><FONT face='Arial' size='1'>
    <xsl:variable name="amount" select="RETURNS/DAY"/>
    <xsl:value-of select="format-number($amount, '#,#00;(#,#00)')"/>
    </FONT></B></TD>
  <TD align='right' bgColor='#ffffff'><B><FONT face='Arial' size='1'>
    <xsl:variable name="amount" select="RETURNS/MTD"/>
    <xsl:value-of select="format-number($amount, '#,#00;(#,#00)')"/>
    </FONT></B></TD>
  <TD align='right' bgColor='#ffffff'><B><FONT face='Arial' size='1'>
    <xsl:variable name="amount" select="BACKLOG/GT_7DAYS"/>
    <xsl:value-of select="format-number($amount, '#,#00;(#,#00)')"/>
    </FONT></B></TD>
  <TD align='right' bgColor='#ffffff'><B><FONT face='Arial' size='1'>
    <xsl:variable name="amount" select="BACKLOG/LT_7DAYS"/>
    <xsl:value-of select="format-number($amount, '#,#00;(#,#00)')"/>
    </FONT></B></TD>
```

continues

Listing 2.29   **Continued**

```
                    <TD align='right' bgColor='#ffffff'><B><FONT face='Arial' size='1'>
                        <xsl:variable name="amount" select="FUTURE_ORDERS/CURRWK"/>
                        <xsl:value-of select="format-number($amount, '#,#00;(#,#00)')"/>
                        </FONT></B></TD>
                    <TD align='right' bgColor='#ffffff'><B><FONT face='Arial' size='1'>
                        <xsl:variable name="amount" select="FUTURE_ORDERS/CURRWK"/>
                        <xsl:value-of select="format-number($amount, '#,#00;(#,#00)')"/>
                        </FONT></B></TD>
                    <TD align='right' bgColor='#ffffff'><B><FONT face='Arial' size='1'>
                        <xsl:variable name="amount" select="FUTURE_ORDERS/WK8-7-00"/>
                        <xsl:value-of select="format-number($amount, '#,#00;(#,#00)')"/>
                        </FONT></B></TD>
                    <TD align='right' bgColor='#ffffff'><B><FONT face='Arial' size='1'>
                        <xsl:variable name="amount" select="FUTURE_ORDERS/WK8-14-00"/>
                        <xsl:value-of select="format-number($amount, '#,#00;(#,#00)')"/>
                        </FONT></B></TD>
                    <TD align='right' bgColor='#ffffff'><B><FONT face='Arial' size='1'>
                        <xsl:variable name="amount" select="FUTURE_ORDERS/WK_GT_8-21-00"/>
                        <xsl:value-of select="format-number($amount, '#,#00;(#,#00)')"/>
                        </FONT></B></TD>
                    <TD align='right' bgColor='#ffffff'><B><FONT face='Arial' size='1'>
                        <xsl:variable name="amount" select="FUTURE_ORDERS/CURR_QTR"/>
                        <xsl:value-of select="format-number($amount, '#,#00;(#,#00)')"/>
                        </FONT></B></TD>
                    </TR>
                </xsl:otherwise>
            </xsl:choose>
        </xsl:template>
    </xsl:stylesheet>
```

These examples should give you plenty to study and should firm up a lot of what we've talked about in this chapter. Most importantly, have fun.

Recap of What Was Discussed in This Chapter

- The real power of XML becomes apparent when XSLT is applied to XML data to create new data, to modify the document structure, and to provide output in several forms, including rearranged XML documents for business-to-business e-commerce.

- XSLT and CSS are different. Although XSLT and CSS are both used to modify documents and both have the word "stylesheet" in their titles, that's about the only semblance of similarity in the languages. CSS can modify appearance, but XSLT also can modify data structure and relationships.

- Navigation of an XML document is guided by the XPath specification. It utilizes an ancestry paradigm of self, parent, child, sibling, ancestor, and descendent.

- XSLT is not a simple language to master. It is composed of many elements and functions.

- XSLT has the capability not only to change the appearance of XML data but to output new attributes and elements for the source XML document. It also can modify existing elements and attributes.

- Just as any other programming language contains elements that perform multi-pass processing (looping), conditional processing (if-then), and formatting of output, so does XSLT provide for these necessities.

- XSLT provides for the output of data in three separate formats: XML, HTML, and plain text with all necessary attributes.

- Coding XSLT stylesheets can be a lengthy process, but when finished, they are manageable, are easily modified to accommodate changes in data, and are easily customized for changes to output appearance. This equates to easier manageability over time.

IIS and Virtual Directories

3

To save yourself time, you can skip this chapter if you do not plan to implement any of the template or schema code examples included later in the book, or if you do not want to test your code. Skipping this chapter won't affect your reading of the rest of the book, but you may have a difficult time understanding some of the concepts presented. (I work with a person who has unbelievable visualization skills, so go for it if you can.)

Again, I assume that you have some familiarity with Microsoft IIS because instruction on the management of this software is beyond the scope of this book.

In this chapter, we will cover the following topics:

- Virtual directories and how they apply to Internet Information Server (IIS)
- System requirements for Virtual Directory Management on IIS
- The (graphical) Virtual Directory Management Utility
- The (programmatic) Virtual Directory Management object model

Virtual Directories

Before we can accomplish anything productive, it is necessary to create a virtual directory from which to work. This directory is also known as the *virtual root* and must be registered on a server running IIS. (The terms virtual root and virtual directory are used synonymously.) The Virtual Directory Management Utility, which creates an association between the virtual root and a Microsoft SQL Server instance, is the tool we'll use.

When you install SQL Server 2000 on your application server, it installs the Configure SQL XML Support in IIS option on the SQL Server menu. This option gives you the capability to create a virtual root for SQL Server 2000. After you create this root, you can configure virtual names and directories used to identify the location of your templates, schemas, and objects through this menu option as well. All current Web servers have the capability to implement virtual directories. These configuration steps only configure SQL Server to point to the virtual root and directories contained in IIS.

If these configuration steps are not completed, then the examples later in this chapter will not work.

You can create the virtual directory using these methods:

- Graphically, with the IIS Virtual Directory Management for SQL Server Utility
- Programmatically, using the IIS Virtual Directory Management for SQL Server Object Model

In this chapter, we cover the IIS Virtual Directory Management Utility, which is installed as part of the SQL Server general installation. Then, we'll move on to the Object Model.

The Virtual Directory Management Utility

A SQL Server virtual root is exactly like a virtual root of a Web server. You can configure a root directory anywhere in the directory structure and access a file in it with a simple URL call to the name of the root directory and file. The main reason for doing this on SQL Server is to point the ISAPI.DLL dynamic library to the proper starting point it needs to access template and schema files. After the virtual root is properly registered and virtual names are set up, it is possible to generate XML documents from data stored in SQL Server 2000 through queries in a URL. It is necessary to specify the names of the IIS and virtual directory in the URL; however, login, password, permissions, and other necessary information are contained in the virtual directory. This information grants us the ability to establish a connection to a predetermined database and execute the query contained in the URL.

Queries that can be contained in the URL include

- Verbatim SQL statements utilizing SELECT.
- *Template files,* valid XML documents consisting of one or more SQL statements that are executed when the template file is specified in the URL.

- XPath queries, queries that produce an XML document. (We'll talk about these in depth in Chapter 6, "Using XPath Queries.")

System Requirements

The IIS Virtual Directory Management for SQL Server Utility runs on any edition of Microsoft Windows NT 4.0 or Microsoft Windows 2000. The following are Windows NT 4.0 requirements:

- Microsoft IIS 4 or higher. (If you are running Windows NT Workstation 4.0, Peer Web Services 4.0 or higher is required.)
- Microsoft Management Console 1.2. (This is installed by the Windows NT Option Pack, or when you install SQL Server 2000.)

Those of you using Microsoft Windows 2000 Professional need to install the Administrative Tools Pack (Adminpak.msi). This file can be found on Windows 2000 Server editions in the %winroot%\System32 directory. Windows 2000 Server itself has no additional requirements.

Virtual Names

A virtual name must be one of three different types:

- template
- schema
- dbobject

This virtual name is the entity that allows a template file, mapping schema, or database object (table or view) to be part of the URL used to generate XML documents. The URL then executes a template file or an XPath query against a mapping schema file, or it directly accesses a database object.

The type of virtual name specified in the URL determines the type of file specified in the URL. For example, `http://IISServer/northwind/TemplateVirtualName/Template.xml` demonstrates that because `TemplateVirtualName` was previously defined as having the virtual name type template, file `Template.xml` is a template file.

The ability to define virtual name types is strictly an enhancement to IIS provided by SQL Server 2000. IIS by itself does not have the capability of doing this, although as mentioned previously, it can create virtual directories.

Creating a Virtual Directory Using the Virtual Directory Management Utility

If you are anything like me, you need to have a concrete example presented before you really understand not only what these new terms mean, but also how they fit together. The next topic, "The Virtual Directory Management Object Model" is difficult to understand if you haven't worked with a virtual root and its associated components and terms. Before we work with a virtual root and its associated components, we have some preparation to accomplish.

This preparation consists of creating a small directory structure to hold our template and schema objects. We must link a virtual root to the directory structure we've created, and then specify where the various file types should be stored.

I've made a couple of assumptions here: first, that your IIS root was installed to your D: drive; and second, that the `Inetpub\wwwroot` directory is located directly off the root of the D: drive. These assumptions establish common ground from which to work. Remember throughout this discussion that you can set up this directory structure wherever you please. Moreover, you can call the directories any name you want.

Now let's get to work. In the `D:\inetpub\wwwroot` directory, create another directory called Nwind. Next, in the Nwind directory, create three more directories called dbobjects, schemas, and templates, respectively. The directory structure should now look like that in Figure 3.1.

This configuration is very simplistic and will work well in a learning environment. The "real world" dictates, however, that the power of virtual directories allows them to be physically anywhere and, for security reasons, virtual directories shouldn't be made a subdirectory of the default Web site.

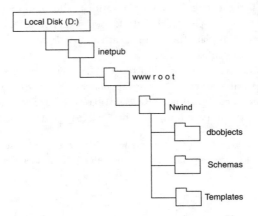

Figure 3.1 Preliminary directory structure setup.

Use the following steps to configure the virtual directory using the Configure SQL XML Support in IIS option.

Starting the Virtual Directory Management Utility

From the Start menu, select Programs, select Microsoft SQL Server, and then click Configure SQL XML Support in IIS (see Figure 3.2).

Figure 3.2 Starting the Virtual Directory Management Utility.

Naming the Virtual Directory

Expand the server you'll be working with, and then right-click the Web site you want to configure. In the drop-down box, select New, and then Virtual Directory to display the General tab of the New Virtual Directory Properties dialog box (see Figure 3.3).

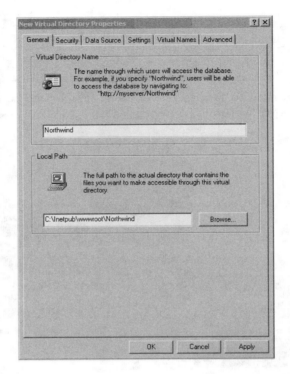

Figure 3.3 The General tab of the Virtual Directory Management Utility.

The options on the General tab are listed in Table 3.1.

Table 3.1 **The General Tab Options**

Option	Description
Virtual Directory Name	The name of the virtual directory.
Local Path	The full path to the physical directory associated with the virtual directory (for example, D:\inetpub\wwwroot\Nwind). The Browse button can be used to navigate to the directory if the virtual root is located on the local computer. The Browse button is not available for a remote virtual directory.

In the Virtual Directory Name box, enter a name for the virtual directory. For this example, type **Northwind**. (Remember you can call it any name you want, but we are using this configuration for all the examples in the book.) Enter the path to the directory Nwind that you created previously (`D:\inetpub\wwwroot\Nwind`). Remember that you also can use the Browse button to point to the directory.

Specifying the Login

Select the Security tab. On this tab, select SQL Server, and enter the valid SQL Server login information. When you go to the next tab, you are asked to confirm this password. See Figure 3.4.

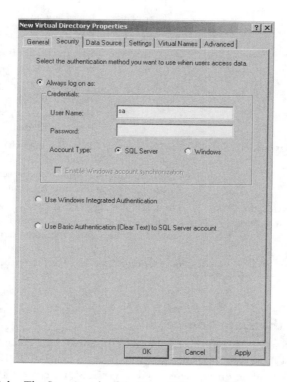

Figure 3.4 The Security tab of the Virtual Directory Management Utility.

The options on the Security tab are given in Table 3.2.

Table 3.2 **The Security Tab Options**

Option	Description
Always log on as	The Windows and SQL Server account type use the anonymous access scheme supplied by IIS authentication security. With this anonymous access, everyone is logged on using the credentials in User Name and Password.

continues

Table 3.2 **Continued**

Option	Description
	If SQL Server is selected, a valid SQL Server logon must be entered. If Windows is selected, the supplied login is used for all users.

■	User Name	User name for the login.
■	Password	A password for the user.
■	SQL Server	Specifies that all users use a SQL Server login.
■	Windows	A Windows account is used for everyone who accesses the directory. By default, the IUSR_Servername is the account used.

Option	Description
Use Windows Integrated Authentication	For NT 4.0, this selects Windows challenge/response authentication. For Windows 2000, this selects Windows Integrated Authentication. SQL Server must allow access for the Windows user accounts.
Use Basic Authentication (Clear Text) to SQL Server Account	Prompts a SQL Server login and password. What actually happens here is that anonymous access is enabled, and during the login, the server tries anonymous access first. If that fails, an error message to the browser causes the login box to appear.

Mapping to the Data Source

Select the Data Source tab. On this tab, in the SQL Server box, enter the name of a server running SQL Server 2000 and the name of an instance of SQL Server 2000, if more than one is running on the designated server. If SQL Server 2000 is running on the local server, you can enter **(local)** here. In the Database box, enter **Northwind** as the name of the default database or select it via the drop-down box (see Figure 3.5).

The options on the Data Source tab are given in Table 3.3.

Table 3.3 **The Data Source Tab Options**

Option	Description
SQL Server	The name of the server (or the instance) you want. With multiple instances of SQL Server running, you can specify the server name and instance.
Database	The name of the default database on the server. The virtual directory maps to this database.

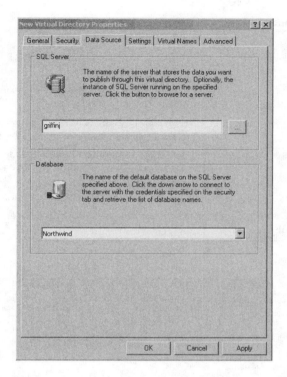

Figure 3.5 The Data Source tab of the Virtual Directory Management Utility.

Specifying the Query Settings

Select the Settings tab. On this tab, select the Allow URL queries, Allow template queries, Allow XPath, and Allow POST options (see Figure 3.6). This enables all forms of submission that are used in the examples.

The options on the Settings tab are given in Table 3.4.

Table 3.4 **The Settings Tab Options**

Option	Description
Allow URL queries	Execute SQL queries directly from the URL.
	Caution: For security reasons, allowing direct execution of queries in a URL is not recommended. You'll want to remove the database details from the user. I recommend that you don't allow this in a production environment. The proper execution method is through the use of template files mentioned next. Better safe than sorry.

continues

Table 3.4 **Continued**

Option	Description
Allow template queries	Execute a template file from the URL. This is enabled by default.
Allow XPath	Execute XPath queries against schemas directly from the URL.
Allow POST	Enable data posting (data writing for you non-HTTPers) to the database. This is not enabled by default.
	Warning: Forgetting to enable this option will bite you and be extremely difficult to troubleshoot if you are planning to write data to the database. If you are not planning to write data, then do not enable it for security reasons.
Maximum size of POST queries (in kilobytes)	Maximum amount of data that you can send to the server per query.

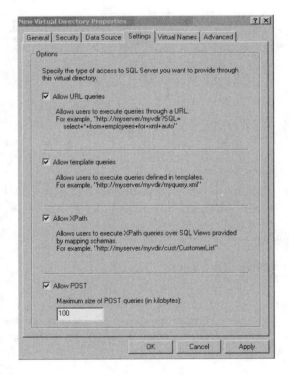

Figure 3.6 The Settings tab of the Virtual Directory Management Utility.

Specifying the Virtual Names

After the virtual root has been configured, we need to create the virtual names that will point to the template files, schema files, and dbobjects, and associate them to the physical directories that house these entities. To accomplish this, perform the following steps:

1. Select the Virtual Names tab. On this tab, click New to create the virtual name for the template type.

The options on the Virtual Names tab are given in Table 3.5.

Table 3.5   The Virtual Names Tab Options

Option	Description
Defined Virtual Names	Specify the virtual name used to access the resource. For example, the virtual name schema in the Virtualroot virtual directory would be accessed with the URL `http://servername/VirtualRoot/schema`.
Type	Specifies the type of query that the virtual name will access.
	• dbobject A database object (table, and so forth).
	• schema An XPath query against a mapping schema.
	• template SQL queries in a template file.
Path	Specifies the directory path where the templates and mapping schemas are located. This can be an absolute or relative path (relative to the physical directory associated with the virtual directory). A virtual name of dbobject type requires no path. The Browse button allows navigation to the directory on a local server, but is not available for remote servers.
	For template or schema mappings, the path can go to a folder or a file. If it goes to a folder, the filename must be in the URL (for example, `http://servername/Virtualroot/schema/schema.xml`). If it goes to a file only, that file can be used.
	URL paths are not allowed because the utility doesn't validate path entries.
New	Click to create a new virtual name.
Delete	Click to delete a mapping from the list of mappings.

In the Virtual Name Configuration dialog box, enter **Template** in the Virtual Name box (you could put any name you want here, but let's use the same name in the example). In the Type list, select Template. In the Path box, enter the physical path to the Templates directory that was created earlier (`D:\inetpub\wwwroot\Nwind\Templates`). See Figure 3.7. Click Save to save the virtual name.

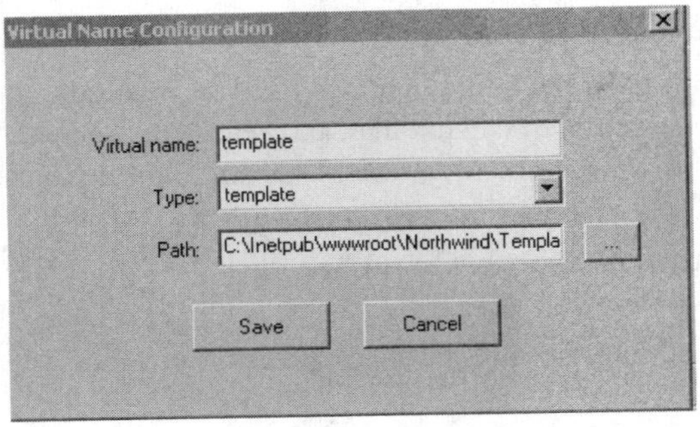

Figure 3.7 The Virtual Name Configuration dialog box of the Virtual Directory Management Utility.

Warning: The program does not check the existence of the directory you enter, so you won't know if there was a mistake until you can't get anything to work. Moral of the story: Double-check your entry! This saves you from a lot of frustration. It's bitten me more than once.

2. Again, select the Virtual Names tab. On this tab, click New to create the virtual name for the schema type.

   In the Virtual Name Configuration dialog box, enter **schema** in the Virtual Name box (again, you could put any name you want here). In the Type list, select schema. In the Path box, enter the physical path to the Templates directory that was created earlier (`D:\inetpub\wwwroot\Nwind\Schemas`). Click Save to save the virtual name.

3. One last time, click New on the Virtual Names tab. On this tab, click New to create the virtual name for the dbobject type.

   In the Virtual Name Configuration dialog box, enter **dbobject** in the Virtual Name box. In the Type list, select dbobject. Click Save to save the virtual name.

4. On the Virtual Names tab, click OK to save the settings.

That's it! You've created the virtual directory Northwind. All queries using the virtual directory will be against the database Northwind.

The Advanced Tab

For our purposes, the only setting that needs to be changed on the Advanced tab is Disable Caching of Mapping Schemas. Experienced developers know that caching in a development environment can cause innumerable headaches by preventing changes from appearing until the cache timeout period expires, so make sure this option is checked, so that changes we make are available immediately (see Figure 3.8).

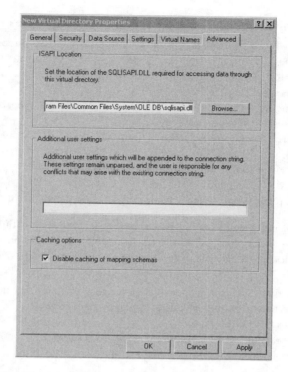

Figure 3.8   The Advanced tab of the Virtual Directory Management Utility.

The options on the Advanced tab are given in Table 3.6.

Table 3.6   **The Advanced Tab Options**

Option	Description
ISAPI Location	Specify the location of the SQLISAPI.DLL file.
Additional user settings	Specify additional optional settings. These settings are passed untouched to the connection string, and passed in to OLE DB.
Caching options	Sqlisapi.dll has a caching option that stores mapping schemas in its memory for subsequent queries. For development purposes, the caching option should be disabled so that schemas are reloaded every time a query is executed against the schema.

URLs, Virtual Directories, and Physical Directories

Let's take one final look at the relationship among URLs, virtual directories, and physical directories. To simplify things, we'll only talk about templates.

Our example has a physical directory defined as the virtual root at

```
D:\inetpub\wwwroot\Northwind
```

with the name nwind. A physical subdirectory of this directory

```
D:\inetpub\wwwroot\Northwind\templates
```

is defined as a virtual directory with the name template. A URL would access a file in this directory with

```
http://IISServername/nwind/template/filename.xml
```

or

```
servername/virtual root name/virtual directory name/filename.xml
```

The TEMPLATES directory holds multiple templates and is physically named TEMPLATES, but the URL calls only one template file (the virtual name was defined as template). This is solely my personal preference. You can name them as you see fit but all the book examples follow this nomenclature.

If we had the virtual root dir3 deeper in the directory structure, for instance,

```
D:\inetpub\wwwroot\dir1\dir2\dir3\virtual directory
```

you would still use the URL

```
D:\inetpub\wwwroot\dir3\virtual directory\filename.xml
```

I hope the example helped to explain this relationship a little better.

The Virtual Directory Management Object Model

All the virtual root and virtual name configuration that we have done in this chapter by utilizing a GUI also can be carried out programmatically. Microsoft has provided an object model called the Virtual Directory Management Object Model to accomplish this. It consists of the following objects:

- SQLVDirControl Object
- SQLVDirs Collection Object
- SQLVDir Object
- VirtualNames Collection Object
- VirtualName Object

The following discussion utilizes VBScript and Active Server Pages to demonstrate some advanced programmatic methods of duplicating what we created earlier with a GUI. Those of you that are not familiar with these technologies may want to skip the remainder of this chapter.

In an object model, the objects contained in an application provide the state, functionality, and characteristics of an application. A collection object, however, contains related objects (a collection). A collection object's `Item` method is usually employed to gain access to one of its objects.

The Web, which utilizes the HTTP protocol, has several collection objects, one of which is the *Form Collection*. How many of you have filled out a form on the Internet and then submitted your information by clicking on a button? What's actually going on is that the names of the form elements that you have put data in are passed to a Web server along with the data itself. The Form Collection contains these names and their associated data. After that collection arrives at the server, the data can be accessed and processed as the developer sees fit. Take a look at Listing 3.1, which shows the relationship of these different entities and how to iterate through all the individual objects contained in the Form Collection via Active Server Pages and VBScript (this code assumes that the user has clicked the Submit button). This example contains both a small portion of HTML code and server-side code.

Listing 3.1 **Collection Object, Objects, and Item**

```
<% for each Item in Request.Form %>    Name = <% =Item %>
    Value = <% =Request.Form(Item) %>
    <BR>
<% Next %>
```

In the Virtual Directory Management Object Model, `SQLVDirControl` is the top-level object or the collection, and the only one that can be directly created. All other objects must be obtained from the `SQLVDirControl` object, or a derivative of it.

A *hierarchy diagram* (object model) illustrates the relative arrangement of objects to one another. The diagram for creating a virtual root is given in Figure 3.9.

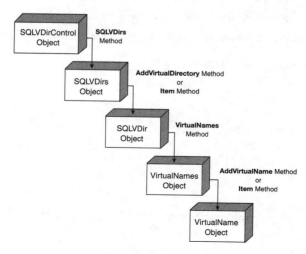

Figure 3.9 Virtual Directory Management Object Model hierarchy.

SQLVDirControl Object

This is the only object in the object hierarchy that can be directly accessed programmatically. All other objects must be accessed through it or derived from it. Table 3.7 gives the SQLVDirControl methods. The rest of this chapter is dedicated to providing examples to accomplish the manipulation of all the other objects.

Table 3.7 *SQLVDirControl* **Methods**

Method	Description
Connect	Connects to a specified IIS server. Parameters: IIS server name, Web site number in the metabase tree.
Disconnect	Closes the last connection made to an IIS server and Web site. There are no parameters. Disconnect must be called after processing is finished and before attempting to connect to another server or Web site. **Note:** Simultaneous connections to multiple servers are not possible. On the other hand, multiple calls to Connect without calling Disconnect are possible when you make more than one connection to different Web sites on the same server.
SQLVDirs	Retrieves the virtual directory collection of the Web site you are connected to. Thus, it provides access to the virtual directory objects.

Listing 3.2 is an example showing server and Web site connection methods and how to connect to the first Web site on a Web server. For a more comprehensive example of the usage of this object, and the other objects in the hierarchy, see the section "Using the Object Model" toward the end of this chapter.

Listing 3.2 **Selecting the Server's First Web Site**

```
Set objDirControl = Server.CreateObject("SQLVDir.SQLVDirControl")  'create the
                                                                   'base object
ObjDirControl.Connect "IISServer", "1"                             'connect to
                                                                   'the first web
                                                                   'site on the
                                                                   'server
                                                                   'IISServer
Set objDirs = objDirControl.SQLVDirs                               'get the
                                                                   'virtual
                                                                   'directory
                                                                   'collection
                                                                   'object

...
ObjDirControl.Disconnect
```

SQLVDirs Collection Object

As seen in the small example provided in the preceding section, the SQLVDirs, which is the collection object of virtual directories, is returned by the SQLVDirControl.SQLVDirs methods as given in Table 3.8. After you have the SQLVDirs collection you can:

- Access a virtual directory with the Item method
- Create a new virtual directory with the AddVirtualDirectory method
- Remove an existing virtual directory with the RemoveVirtualDirectory method

Table 3.8 *SQLVDirs* **Methods**

Method	Description
Next	Retrieves the next virtual directory or directories. An integer specified for Next indicates how many directories to retrieve.
Skip	Skips the virtual directory. An integer specified for Skip indicates how many directories to skip.
Reset	Resets the collection index to the first virtual directory.
Clone	Returns a copy of the SQLVDirs collection object.
Count	Returns the number of virtual directories present.
Item	Retrieves one virtual directory, which can be specified with an integer (0 is the first virtual directory), or with a name.
AddVirtualDirectory	Needs the virtual directory name as a parameter. Creates a new virtual directory with all the default values. Some properties are not set (for example, Default database).
RemoveVirtualDirectory	Deletes the virtual directory from IIS.

Listing 3.3 shows an example of connecting to a Web site and accessing the first virtual directory object.

Listing 3.3 **Accessing the First Virtual Directory Object, Item(0)**

```
Set objDirControl = Server.CreateObject("SQLVDir.SQLVDirControl")   'create the
                                                                    'base object
ObjDirControl.Connect "IISServer", "1"                              'connect to
                                                                    'the first
                                                                    'web site on
                                                                    'the server
                                                                    'IISServer
Set objDirs = objDirControl.SQLVDirs                               'get the
                                                                    'virtual
```
continues

Listing 3.3   **Continued**

```
                                              'directory
                                              'collection object
Set objDir  = objDirs.Item(0)                 'get the first virtual
                                              'directory object. You
                                              'could say objDirs(0)
                                              'since Item() is the
                                              'default

...
ObjDirControl.Disconnect
```

SQLVDir Object

The SQLVDir object is obtained by calling the Item method, the SQLVDirs object, and the AddVirtualDirectory method when creating a new virtual directory.

The SQLVDir object has the following properties, as given in Table 3.9, all of which are read/write (you can set or get them), except Password. Password is write only (it can only be set).

Table 3.9   *SQLVDir* Object Properties

Property	Description
Name	The name of the virtual directory.
PhysicalPath	The full physical path to the physical directory associated with the virtual directory.
ServerName	The name of the server running SQL Server 2000 (the data source).
DatabaseName	The default database used in queries against the virtual directory.
UserName	The user login that connects to the data source.
Password	The user password that connects to the data source.
SecurityMode	The login authentication method used with the virtual directory. The following values can be used:

	Value	Description
	1	SQL Server login
	2	Microsoft Windows anonymous login
	4	Basic authentication
	8	Windows Integrated Authentication

AllowFlags	Provides the type of access allowed through this virtual directory. The following values can be used:

	Value	Description
	1	URL queries
	8	Template access
	4	XPath queries

Property	Description
	Programmatically, to specify more than one type, simply add the values together. To allow both XPath queries and template access, the value specified would be 64 + 8, or 72. (This is a programmer preference, and I don't want to start a religious war here.) See the complete example at the end of the chapter.
	Caution: If you are changing the connection settings (server name, database name, user name, password, or the security mode), disallow virtual directory access by setting the `AllowFlags` property to 0. After you are finished, be sure to re-enable access by setting the `AllowFlags` property back to its original value.
EnablePasswordSync	Specifies whether or not IIS handles anonymous password synchronization. I recommend that this be enabled.
DLLPath	Provides the full path to the `Sqlisapi.dll` file.
AdditionalSettings	User defined settings appended to the OLE DB connection string.

In addition to these properties, the `SQLVDir` object supports the `VirtualNames` method. This method returns the collection of virtual names for the virtual directory.

Listing 3.4 shows an example of connecting to a Web site and setting the `PhysicalPath` property of the first virtual directory object.

Listing 3.4   **Setting the *PhysicalPath* Property**

```
Set objDirControl = Server.CreateObject("SQLVDir.SQLVDirControl")  'create the
                                                                   'base object
ObjDirControl.Connect "IISServer", "1"                             'connect to
                                                                   'the first web
                                                                   'site on the
                                                                   'server
                                                                   'IISServer
Set objDirs = objDirControl.SQLVDirs                               'get the
                                                                   'virtual
                                                                   'directory
                                                                   'collection
                                                                   'object

Set objDir  = objDirs.Item(0)                                      'get the first
                                                                   'virtual
                                                                   'directory
                                                                   'object. You
                                                                   'could say
                                                                   'objDirs(0)
                                                                   'since Item()
```

continues

Listing 3.4   **Continued**

```
                                                    'is the
                                                    'default
objDir.PhysicalPath = "C:\"                         'these two lines
                                                    'just show two
objDir.PhysicalPath = objDir.PhysicalPath & "inetpub"  'different ways
                                                    'of setting the
                                                    'value.  It can
                                                    'be done either
                                                    'way


ObjDirControl.Disconnect
```

VirtualNames Collection Object

The VirtualNames collection object is a collection of virtual names in the virtual directory object. It is similar to the SQLVDirs object (a collection of virtual roots).

The VirtualNames collection object contains the following methods given in Table 3.10.

Table 3.10   *VirtualNames* **Methods**

Method	Description
Next	Retrieves the next virtual name or names. An integer specified for Next indicates how many virtual names to retrieve.
Skip	Skips the virtual name or names. An integer specified for Skip indicates how many names to skip.
Reset	Resets the collection index to the first virtual name.
Clone	Returns a copy of the VirtualNames collection object.
Count	Returns the number of virtual names present.
Item	Retrieves one virtual name that can be specified with an integer (0 is the first virtual name), or with the name of the virtual name.
AddVirtualName	Requires the name, type, and directory path of the virtual name to create as parameters. The AddVirtualName method or Item method returns an interface to a VirtualName object that represents the virtual name.
RemoveVirtualName	Removes the specified virtual name.

Listing 3.5 provides the steps required to access a VirtualNames collection object.

Listing 3.5   **Accessing a *VirtualNames* Collection Object**

```
Set objDirControl = Server.CreateObject("SQLVDir.SQLVDirControl")    'create the
                                                                     'base object
ObjDirControl.Connect "IISServer", "1"                              'connect to
                                                                     'the first
                                                                     'web site on
                                                                     'the server
                                                                     'IISServer
Set objDirs = objDirControl.SQLVDirs                                'get the
                                                                     'virtual
                                                                     'directory
                                                                     'collection
                                                                     'object

Set objDir  = objDirs.Item(0)                                       'get the first
                                                                     'virtual
                                                                     'directory
                                                                     'object. You
                                                                     'could say
                                                                     'objDirs(0)
                                                                     'since Item()
                                                                     'is the
                                                                     'default
Set objNames = objDir.VirtualNames                                  'get the
                                                                     'Virtualnames
                                                                     'collection

ObjDirControl.Disconnect
```

VirtualName Object

The VirtualName object is obtained by calling the Item method (or the AddVirtualName object if you are creating a new virtual name). Listing 3.6 demonstrates this.

The VirtualName collection object contains the following properties given in Table 3.11.

Table 3.11   *VirtualName* **Properties**

Property	Description
Name	The name of the virtual name being created.
Path	The directory path (absolute or relative) of the virtual name.
Type	The virtual name type that can have one of the following values.

	Value	Description
	1	Virtual name of type dbobject.
	2	Virtual name of type schema.
	4	Virtual name of type template.

Listing 3.6 **Accessing a *VirtualName* Object and Setting Attributes**

```
Set objDirControl = Server.CreateObject("SQLVDir.SQLVDirControl")  'create the base
                                                                    'object
ObjDirControl.Connect "IISServer", "1"                              'connect to the
                                                                    'first web site
                                                                    'on the server
                                                                    'IISServer

Set objDirs = objDirControl.SQLVDirs                                'get the virtual
                                                                    'directory
                                                                    'collection
                                                                    'object

Set objDir  = objDirs.Item(0)                                       'get the first
                                                                    'virtual
                                                                    'directory
                                                                    'object. You
                                                                    'could say
                                                                    'objDirs(0)
                                                                    'since Item() is
                                                                    'the default

Set objNames = objDir.VirtualNames                                  'get the
                                                                    'Virtualnames
                                                                    'collection
Set objName1 = objNames.Item(0)                                     'get the first
                                                                    'virtual name
                                                                    'object

ObjNamem1.Type = 2                                                  'set the
                                                                    'properties of
                                                                    'the virtual
ObjNamem1.Name = "MySchema"                                         'name object
                                                                    'obtained above
ObjNamem1.Path = "C:\inetpub\schema"
...
ObjDirControl.Disconnect
```

To create a new virtual name, do something similar to this:

```
Set NewVName = objNames.AddVirtualName "MyNewSchema", 2, "C:\inetpub\schema"
```

Creating a Virtual Directory Using the Object Model

Using the physical directory structure we created earlier and incorporating the code snippets presented to this point, we can now work through a complete example to create all the components we have talked about in this chapter. This example is Listing 3.7. If you need to, refer to the comments of the code snippets to explain what's going on.

Listing 3.7   **Complete Example of Creating a Virtual Directory**

```
Set ObjXML = Server.CreateObject("SQLVDir.SQLVDirControl")
ObjXML.Connect                     'Connect to the local computer and Web site
"1"

Set ObjDirs = ObjXML.SQLVDirs
Set ObjDir = ObjDirs.AddVirtualDirectory("northwind")

'General tab in UI
ObjDir.PhysicalPath = "C:\Inetpub\wwwroot\northwind"

'Security tab in UI
ObjDir.UserName = "sa" 'SQL Server login
ObjDir.Password = ""    'SQL Server Password (blank by default)

'Data source tab in UI
'(local) is default for the SQL Server
ObjDir.DatabaseName = "Northwind"

'Settings tab in UI
objDir.AllowFlags = 73 'URL_QUERIES OR TEMPLATES OR XPath

'Virtual Name Configuration tab in the UI
Set objNames = objDir.VirtualNames
objNames.AddVirtualName "dbobject", 1, ""
objNames.AddVirtualName "schema", 2, "C:\Inetpub\wwwroot\northwind\schema"
objNames.AddVirtualName "template", 4 , "C:\Inetpub\wwwroot\northwind\template"

objXML.Disconnect    'Disconnect from the server.

msgbox "Done."
```

Recap of What Was Discussed in This Chapter

- Virtual Directories are created graphically through the Virtual Directory
  Management Utility or programmatically through the Virtual Directory
  Management Object Model. These directories are the *holding pens* for XML template files and XDR schema files. In the case of a dbobject, specifying a virtual
  directory name provides direct access to a database object such as a table or view.

- The IIS Virtual Directory Management for SQL Server Utility runs on any edition of Microsoft Windows NT 4.0 or Microsoft Windows 2000. Minor changes
  may have to be made depending on what version you are running.

- SQL Server 2000 comes with a graphical user interface utility that allows setting
  up of all aspects of virtual directories and virtual names.

- SQL Server 2000 provides a programmatic interface that allows access to and
  creation of all components associated with virtual directories and virtual names.

4

Accessing SQL 2000 via HTTP

IN THE FIRST THREE CHAPTERS, WE COVERED THE XML specification, Extensible Stylesheet Language Transformations (XSLT), and the necessary setup steps for virtual roots on SQL Server. In this chapter, we'll first discuss client/server architecture to give you a feel for how the different system components, application servers, database servers, and so on interact with each other. Then we'll look at how to utilize the HTTP protocol in various ways to execute SQL statements against SQL Server. This includes the use of template files to generate XML data. Utilizing the HTTP protocol via URLs will simplify our tasks because most people in the computer industry are very familiar with this process.

This chapter will cover the following topics:

- General client/server architecture in two-, three-, and n-tiered configurations
- SQL Server 2000's HTTP capabilities
- Entities in XML and URLs
- Generating XML documents by querying SQL Server via HTTP
- Generating XML documents utilizing XML template files
- Generating XML documents utilizing stored procedures

I think it's about time to define this *template file* that we've been talking about. It's not some new language you'll have to learn, so you can relax. It also has nothing to do with the template elements of XSLT that we learned about in Chapter 2, "XSLT Stylesheets." Simply put, these templates are just XML files that contain one or more SQL statements. When these templates are applied to a database through mechanisms you'll learn about in this chapter, they help produce results in XML format.

Let's take one last look at the XML process diagram that we used in Chapter 1, "Database XML," and Chapter 2 (see Figure 4.1).

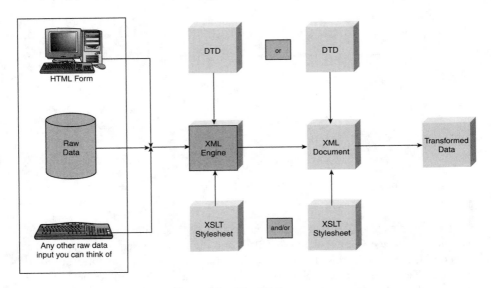

Figure 4.1   The XML process.

Yes, that's right; this is the last look. We've covered all the components in the diagram and will remain at the XML engine component for the rest of this book. The XML engine is SQL Server 2000.

Two-, Three-, and N-Tiered Architectures

To get a better understanding of how client/server components function together and therefore a better understanding of system extensibility and capability, we need to have a brief discussion of client/server architecture.

Each component of a client/server system performs one or more specific logical functions. We'll begin this discussion by defining these functions, and then we'll show you how they are distributed throughout a client/server system. These four functions are the basic building blocks of any application:

- **Data storage logic.** Most applications need to store data, whether it's a small memo file or a large database. This covers such topics as input/output (I/O) and data validation.

- **Data access logic.** This is the processing required to access stored data, which is usually in the form of SQL queries (whether they are issued from the command line of Query Analyzer or from a stored procedure).

- **Application logic.** This is the application itself, which can be simple or complex. Application logic is also referred to as a company's *business rules*.

- **Presentation logic.** This is the projection of information to the user and the acceptance of the user's input.

With these different *functional processes* now defined, we can look at how different client/server configurations split these functions up and what effect they have on extensibility. We'll begin with two-tier architecture, followed by three-tier and then n-tier architecture. Finally, we'll talk briefly about a sample SQL Server and IIS configuration.

Two-Tier Client/Server Architecture

In its simplest form, client/server architecture is a two-tier structure consisting of, believe it or not, a client component and a server component. A static Web site is a good two-tier example (see Figure 4.2).

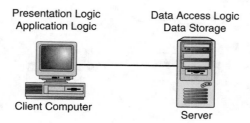

Presentation Logic
Application Logic

Data Access Logic
Data Storage

Client Computer

Server

Figure 4.2 Two-tier client/server architecture.

In this configuration, the client accepts user requests and performs the application logic that produces database requests and transmits them to the server. The server accepts the requests, performs the data access logic, and transmits the results to the client. The client accepts the results and presents them to the end user.

Three-Tier Client/Server Architecture

The next step up is three-tier architecture. Take a look at Figure 4.3.

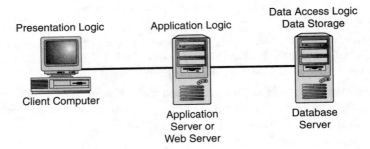

Figure 4.3   Three-tier client/server architecture.

This design utilizes three different focus points. In this case, the client is responsible for presentation logic, an application server is accountable for application logic, and a separate database server is responsible for data access logic and data storage. Many large-scale Web sites with database servers separate from Web servers are examples of this.

N-Tier Client/Server Architecture

Last but not least, there is the n-tier client/server architecture. This configuration is basically open ended (see Figure 4.4).

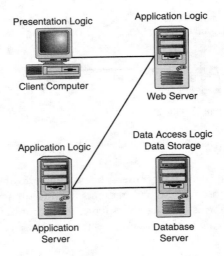

Figure 4.4   N-tier client/server architecture.

In this figure, there are more than three focus points. The client is responsible for presentation logic, a database server(s) is responsible for data access logic and data storage, and application logic is spread across two or more different sets of servers. In our example, one of the application servers is a Web server, and the other is a non-Web server. This isn't required for the architecture. Any combination of two or more types of application servers is all right.

The primary advantage of n-tiered client/server architecture, as compared to a two-tiered architecture (or a three-tiered to a two-tiered), is that it prepares an application for *load balancing*, distributing the processing among multiple servers. Also, a proper n-tier setup enables better integration with other components and ease of development, testing, and management.

Typical Microsoft Three-Tier Architecture for IIS and SQL 2000

Looking at Figure 4.5, you'll see that I have diagrammed it in a slightly different way to illustrate some important points. At first glance, you'll see that it represents three-tier client/server architecture. Nothing is new here; the client is responsible for presentation logic, a SQL Server 2000 server(s) is responsible for data access logic and data storage, and IIS contains the application logic. It's the internal workings of IIS in this instance that I want to explain a little more deeply.

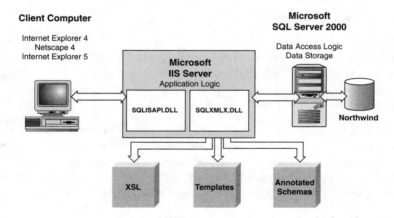

Figure 4.5   Typical Microsoft client/server architecture.

When a URL-type query is passed to IIS, it examines the virtual root contained in the URL and ensures that the SQLISAPI.DLL has been registered for this virtual root. This should have been done when the virtual root was configured via one of the two configuration methods covered in Chapter 3, "Internet Information Server and Virtual Directories."

SQLISAPI.DLL, in conjunction with other DLLs, establishes a connection with the SQL Server identified in the virtual root. After the connection is established and it is determined that the command in the URL is an XML command, the command is passed to SQLXMLX.DLL. SQLXMLX.DLL executes the command, and the results are returned. All XML functionality is contained in SQLXMLX.DLL.

> If you take into account what we have just discussed and look back to Chapter 3's section "The Advanced Tab," you'll see why the configuration of the Advanced tab is so important. If the SQLISAPI.DLL file can't be found, nothing works.

As you can see in Figure 4.5, template files, schema files, and XSLT stylesheets all reside on the IIS server.

What Are Our Capabilities When Utilizing HTTP?

Now let's take a quick look at what we can accomplish by using the HTTP protocol. The rest of this chapter will then go into each of these functions in depth.

Placing a SQL Query Directly in a URL

Take a look at the following:

```
http://IISServer/Nwind?sql=SELECT+*+FROM+Employees+FOR+XML+AUTO&root=root
```

Placing a SQL query in a URL like this is simple enough, don't you think? After the URL, which points to the Nwind virtual directory, insert a question mark followed by `sql=` and then the SQL query itself. Separate all words in the query with a plus (+) sign. We'll explain the `&root` parameter in the upcoming section "Well-Formed Documents, Fragments, and `&root`."

> FOR XML AUTO is a new extension to the SELECT statement making its appearance with SQL Server 2000. It will be covered in depth in Chapter 8, "OPENXML." For now, it's only necessary to know that it returns the results of the SQL statement as an XML document instead of as a standard rowset, as you're probably used to. You might also see it as FOR XML RAW or FOR XML EXPLICIT. Hang in there for now; we'll get to it. If you try leaving out the FOR XML statement with code similar to the following:
>
> ```
> http://griffinj/Nwind/?sql=select+*+from+Employees&root=root
> ```
>
> You'll see an error message in your browser that's very similar to what is shown in Listing 4.1.

Listing 4.1   **Error Generated by Missing FOR XML Statement**

```
<?xml version="1.0" encoding="utf-8" ?>
<root>
  <?MSSQLError HResult="0x80004005" Source="Microsoft XML Extensions to
SQL Server" Description="Streaming not supported over multiple column
result"?>
</root>
```

Specifying a Template Directly in a URL

Here's an example of specifying a template directly:

```
http://IISServer/Nwind?template=<ROOT+xmlns:sql="urn:schemas-
microsoft-com:xml-sql"><sql:query>SELECT+*+FROM+Employees+FOR+XML+AUTO
</sql:query></ROOT>
```

Now you see an example of a template file. It is in the form of an XML document and contains one or more SQL statements.

Templates allow the data to be returned as a well-formed XML document. As you'll see shortly, this isn't necessarily so when specifying a SQL statement directly in a URL. Also, some SQL query statements can become quite long. If they were in a template file, they would be easier to read than in a URL with all the additional markup needed (the plus [+] signs).

Declaring a Template File in a URL

Rather than writing a very long URL statement similar to the one in the preceding section, we could put the SQL query in a template file and refer to it in the URL like this:

```
http://IISServer/Nwind/TemplateVirtualName/template.xml
```

Remember that the TemplateVirtualName was specified with the Virtual Directory Management utility.

This also provides for better security by keeping the user away from the details of the database.

Specifying an XPath Query Against a Schema File in a URL

The following example shows how this would look:

```
http://IISServer/Nwind/SchemaVirtualName.schemafile.xml/
Employee[@EmployeeID=6]
```

Here the SchemaVirtualName was specified with the Virtual Directory Management Utility, and Employee[@EmployeeID=6] is the XPath query executed against schemafile.xml.

Specifying Database Objects Directly in a URL

Database objects such as tables and views can be specified in a URL, and then an XPath query can be issued against it to produce results as shown in the following example:

```
http://IISserver/Nwind/dbobjectVirtualName/XpathQuery
```

The XPath query is placed as the last entity in the URL, directly after the VirtualDirectoryName.

Entities

When we talked about XML documents in Chapter 1, we mentioned certain special characters that must be treated differently than other characters because they are interpreted differently depending on their location in documents. For more information, go to http://www.landfield.com/rfcs/rfc1738.html.

We must also be concerned now about special characters in URLs. Certain characters have a functionality all their own when used in URLs.

Entities in XML

The characters listed in Table 4.1 should not be used between tags in an XML document. These characters have special meaning to XML and will cause misinterpretation during parsing. The appropriate substitution entities that should be used in their place are provided in the table.

> For a more thorough discussion of these characters and why they affect things the way they do, see RFC 2396. This RFC is freely available on the Internet at http://www.landfield.com/rfcs/rfc2396.html.

Table 4.1   **Entity Substitutions**

Character	Entity
& (ampersand)	Use &
' (apostrophe)	Use '
< (less than)	Use <
> (greater than)	Use >
" (quote)	Use "

Let's look at the sample template file in Listing 4.2. You'll see why these entities are necessary. Listing 4.3 shows the result.

Listing 4.2   **Entities in Template Files**

```
<ROOT xmlns:sql="urn:schemas-microsoft-com:xml-sql">
    <sql:query>
      SELECT CustomerID, OrderDate, Freight
      FROM    Orders
      WHERE   Freight &gt; 800              <!--&gt; substituted for '>' -->
      FOR XML AUTO
    </sql:query>
</ROOT>
```

Listing 4.3   **Results of Entity Substitution**

```
<ROOT xmlns:sql="urn:schemas-microsoft-com:xml-sql">
    <Orders CustomerID="QUEEN" OrderDate="1996-12-04T00:00:00"
     Freight="890.78" />
    <Orders CustomerID="QUICK" OrderDate="1997-05-19T00:00:00"
     Freight="1007.64" />
    <Orders CustomerID="QUICK" OrderDate="1997-10-03T00:00:00"
     Freight="810.05" />
    <Orders CustomerID="SAVEA" OrderDate="1998-04-17T00:00:00"
     Freight="830.75" />
</ROOT>
```

Entities in URLs

When executing a query in a URL, you must be careful when using the characters listed in Table 4.2. They are interpreted according to the description in the table. All these characters are required at one point or another in the interpretation of URLs. Again, RFC 2396 discusses these characters in greater detail.

Table 4.2   **Special Characters in URLs**

Character	Description	Hexadecimal Value
+	Indicates a space (spaces cannot be used in a URL).	%20
/	Separates directories and subdirectories.	%2F
?	Separates the URL from the parameters.	%3F
%	Specifies special characters.	%25
#	Indicates bookmark anchors.	%23
&	Separates parameters specified in the URL.	%26

Here's an example of a direct SQL query in a URL:

```
http://IISServer/Nwind?sql=SELECT+*+FROM+Employees+WHERE+LastName+LIKE+
'D%'FOR+XML+AUTO&root=root
```

Here we are trying to retrieve all information concerning employees whose last names start with D. Because the % character is one of the special characters for URLs, trying this query directly in a URL results in several errors. To fix the problem, you need to substitute the hexadecimal value of the special character in its place, like this:

```
http://IISServer/Nwind?sql=SELECT+*+FROM+Employees+WHERE+LastName+LIKE+
'D%25'+FOR+XML+AUTO&root=root
```

There's one more point to make here. There are instances when it might become necessary to use a combination of XML and URL special characters. Look at the following sample template that could be specified directly in a URL. See if you can spot the problem.

```
<ROOT xmlns:sql="urn:schemas-microsoft-com:xml-sql"><sql:query>SELECT+
CustomerID,OrderDate,Freight+FROM+Orders+WHERE+Freight+>+800+FOR+XML+AUTO
</sql:query></ROOT>
```

Hopefully, by now you know that the > character won't work here, so we'll change it to the required XML entity.

```
<ROOT xmlns:sql="urn:schemas-microsoft-com:xml-sql"><sql:query>SELECT+
CustomerID,OrderDate,Freight+FROM+Orders+WHERE+Freight+&gt;+800+FOR+XML+
AUTO</sql:query></ROOT>
```

Did you make it this far? If so, good; but if you stopped here, you didn't go quite far enough. The & character is a URL special character, and a substitution needs to be made here also. Replace the & with the hexadecimal value %26.

```
<ROOT xmlns:sql="urn:schemas-microsoft-com:xml-sql"><sql:query>SELECT+
CustomerID,OrderDate,Freight+FROM+Orders+WHERE+Freight+%26gt;+800+FOR+XML
+AUTO</sql:query></ROOT>
```

Executing SQL via HTTP

Up to this point, we've given a lot of examples to show how the HTTP protocol is used to request XML documents from SQL Server. We've never really given a formal definition of the syntax. Table 4.3 gives the formal definition. We'll also cover some more details of querying via a URL, such as stored procedures, templates in depth, utilizing XSLT stylesheets, and so on.

Here's the formal syntax for URL access accepted by the SQL ISAPI extension:

```
http://iisserver/virtualroot/virtualname[/pathinfo][/XPathExpression]
[?param=value[&param=value]...n]
```

or:

```
http://iisserver/virtualroot?{sql=SqlString | template=XMLTemplate}
[&param=value[&param=value]...n]
```

Table 4.3   **HTTP Syntax Explanation**

Keyword	Description
iisserver	The IIS server to access.
	For example: www.newriders.com.
virtualroot	The virtual root configured with the Virtual Directory Management utility (graphically or programmatically).
virtualname	A virtual name defined when the virtual root was configured. It will be one of three types: template, schema, or dbobject.
[/pathinfo]	Path information to locate template or schema files in addition to the path information specified during virtualname configuration. Not needed for a dbobject type.
[/XPathExpression]	Specified if necessary for schema files or dbobject types.
?sql	Delimits an SQL query string.
SqlString	An SQL query or stored procedure name. Usually contains the FOR XML extension unless the returned data is already in XML format. For example, a stored procedure that returns XML data.
?template	Delimits a SQL query string formatted as an XML document.
param	This is either a parameter name or one of the following:
	contenttype	Specifies the content format of the returned document to allow a Web browser to pick the proper display method. Specified in two parts, the contenttype and subtype. It's sent in the HTTP header to become the MIME type of the document. text/XML, text/HTML, and image/gif designate an XML document, an HTML document, and a GIF image, respectively.
	outputencoding	The character set used to render the generated XML document. The default is UTF-8. Templates specified directly in a URL via template= are rendered in Unicode. Template files can specify the outputencoding themselves because they are XML documents.

continues

Table 4.3   **Continued**

Keyword	Description
root	When specified, the returned data is bracketed with the element name given to generate a well-formed XML document.
xsl	The URL of an XSLT stylesheet used to process the returned data. By default, output documents are UTF-8 encoded unless overridden by an encoding instruction in the XSL file. If outputencoding is specified, it overrides the XSL specified encoding.

Character encodings are specified with the encoding= attribute in the XML declaration. The XML specification explicitly says XML uses ISO 10646, the international standard 31-bit character repertoire that covers most human languages. It is planned to be a superset of Unicode and can be found at http://www.iso.ch.

The spec says (2.2) "All XML processors must accept the UTF-8 and UTF-16 encodings of ISO 10646... ." UTF-8 is an encoding of Unicode into 8-bit characters: The first 128 are the same as ASCII; the rest are used to encode the rest of Unicode into sequences of between 2 and 6 bytes. UTF-8 in its single-octet form is therefore the same as ISO 646 IRV (ASCII), so you can continue to use ASCII for English or other unaccented languages using the Latin alphabet. Note that UTF-8 is incompatible with ISO 8859-1 (ISO Latin-1) after code point 126 decimal (the end of ASCII). UTF-16 is like UTF-8 but with a scheme to represent the next 16 planes of 64k characters as two 16-bit characters.

Regardless of the encoding used, any character in the ISO 10646 character set can be referred to by the decimal or hexadecimal equivalent of its bit string. So, no matter which character set you personally use, you can still refer to specific individual characters by using &#dddd; (decimal character code) or &#xHHHH; (hexadecimal character code in uppercase). The terminology can get confusing, as can the numbers: See the ISO 10646 Concept Dictionary at http://www.cns-web.bu.edu/djohnson/web_files/i18n/ISO-10646.html.

Well-Formed Documents, Fragments, and &root

As promised, the &root=root parameter used in some of the URLs and template files in the previous section requires a little explanation.

Think back to our discussion of well-formedness and XML documents. One of the conditions that must be met for an XML document to be well-formed is that it must contain a single top-level element. Remember our RESUMES shown in the following example:

```
<RESUMES xmlns='http://www.myorg.net/tags'>
  <PERSON PERSONID="p1">
    <NAME>
...
</RESUMES>
```

Our document contains the single top-level element `<RESUMES>`. Although there are other requirements for well-formed documents, if this one isn't met, the document fails the test.

How does this relate to the `&root` parameter in the URL? The `&root` parameter specifies the name of the document ROOT element. The result is an XML document with that all-important single top-level element. Let's look at some examples by reusing some of the code we have given previously:

```
http://IISServer/Nwind?sql=SELECT+*+FROM+Employees+FOR+XML+AUTO&root=root
```

Here we specify `&root=root`. This will generate a document that contains that single top-level element, and the element will be `<ROOT>`. In the following example, you would expect a document fragment to be returned because no root element is specified. You actually receive an error message stating, "Only one top-level element is allowed in an XML document." Because the root element is missing, all employee elements are assumed to be at the top level, which isn't allowed.

```
http://IISServer/Nwind?sql=SELECT+*+FROM+Employees+FOR+XML+AUTO
```

When template files are used, the same conditions hold true. Let's say we have the template file shown in Listing 4.4.

Listing 4.4   **Template File Without a Root Element**

```
<ROOT XMLNS:SQL="urn:schemas-microsoft-com:xml-sql">
  <sql:query>
    SELECT   *
    FROM     Employees
    FOR XML AUTO
  </sql:query>
</ROOT>
```

Let's say we employ this template file via this URL:

```
http://IISServer/Nwind/TemplateVirtualName/template.xml
```

The template file will provide the single top-level element via the `<ROOT>` element declaration.

Just to make sure we understand the root declaration, if I make the specification root=EMPS in the template file, the following fragment shows how the resulting document's root element has changed.

```
<EMPS xmlns:sql="urn:schemas-microsoft-com:xml-sql">
  <Employees EmployeeID="1" LastName="Davolio" ...
...
</EMPS>
```

Queries on Multiple Tables

Querying multiple tables has implications that you need to consider carefully if you want to generate your resulting documents with the proper element order. Here's the rule of thumb: "The order in which tables are specified in the SQL query determines the element nesting order." We'll take a look at the Orders and Employees tables in Northwind in a couple of ways (also refer to Appendix A, "Northwind Database Schema").

Here's the first query:

```
http://iisserver/Nwind?sql=SELECT+TOP+2+Orders.OrderID,+Employees.
LastName,+Orders.ShippedDate+FROM+Orders,+Employees+WHERE+Orders.
EmployeeID=Employees.EmployeeID+Order+by+Employees.EmployeeID,
OrderID+FOR+XML+AUTO&
root=ROOT
```

This returns the results in Listing 4.5.

Listing 4.5   **Results of Querying Multiple Tables**

```
<?xml version="1.0" encoding="utf-8" ?>
<ROOT>
  <Orders OrderID="10258" ShippedDate="1996-07-23T00:00:00">
    <Employees LastName="Davolio" />
  </Orders>
  <Orders OrderID="10270" ShippedDate="1996-08-02T00:00:00">
    <Employees LastName="Davolio" />
  </Orders>
</ROOT>
```

Let's do this again with three tables, this time adding the Order Details table.

```
http://iisserver/Nwind?sql=SELECT+TOP+2+Orders.OrderID,+Employees.
LastName,+Orders.ShippedDate,+[Order+Details].UnitPrice,+[Order+
Details].ProductID+FROM+Orders,+Employees,+[Order+Details]+WHERE+Orders.
EmployeeID=Employees.EmployeeID+AND+Orders.OrderID=[Order+Details].OrderID
+Order+by+Employees.EmployeeID,Orders.OrderID+FOR+XML+AUTO&root=ROOT
```

Listing 4.6 shows the results of this query.

Listing 4.6 **Results of Querying Three Tables**

```xml
<?xml version="1.0" encoding="utf-8" ?>
<ROOT>
  <Orders OrderID="10258" ShippedDate="1996-07-23T00:00:00">
    <Employees LastName="Davolio">
      <Order_x0020_Details UnitPrice="15.2" ProductID="2" />
      <Order_x0020_Details UnitPrice="17" ProductID="5" />
    </Employees>
  </Orders>
</ROOT>
```

Listing 4.7 shows the results obtained when we execute the same SQL expression but move the `Employees.LastName` element to the last element specified.

Listing 4.7 **Results of Moving *Employees.LastName* to the Last Element**

```xml
<?xml version="1.0" encoding="utf-8" ?>
<ROOT>
  <Orders OrderID="10258" ShippedDate="1996-07-23T00:00:00">
    <Order_x0020_Details UnitPrice="15.2" ProductID="2">
      <Employees LastName="Davolio" />
    </Order_x0020_Details>
    <Order_x0020_Details UnitPrice="17" ProductID="5">
      <Employees LastName="Davolio" />
    </Order_x0020_Details>
  </Orders>
</ROOT>
```

The key point I want you to grasp here is that the placement of elements in the result XML document depends on their placement in the SQL expression. This should be especially evident in the difference between Listings 4.6 and 4.7.

Passing Parameters

It is possible to pass parameters to SQL queries in URLs. This is known as *run-time* substitution as opposed to *design-time* substitution. In this case, we use a placeholder to specify the location where the parameter is to be substituted at execution time. The placeholder is a ?, which must be specified as %3F in a URL. Here's an example:

```
http://iisserver/Nwind?sql=SELECT+TOP+4+OrderID+FROM+Orders+WHERE+
EmployeeID=%3F+FOR+XML+AUTO&EmployeeID=5&root=ROOT
```

Listing 4.8 is the resulting document.

Listing 4.8   **Results of Parameter Substitution in Our URL**

```
<?xml version="1.0" encoding="utf-8" ?>
<ROOT>
  <Orders OrderID="10248" />
  <Orders OrderID="10254" />
  <Orders OrderID="10269" />
  <Orders OrderID="10297" />
</ROOT>
```

Passing multiple parameters would just consist of more than one item with a question mark and a separate parameter for each. This URL passes two parameters:

```
http://iisserver/Nwind?sql=SELECT+TOP+4+OrderID+FROM+Orders+WHERE+
EmployeeID%3F+AND+CustomerID%3F+FOR+XML+AUTO&EmployeeID=5&CustomerID=
'VINET'&root=ROOT
```

This might not seem like a big deal here, and perhaps it's not to you, but wait until we start specifying template files in URLs that have parameters queries designed into them. We'll get to these shortly.

The XSL Keyword

Now we get to make use of what we learned in Chapter 2. Utilizing XSLT stylesheets gives us the much-needed flexibility to manipulate the XML output we generate. We can create HTML on-the-fly for immediate or later display, or we can change the returned XML document to a different one for further processing. The latter occurs more often than you would think, as with Electronic Data Interchange (EDI) related messages. Let's take the following SQL query and generate an HTML page:

```
http://iisserver/Nwind?sql=SELECT+TOP+4+OrderID,EmployeeID,Shipname+FROM+
Orders+WHERE+EmployeeID=5+FOR+XML+AUTO&xsl=order.xsl &root=ROOT
```

In this example, the XSL file is located in the virtual root directory. The resulting XML document is given in Listing 4.9, followed by the XSLT stylesheet in Listing 4.10.

Listing 4.9   **XML Document Containing Order Information**

```
<?xml version="1.0" encoding="utf-8" ?>
<ROOT>
  <Orders OrderID="10248" EmployeeID="5" Shipname="Vins et alcools
  Chevalier" />
  <Orders OrderID="10254" EmployeeID="5" Shipname="Chop-suey Chinese" />
  <Orders OrderID="10269" EmployeeID="5" Shipname="White Clover Markets"
/>
  <Orders OrderID="10297" EmployeeID="5" Shipname="Blondel père et fils"
/>
</ROOT>
```

Listing 4.10 **XSLT Stylesheet to Apply to Order Information**

```xml
<?xml version='1.0'?>
<xsl:stylesheet xmlns:xsl='http://www.w3.org/XSL/Transform/1.0'>
<xsl:output media-type="text/html"/>

  <xsl:template match="/">
    <HTML>
    <BODY>
      <TABLE width='400' border='1'>
      <TR>
      <TD><B>Order ID</B></TD>
      <TD><B>Ship Name</B></TD>
      </TR>
      <xsl:apply-templates/>
      </TABLE>
    </BODY>
    </HTML>
  </xsl:template>

  <xsl:template match="Orders">
    <TR>
      <TD>
        <xsl:value-of select="@OrderID"/>
      </TD>
      <TD>
        <xsl:value-of select="@Shipname"/>
      </TD>
    </TR>
  </xsl:template>
</xsl:stylesheet>
```

This results in a simple table of Order ID versus Shipname, as shown in Table 4.4.

Table 4.4 **HTML Table of Results**

Order ID	Shipname
10248	Vins et alcools Chevalier
10254	Chop-suey Chinese
10269	White Clover Markets
10297	Blondel per`e et fils

Again, the result in this case might be simple, but the potential is enormous. Data can be retrieved from a database and presented in real-time to the viewer via a thin–client browser. Static pages can be generated and stored for viewing as needed by the client. In this case, the XSLT stylesheet functions as an HTML template. (Templates are much easier to maintain than rewriting HTML documents.) Business-to-business e-commerce documents can be generated from existing queries without having to modify the query itself. The XSLT stylesheet can manipulate the data in any way desired to create the required new XML document.

Next we change our focus to using template files to generate XML documents. We'll discuss them in a lot more detail than we have so far.

Executing Template Files via HTTP

If you look back at some of the queries we wrote in the previous section, you'll see that they can be pretty difficult to read sometimes. Take a look at the query that generated Listings 4.6 and 4.7 and tell me that you immediately know exactly what the query is doing. I doubt you can.

Template files have the same functionality as SQL queries written directly in URLs. Template files can do the following:

- Specify SQL queries or XPath queries
- Define parameters that can be passed to these queries
- Specify a top-level (root) element for the XML document
- Declare namespaces
- Specify an XSLT stylesheet to apply to the results

Template files have the added benefits of being easier to read and some say easier to write. In addition, they remove the database details from the general user for added security. Editing a file can be made impossible for the user, but because he can see a URL, he can change it or write his own and obtain information you might not want him to see or have. Also, there are fewer training requirements because the user only needs to know the filename and any parameters that might need to be passed.

Using XML Templates

Up to this point, when we've written a template file, we've used only the `<sql:query>` element to specify what the statement is to execute. In addition to this `<sql:query>` element, there are four other elements that can appear in a template file. Listing 4.11 shows the general format of a template file and is followed by an explanation of each of the elements in Table 4.5.

Listing 4.11 **XML Template Format**

```
<ROOT xmlns:sql="urn:schemas-microsoft-com:xml-sql"
      sql:xsl="XSL FileName" >
  <sql:header>
    <sql:param>..</sql:param>
    <sql:param>..</sql:param>...n
  </sql:header>
```

```
<sql:query>
   sql statement(s)
</sql:query>
<sql:xpath-query mapping-schema="SchemaFileName.xml">
   XPath query
</sql:xpath-query>
</ROOT>
```

Table 4.5 **XML Template Elements**

Element	Description
`<ROOT>`	This tag provides a single top-level element (also referred to as the *root tag*) for the resulting XML document. It can have any name.
`<sql:header>`	This tag is used to hold any header values. In the current implementation of SQL Server 2000, only the `<sql:param>` element can be specified in this tag. The `<sql:header>` tag acts as a containing tag, enabling you to define multiple parameters. This provides greater efficiency because all the parameter definitions are in one place. This is similar to declaring variables at the start of a T-SQL stored procedure.
`<sql:param>`	This element defines parameters that are passed to the queries inside the template. Each `<param>` element defines one parameter. Multiple `<param>` elements can be specified in the `<sql:header>` tag.
`<sql:query>`	This element specifies SQL queries. You can have multiple `<sql:query>` elements in a template.
	If there are multiple `<sql:query>` tags in the template and one fails, the others will proceed.
`<sql:xpath-query>`	This element specifies an XPath query. The schema filename must be specified using the `mapping-schema` attribute.
	If there are multiple `<sql:XPath-query>` tags in the template and one fails, the others will proceed.
`<sql:xsl>`	Specifies an XSLT stylesheet to be applied to the result document. A relative or absolute path can be given for the file. If a relative path is given, it is relative to the directory that was defined as the Template directory with the Virtual Directory Management utility.
`mapping-schema`	If you are executing an XPath query in a template, this attribute identifies the associated XDR schema. It can have a specified path identical to the path requirements of the `sql:xsl` element.

Here are some examples of using templates and template files in URLs. I'll reuse some of the earlier examples of URL SQL queries to illustrate the differences.

Here is a simple SELECT statement on a single table specified directly in a URL:

```
http://iisserver/Nwind?template=<ROOT+xmlns:sql="urn:schemas-microsoft-
com:xml-sql"><sql:query>SELECT+LastName,FirstName+FROM+Employees+
FOR+XML+AUTO</sql:query></ROOT>
```

Here is the result in Listing 4.12.

Listing 4.12 **Specifying a Template Directly in a URL**

```
<ROOT xmlns:sql="urn:schemas-microsoft-com:xml-sql">
  <Employees LastName="Davolio" FirstName="Nancy" />
  <Employees LastName="Fuller" FirstName="Andrew" />
  <Employees LastName="Leverling" FirstName="Janet" />
  <Employees LastName="Peacock" FirstName="Margaret" />
  <Employees LastName="Buchanan" FirstName="Steven" />
  <Employees LastName="Suyama" FirstName="Michael" />
  <Employees LastName="King" FirstName="Robert" />
  <Employees LastName="Callahan" FirstName="Laura" />
  <Employees LastName="Dodsworth" FirstName="Anne" />
</ROOT>
```

Taking the same template and making it a template file enables us to write it in a manner that is much easier to read (see Listing 4.13).

Listing 4.13 **SQL Query Rewritten into a Template Format**

```
<ROOT xmlns:sql="urn:schemas-microsoft-com:xml-sql">
  <sql:query>
    SELECT LastName, FirstName
    FROM Employees
    FOR XML AUTO
  </sql:query>
</ROOT>
```

Assuming that this template would be saved as the file template1.xml and saved to the directory with the virtual name templates, we would execute this template using the following URL:

```
http://iisserver/Nwind/templates/template1.xml
```

Let's look at one more example. When we queried a combination of three tables, we ended up with the following URL:

```
http://iisserver/Nwind?sql=SELECT+TOP+2+Orders.OrderID,+Employees.
LastName,+Orders.ShippedDate,+[Order+Details].UnitPrice,+[Order+
Details].ProductID+FROM+Orders,+Employees,+[Order+Details]+WHERE+Orders.
EmployeeID=Employees.EmployeeID+AND+Orders.OrderID=[Order+Details].
OrderID+Order+by+Employees.EmployeeID,Orders.OrderID+FOR+XML+AUTO&root=ROOT
```

Converting this to a template file gives us Listing 4.14.

Listing 4.14   **Long SQL Query Rewritten in a Template File**

```
<ROOT xmlns:sql="urn:schemas-microsoft-com:xml-sql">
  <sql:query>
    SELECT TOP 2
      Orders.OrderID,
      Employees.LastName,
      Orders.ShippedDate,
      [Order Details].UnitPrice,
      [Order Details].ProductID
    FROM
      Orders, Employees, [Order Details]
    WHERE
      Orders.EmployeeID=Employees.EmployeeID
    AND
      Orders.OrderID=[Order Details].OrderID
    ORDER BY
      Employees.EmployeeID,Orders.OrderID
    FOR XML AUTO
  </sql:query>
</ROOT>
```

This template file will produce the same results as those shown in Listing 4.6, but don't you think this is easier to read than the URL method?

Passing Template Parameters

Just as we passed parameters to SQL queries, we can also pass them to templates. The `<sql:header>` element is used to define the parameters, which also can be assigned default values. These default values are used for parameters at run-time if values are not explicitly specified.

Explicit Default Values and Parameter Passing

In this example, we want the CustomerID, OrderID, RequiredDate, and freight costs for a CustomerID we specify in the URL. Take a close look at the template file in Listing 4.15. We have our query stated in the `<sql:query>` element as we would expect. In addition, we have explicitly specified a default value of VINET for the CustomerID. The `<sql:param>` element accomplishes this. The `sql:header` element holds all parameters and their values.

The item in the query that is the parameterized quantity is specified by prepending the @ symbol to the quantity name. In this case, it is CustomerID. Don't confuse this @ symbol usage with the XML attribute usage of @. In this case, they are different entities altogether. This usage is specific to Microsoft parameterized expressions. If we execute this template file with the following URL, we will generate the result given in Listing 4.16.

```
http://iisserver/Nwind/templates/customer.xml
```

Listing 4.15 **Customer.xml**

```
<ROOT xmlns:sql='urn:schemas-microsoft-com:xml-sql'>
  <sql:header>
    <sql:param name='CustomerID'>VINET</sql:param>
  </sql:header>
  <sql:query>
    SELECT CustomerID,OrderID,RequiredDate,Freight
    FROM Orders
    WHERE CustomerID=@CustomerID
    FOR XML AUTO
  </sql:query>
</ROOT>
```

Listing 4.16 **Customer.xml Results with no CustomerID Passed**

```
<ROOT xmlns:sql="urn:schemas-microsoft-com:xml-sql">
  <Orders CustomerID="VINET" OrderID="10248" RequiredDate="1996-08-
    01T00:00:00" Freight="32.38" />
  <Orders CustomerID="VINET" OrderID="10274" RequiredDate="1996-09-
    03T00:00:00" Freight="6.01" />
  <Orders CustomerID="VINET" OrderID="10295" RequiredDate="1996-09-
    30T00:00:00" Freight="1.15" />
  <Orders CustomerID="VINET" OrderID="10737" RequiredDate="1997-12-
    09T00:00:00" Freight="7.79" />
  <Orders CustomerID="VINET" OrderID="10739" RequiredDate="1997-12-
    10T00:00:00" Freight="11.08" />
</ROOT>
```

Because no value for the parameter CustomerID was passed in the URL, the template file will use the default value VINET. If we pass a parameter value of WELLI, we obtain the results in Listing 4.17. Here's the URL:

```
http://iisserver/Nwind/templates/customer.xml?CustomerID=WELLI
```

Listing 4.17 shows the results.

Listing 4.17 **Partial Results with Parameter of *CustomerID=WELLI***

```
<ROOT xmlns:sql="urn:schemas-microsoft-com:xml-sql">
  <Orders CustomerID="WELLI" OrderID="10256" RequiredDate="1996-08-
    12T00:00:00" Freight="13.97" />
  <Orders CustomerID="WELLI" OrderID="10420" RequiredDate="1997-02-
    18T00:00:00" Freight="44.12" />
  <Orders CustomerID="WELLI" OrderID="10585" RequiredDate="1997-07-
    29T00:00:00" Freight="13.41" />
  ...
</ROOT>
```

Passing Multiple Parameters

You would think that multiple parameter passing would present no new problems, and you would be right. The parameters can just be individually listed in the `<sql:header>` element and be given default values. See Listing 4.18 and the result in Listing 4.19.

Listing 4.18 **Shipvia.xml—Multiple Parameters in a Template**

```
<ROOT xmlns:sql='urn:schemas-microsoft-com:xml-sql'>
  <sql:header>
    <sql:param name='ShipVia'>1</sql:param>
    <sql:param name='ShipCountry'>France</sql:param>
  </sql:header>
  <sql:query>
    SELECT TOP 4 CustomerID,OrderID,Freight
    FROM Orders
    WHERE ShipVia=@ShipVia
    AND ShipCountry=@ShipCountry
    ORDER BY OrderID
    FOR XML AUTO
  </sql:query>
</ROOT>
```

Listing 4.19 **Results of Listing 4.18**

```
<ROOT xmlns:sql="urn:schemas-microsoft-com:xml-sql">
  <Orders CustomerID="VICTE" OrderID="10251" Freight="41.34" />
  <Orders CustomerID="BLONP" OrderID="10265" Freight="55.28" />
  <Orders CustomerID="VINET" OrderID="10274" Freight="6.01" />
  <Orders CustomerID="BONAP" OrderID="10331" Freight="10.19" />
</ROOT>
```

Executing the URL `http://iisserver/Nwind/templates/shipvia.xml`, which calls the template in Listing 4.18, gives the results in Listing 4.19 because no parameters were passed and the default values of 1 for `ShipVia` and `France` for `ShipCountry` were used. You could also pass just one of the parameters. It would be substituted for the default value, and the other parameter would use the default value provided.

Specifying an XSL Stylesheet

There also is really nothing new when you want to apply an XSLT stylesheet to the results of a template file. Just specify the stylesheet name in the `sql:xsl` attribute of the `ROOT` element. Let's take the example from "The XSL Keyword" section earlier in this chapter that illustrated using an XSLT stylesheet.

Stylesheets are developed utilizing some third-party (relative to SQL server) application using a model of the document it is supposed to transform. If everything is tested during development, the only error conditions that usually happen are a blank HTML document, garbled HTML output, or an attempted transformation of an XML document that ends up blank. Because the XSLT stylesheet and query are properly tested in development, almost all these errors are traceable to a bad XML document or bad data.

Listing 4.20 gives the template file XSLDemo.xml.

Listing 4.20 **XSLDemo.xml**

```
<ROOT xmlns:sql='urn:schemas-microsoft-com:xml-sql'
sql:xsl='XSLDemo.xml'>
  <sql:query>
    SELECT TOP 4 OrderID,EmployeeID,Shipname
    FROM Orders
    WHERE EmployeeID=5
    FOR XML AUTO
  </sql:query>
</ROOT>
```

The stylesheet to apply is given in Listing 4.9, and the results are given in Listing 4.10. These result in Table 4.4.

Executing Stored Procedures

So far, everything we've done has been either SQL queries or templates in a URL or template files accessed via a URL. There has been one glaring omission here, however: *stored procedures* and how we execute them. In essence, we've been mimicking stored procedures through the use of template files. Now we'll use stored procedures as they should be used. (No doubt we'll be required to know how to do this in both URL queries and template files.)

Granting users the capability to write and execute stored procedures against a database is not the most secure way of doing business. Administrators should allow the user to read and execute stored procedures written by developers but not to write files to the TemplateVirtualDirectory. You would be leaving yourself open to all sorts of problems otherwise.

Listing 4.21 gives the stored procedure we'll use throughout this discussion.

Listing 4.21 **Example Stored Procedure**

```
IF EXISTS (SELECT name FROM sysobjects
    WHERE name = 'OrderInfo' AND type = 'P')
    DROP PROCEDURE OrderInfo
GO
```

```
CREATE PROCEDURE OrderInfo
AS
    SELECT OrderID, CustomerID
    FROM   Orders
    WHERE  CustomerID='CHOPS'
FOR XML AUTO
GO
```

This stored procedure can be executed using this URL:

```
http://IISServer/Nwind?sql=EXECUTE+OrderInfo&root=ROOT
```

Listing 4.22 gives the result file.

Listing 4.22 **Results of Calling the Example Stored Procedure**

```
<?xml version="1.0" encoding="utf-8" ?>
<ROOT>
  <Orders OrderID="10254" CustomerID="CHOPS" />
  <Orders OrderID="10370" CustomerID="CHOPS" />
  <Orders OrderID="10519" CustomerID="CHOPS" />
  <Orders OrderID="10731" CustomerID="CHOPS" />
  <Orders OrderID="10746" CustomerID="CHOPS" />
  <Orders OrderID="10966" CustomerID="CHOPS" />
  <Orders OrderID="11029" CustomerID="CHOPS" />
  <Orders OrderID="11041" CustomerID="CHOPS" />
</ROOT>
```

Passing parameters is accomplished by utilizing the @ symbol again for the parameter expression in the stored procedure, as shown in Listing 4.23.

Listing 4.23 **Passing a Parameter to a Stored Procedure**

```
...
    SELECT OrderID,CustomerID
    FROM   Orders
    WHERE  CustomerID=@CustomerID
    FOR XML AUTO
...
```

The stored procedure can then be called via a URL in one of two ways. The first method is as follows:

```
http://iisserver/Nwind?sql=execute+OrderInfo+CHOPS
```

This method provides the value CHOPS by virtue of its position. If two parameters were being passed, you could just put them one right after the other, and they would be correctly passed.

The second method is as follows:

```
http://iisserver/Nwind?sql=execute+OrderInfo+@CustomerID=CHOPS
```

This method provides the value CHOPS by name, which is the method we are most used to.

Accessing Database Objects via HTTP

There is one entity left that we need to understand how to access. We've covered direct SQL queries and direct templates in URLs and the use of template files. Now we'll take a look at accessing dbobjects (tables, views, and so on).

Posting Templates via HTML Forms

As a final exercise for this chapter, we are going to show how to post a template file using an HTML form. In a Web environment, this would probably be the most common way of executing template files. Let's face it; users are comfortable and familiar with HTML forms. They see them just about every time they access the Internet and on their company intranet if there is one. Forms are easy to generate and provide a high level of interaction.

This template file has one parameter passed to the query. It would be a simple exercise to add multiple parameters. This template file would be saved as an HTML file and placed in a directory other than the virtual root tree. The SQLISAPI.DLL file is not expecting an HTML file and will not function correctly if placed in its directory tree.

Let's look at the HTML form itself, as shown in Listing 4.24.

Listing 4.24   **Posting a Template via an HTML Form**

```
<head>
<TITLE>Sample Form </TITLE>
</head>
<body>
For a given customer ID, order ID, order date and freight costs is
retrieved.
<form action="http://griffinjnt4s/nwind" method="POST">
<B>Customer ID</B>
<input type=text name=CustomerID value='VINET'>
<input type=hidden name=contenttype value=text/xml>
<input type=hidden name=template value='
<ROOT xmlns:sql="urn:schemas-microsoft-com:xml-sql" >
<sql:header>
    <sql:param name="CustomerID">VINET</sql:param>
</sql:header>

<sql:query>
  SELECT OrderID, OrderDate, Freight
  FROM    Orders
  WHERE     CustomerID=@CustomerID
```

```
    FOR XML AUTO
</sql:query>
</ROOT>
'>

<p><input type="submit">
</form>
</body>
```

Here, the HTML text box supplies the value that is passed to the query. The query then returns the order ID, date ordered, and freight cost.

It is also possible to give the user a choice of what XSLT stylesheet to apply to the data. Add the following lines in Listing 4.25 to Listing 4.24.

Listing 4.25   **Additional HTML Code for the Drop-Down Box**

```
<br>
Select a Stylesheet to apply:
<select name='stylesheets' size='1'>
  <option value=''></option>
  <option value='ss1.xsl'>Stylesheet 1</option>
  <option value='ss2.xsl'>Stylesheet 2</option>
  <option value='ss3.xsl'>Stylesheet 3</option>
</select>
```

This adds a drop-down list of stylesheets for the user to choose from (see Figure 4.6).

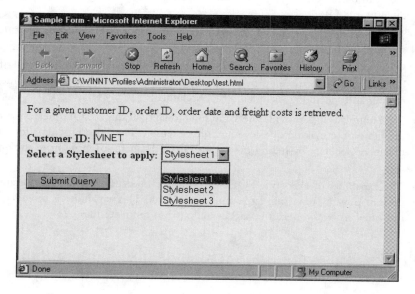

Figure 4.6   Adding an XSLT stylesheet selection drop-down box.

Also add an additional input field and parameter field like this:

```
<input type="text" name="stylesheet" value="ss1.xsl">
```

```
sql:param name="stylesheet">ss1</sql:param>
```

Finally, modify the <root> statement to this:

```
<root xmlns:sql="urn:schemas-microsoft-com:xml-sql"
sql:xsl="@stylesheet">
```

That finishes this chapter. One thing you should have noticed in this chapter is that the documents we generated are what are known as *attribute-centric documents*. All data is assigned to attributes of the elements of the document. The opposite of this is *element-centric documents*. All data is returned as a series of nested elements, which is probably the way you expected the data to be returned in the first place. SQL Server 2000 does provide ways to generate element-centric documents, and we will learn about them when we cover the FOR XML clause in detail in Chapter 8.

Recap of What Was Discussed in This Chapter

- Client/server is an open-ended architecture that provides for enhanced extensibility. It usually is implemented in two-tier, three-tier, or n-tier configurations and is based on the organization of data, application, and client logic.

- SQL Server 2000 provides several methods for generating XML documents directly from relational data. SQL queries can be placed directly in a URL, and they can be placed in template files. Templates themselves also can be placed directly in a URL.

- There are several special characters that, if placed in a URL, must be rewritten so they will be interpreted correctly.

- SQL queries in URLs provide much functionality. In addition to providing for document well-formedness by furnishing a ROOT element, they allow parameter passing and specifying included XSLT stylesheets.

- SQL template files provide the same functionality as direct SQL queries while at the same time making queries much more legible. They also provide a level of enhanced security by hiding the details of the database structure from the end user.

- The capability of executing SQL Server–stored procedures is very important to prevent possibly rewriting large amounts of code. This capability is provided for not only via SQL queries in URLs but also via template files.

5

Creating XML Views
with XDR Schemas

THINK BACK TO CHAPTER 4, "ACCESSING SQL 2000 VIA HTTP," and you'll realize that we covered a large amount of information and coding techniques in that chapter. This information enables us to generate XML documents in several ways: by calling stored procedures, by calling template files, and by directly stating SQL in URLs. The template file's contents also can be listed directly in a URL. In addition, we can modify the returned document to suit our requirements by employing XSLT stylesheets.

Even though we learned how to accomplish all this, we still have the full version of the XPath expression and queries to learn, along with the FOR XML and OPENXML Microsoft extensions and Microsoft's version of schemas, XML-Data Reduced (XDR) schemas. We tackle the latter subject matter, XDR schemas, in this chapter.

In Chapter 1, "XML," I mentioned that Microsoft's version on XML schemas differs from the schemas documented in the W3C specification. This came about from Microsoft taking the initial specification, immediately adopting it, modifying it accordingly, and not paralleling the W3C specification. In this chapter, you'll see just how different the two specifications are.

This chapter will cover the following topics:

- A thorough canvass of Microsoft's XDR schema
- Microsoft's BizTalk Framework and what it attempts to accomplish

- Annotations to Microsoft's XDR schema and how they are used to map XML to relational databases
- Data types and how they map between XML and XDR schemas

Overview

With relational database management systems, it is common practice to create a *view* of a database and then query that view using SQL. XDR schemas perform the similar function of creating XML views of relational data, which can then be queried via XPath expressions.

As we saw in Chapter 1, XML schemas describe XML document structure and are capable of placing constraints on the data in the document. SQL Server 2000 uses the XML-Data Reduced language to create schemas. This language is similar but *only* similar to the W3C specification for a schema language, which is located at `http://www.w3.org/TR/2000/CR-xmlschema-0-20001024/`. Although the two methods accomplish basically the same thing, the languages are very, very different. Now let's take a look at XDR schemas and the XDR language as a whole.

XDR Schemas

The XDR language is a subset of ideas described in the XML-Data specification. Microsoft's XML Parser (MSXML) implementation utilizes the XML-Data Reduced language specification, which is based on the XML-Data Note posted by the W3C in January 1998. It is still available at `http://www.w3.org/TR/1998/NOTE-XML-data-0105/`. The parser implementation is also based on the Document Content Description (DCD) for XML, available at `http://www.w3.org/TR/NOTE-dcd`. XML schemas in Microsoft Internet Explorer 5.0 and later provide support for the subset of XML-Data that coincides directly with the functionality expressed in this DCD, although in a slightly different XML grammar.

Elements and Attributes

Just as in the W3C schema specification, specifying `<ElementType ...>` and `<AttributeType ...>` defines the elements and attributes contained in an XDR schema, respectively. These provide the definition and type of the elements and attributes. Then an instance of an element or an attribute is declared using `<element ...>` or `<attribute ...>` tags.

Consider the XDR schema shown in Listing 5.1.

Listing 5.1 **Sample XDR Schema**

```
<?xml version="1.0"?>
<Schema xmlns="schemas-microsoft-com:xml-data">
  <ElementType name="title" />
  <ElementType name="author" />
  <ElementType name="pages" />
  <ElementType name="book" model="closed">
    <element type="title" />
    <element type="author" />
    <element type="pages" />

    <AttributeType name="copyright" />
    <attribute type="copyright" />
  </ElementType>
</Schema>
```

The schema defines four elements—<title>, <author>, <pages>, and <book>—using the <ElementType> element. The <book> element specifies the individual elements and attributes that make it up. In other words, it describes the content model for the element. There is much more to the content model than this simple example shows, and we will discuss the additional components in the next section.

This example shows that each book element contains title, author, and pages child elements. This content model is specified using the element element, along with the type attribute that references the element type defined earlier.

There is also support for global attributes that enable multiple elements to share the definition of a common attribute. Take a look at Listing 5.2. This schema declares an attribute, copyright, for the book element. This is done using the <AttributeType> element, which defines an attribute type, and then declaring it using attribute element. You specify the <AttributeType> element globally by placing it outside the context of any <ElementType>.

Listing 5.2 **Sample of Global Attribute Declaration**

```
<Schema xmlns:s="urn:schemas-microsoft-com:xml-data">
  <ElementType name="title" content="textOnly"/>
  <ElementType name="authors" content="textOnly"/>
  <AttributeType name="pages" content="textOnly"/>
  <ElementType name="book" order="seq" content="eltOnly">

    <attribute type="pages" />
    <element type="title" />
    <element type="authors" />
  </ElementType>
</Schema>
```

The Content Model

The content model describes the structure of elements and attributes in the XML document. To do this, you use various attributes such as `model`, `minOccurs`, `maxOccurs`, `order`, `content`, and so on. We'll look at the content model of an element first and then at the content model of an attribute.

For the rest of this content model discussion, I would like you to keep in mind that choices made concerning these elements and attributes and the attributes' values are strictly and completely governed by a company's business rules. These are not arbitrary decisions.

Look back at Listing 5.2. As we saw in the preceding section, the content model for the `title`, `author`, and `pages` elements is pretty straightforward. Because the `content` attribute specifies the elements as `textOnly`, these elements contain text and nothing else (no child elements).

The content model for the `book` element is a little more complex. The `content` attribute for the `book` element is `eltOnly`. This means that the `book` element can contain only the elements specified (`title`, `author`, and `pages`). Furthermore, for each `book` element instance, the child elements must be in the order specified in the schema. See Listing 5.3 for a sample instance document that conforms to the schema in Listing 5.2.

Listing 5.3 **A Valid Instance Document of the Schema in Listing 5.2**

```
<msx:book xmlns:msx="x-schema:BookSchema.xml">
  <msx:pages>522</msx:pages>
  <msx:title>Java and XML: A Marriage That Works</msx:title>
  <msx:authors>John Griffin</msx:authors>
<msx:/book>
```

Let's now take a look at the different attributes used by the content model.

The *model* Attribute (Open and Closed Content Models)

An element's content model can have the property of being either *open* or *closed*. In an open content model, an element can have additional child elements and attributes that are not declared in the schema that the document references. With the opposite, a closed model, the document cannot include any data that does not follow the rules of the referenced schema.

The default value for an XDR schema content model is open. This provides extensibility for an XDR schema that is not present in a Document Type Definition (DTD), which is a closed model. A DTD disallows including any information that does not follow its rules.

Listing 5.4 is a fragment of our earlier XML document in Listing 5.2.

Listing 5.4 *BookSchema* **Fragment**

```
<msx:book xmlns:msx="x-schema:BookSchema.xml"
          xmlns:msy="urn:some-new-namespace">
  <msx:title msy:id="123"> Java and XML: A Marriage That Works
</msx:title>
  <msx:authors> John Griffin </msx:authors>
  <msx:pages>474</msx:pages>
  <msy:publisher>New Rider's Publishing</msy:publisher>
</msx:book>
```

By default, this schema specifies an open content model. This fragment is valid even though it has additional elements and attributes not specified in the schema (such as the id attribute in the title element and the publisher child element, both of which are defined in the "urn:some-new-namespace" namespace).

Even though the open content model allows some freedom and enables us to do some things that we can't do in a DTD, there are constraints that must be met:

- Content cannot be inserted or deleted, thereby breaking the existing content model. For example, our schema defines the book element as a sequence of three elements. Therefore, you must provide that exact element sequence before adding any open content. So the pages element cannot be removed, nor can there be two title elements next to each other.

- Undeclared elements can be added as long as they are defined in a different namespace.

- After the schema content model is satisfied, other elements can be added. For example, an XML document will validate even if you add a second title element after the pages element.

The following example specifies a closed content model:

```
<x:ElementType name="book" model="closed">
```

This indicates that a book element can only contain the title, author, and pages elements, as the schema dictates. In this case, utilizing the extended elements in the preceding XML fragment would invalidate the document.

The *content* Attribute

The content attribute describes exactly what an element can contain. Its possible values are listed in Table 5.1.

Table 5.1   **The *content* Attribute**

Value	Description
textOnly	The element can contain only text.
eltOnly	The element can contain only other elements.
mixed	The element can contain a mixture of text and elements.
empty	The element must be empty.

Going back to our book example in Listing 5.4, as we've said, this XDR schema defines a book element that contains three child elements: title, author, and pages. These child elements can contain only text because the content attribute for each of these elements is textOnly. The book element, however, can contain only elements and no text because its content attribute is eltOnly. Listing 5.5 shows our entire schema again.

Listing 5.5   **The Book XDR Schema**

```
<?xml version="1.0"?>
<Schema xmlns:s="schemas-microsoft-com:xml-data">
  <s:ElementType name="title" content="textOnly" />
  <s:ElementType name="author" content="textOnly" />
  <s:AttributeType name="pages" content="textOnly" />
  <s:ElementType name="book"  content="eltOnly" model="closed">
    <s:element type="title" />
    <s:element type="author" />
    <s:attribute type="pages" />

    <s:AttributeType name="copyright" />
    <s:attribute type="copyright" />
  </s:ElementType>
</Schema>
```

Notice also that the book element uses a *closed* content model (model="closed"). This means the book element can contain only these three child elements and no text or additional child elements and attributes.

An *empty* content attribute specifies that the element cannot contain any text or child elements; conversely, it can contain attributes. A *mixed* element, on the other hand, *can* contain text and child elements.

The *minOccurs* and *maxOccurs* Attributes

The minOccurs and maxOccurs attributes are constraint rules that specify how many times a child element can appear within its parent element. A complete description of these attributes is given in Table 5.2. You specify it like this:

```
<element type="Item" maxOccurs="*" />
```

Table 5.2 **The Constraint Rules**

Attribute	Description	Valid Value	Interpretation	Default
maxOccurs	Specifies the maximum number of times that a child element may appear within a parent element.	"1"	One and only one instance of this child element may appear.	"1" unless the content= "mixed"; if this is the case, then the default value is "*".
	"*"		Any number of this child element may appear.	n/a
minOccurs	Specifies the minimum number of times that a child element may appear within a parent element.	"0"	In effect, specifying "0" for minOccurs makes an occurrence of the child element optional.	minOccurs' default value is "1".
		"1"		n/a

In the schema in Listing 5.6, the author element sets maxOccurs to "*", while the pages element sets the minOccurs attribute to "0".

Listing 5.6 **A Schema with Both *maxOccurs* and *minOccurs***

```
<?xml version="1.0"?>
<Schema xmlns:s="schemas-microsoft-com:xml-data">
  <s:ElementType name="title" content="textOnly" />
  <s:ElementType name="author" content="textOnly" />
  <s:ElementType name="pages" content="textOnly" />
  <s:ElementType name="book"  content="eltOnly" model="closed">
    <s:element type="title" />
    <s:element type="author" maxOccurs="*" />
    <s:element type="pages" minOccurs="0" />
  </s:ElementType>
  <s:ElementType name="root" >
    <s:element type="book" />
  </s:ElementType>
</Schema>
```

The schema in Listing 5.6 makes the document in Listing 5.7 a valid XML document.

Listing 5.7 **A Valid Document Based on the Listing 5.6 Schema**

```
<root>
  <book>
    <title>C Programming</title>
    <author>Author A</author>
    <author>Author B</author>
    <pages>300</pages>
  </book>
  <book>
    <title>Java Programming</title>
    <author>Author C</author>
  </book>
</root>
```

The *minLength* and *maxLength* Attributes

The "urn:schemas-microsoft-com:datatypes" namespace specifies an element or attribute's data type. The minLength and maxLength attributes defined in this namespace are used to constrain the length of a string, number, bin.hex, or bin.base64 data type. These attributes are enforced at parse-time and run-time, and they have valid parent elements of <ElementType/>, <AttributeType/>, and <dataType/>.

For string and number data types, maxLength specifies the maximum number of characters allowed, and minLength specifies the minimum number of characters.

For bin.hex and bin.base64, maxLength sets the maximum number of bytes of the binary object, and minLength sets the minimum number of bytes.

Here's an example of how to use these length attributes. The following schema (see Listing 5.8) specifies the content model for the userID, password, and LoginInfo elements. The password element specifies a minimum length of six characters and a maximum length of eight characters. dt:type and its uses will be explained later in this chapter in the "Data Type Coercions" section. For now, we'll just say that it specifies an element's data type.

Listing 5.8 **Sample Schema Using *minLength* and *maxLength***

```
<?xml version="1.0"?>
<Schema xmlns:s="schemas-microsoft-com:xml-data"
        xmlns:dt="urn:schemas-microsoft-com:datatypes" >
  <s:AttributeType name="userID"
        xmlns:dt="urn:schemas-microsoft-com:datatypes"
        dt:type="string" />
```

```
    <s:AttributeType name="password"
              dt:type="string"
              dt:minLength="6"
              dt:maxLength="8"/>
    <s:ElementType name="LoginInfo" >
      <s:attribute type="userID" />
      <s:attribute type="password" />
    </s:ElementType>
  </Schema>
```

Here are two examples of valid instance documents of the preceding schema.

```
  <LoginInfo userID="1" password="xyz123" />
  <LoginInfo userID="2" password="" />
```

Although the `password` attribute value in the second instance is less than the `minLength`, the instance is still valid because a `password` value specified as `""` is treated the same as if the `password` attribute is not specified.

The *order* Attribute

The `order` attribute specifies how sequences of elements appear in a document instance. The `order` attribute can have any one of these values: `"seq"`, `"one"`, or `"many"`.

An `order` attribute value of `"seq"` indicates that the enclosed elements must appear in the same order in the instance document as they appear in the schema. See the schema fragment in Listing 5.9.

Listing 5.9 **An Example of *order="seq"***

```
<ElementType name="PurchaseOrder" order="seq">
  <element type="PONumber" />
  <element type="PODate" />
  <element type="ShipAddress" />
</ElementType>
```

An `order` attribute value of `"one"` specifies the `"either/or"` combination. Put another way, only one of the child elements defined in an `<ElementType>` can appear in an instance document. So to specify that an `Item` element can contain *either* a `product` element *or* a `backOrderedProduct` element but not both, the schema can be specified as in the following schema fragment:

```
<ElementType name="Item" order="one">
  <element type="product" />
  <element type="backOrderedProduct" />
</ElementType>
```

An `order` attribute value of `"many"` specifies that the child elements can appear in any order and in any quantity.

The default value for the order attribute depends on the content model in use. With a content attribute of "eltOnly", the default value for order is "seq". With a content attribute of "mixed", the default value for order is "many".

The order attribute is valid for either an <ElementType> or group element.

The *group* Element

The group element enables us to specify constraints on a subset of child elements. This capability can be quite useful.

The group element can have the order, minOccurs, and maxOccurs attributes.

Let's look at another example in Listing 5.10. The following schema defines the Item element as containing a group element with two child elements, product and backOrderedProduct. Because the group element has an order attribute of "one", only one of these children elements can appear in the Item element. This way, you won't have an Item element with both a product and a backOrderedProduct element (that wouldn't work so well). Only one of these child elements can be present.

Listing 5.10   **An Example of the** *<group>* **Element**

```
<ElementType name="Item">
    <group order="one">
        <element type="product" />
        <element type="backOrderedProduct" />
    </group>
    <element type="quantity"/>
    <element type="price"/>
</ElementType>
```

This schema validates the document in Listing 5.11.

Listing 5.11   **Document Conforming to Schema in Listing 5.10**

```
<Item>
  <product>CD</product>
  <quantity>100</quantity>
  <price>10</price>
</Item>
<Item>
  < backOrderedProduct >FloppyDisk</ backOrderedProduct >
  <quantity>100</quantity>
  <price>1</price>
</Item>
```

An Attribute's Content Model

The `<AttributeType>` element specifies the type of attribute used within elements. Required attributes are specified with the `required` keyword, as in the following:

```
<AttributeType name="shipTo" dt:type="idref" required="yes"/>
```

The `<attribute>` element specifies instances of an attribute defined within the `<AttributeType>` element. It is used within an `<ElementType>` element.

In some ways, attributes are more limited than elements:

- Attributes cannot contain child elements.
- Attributes have no "either/or" alternative.
- Attribute order cannot be specified.
- Attributes can appear only once per element (although you can specify `required`).

At the same time, attributes can do some things that elements cannot:

- Attributes can limit their legal values to a small set of strings, like this:
  ```
  <AttributeType name="priority" dt:type="enumeration" dt:values="high
  medium low" />
  ```

- Attributes have a default value, as in the following example:
  ```
  <AttributeType name="quantity" dt:type="int">
  <attribute type="quantity" default="1"/>
  ```

Although different element types can have attributes with the same name, these attributes are independent and unrelated.

Specifying an Attribute's Default Value

The `default` attribute specifies an attribute's default value. It is specified in the `<AttributeType>` and `<attribute>` elements in the schema.

For example, the schema in Listing 5.12 assigns the default value of `"Seattle"` to the `City` attribute.

Listing 5.12 **Specifying a Default Value for an Attribute**

```
<?xml version="1.0" ?>
<Schema xmlns="urn:schemas-microsoft-com:xml-data" >
<ElementType name="Customer" >
    <AttributeType name="CustomerID" />
    <AttributeType name="ContactName" />
    <AttributeType name="City" default="Seattle" />

    <attribute type="CustomerID" />
    <attribute type="ContactName" />
    <attribute type="City"  />
</ElementType>
</Schema>
```

Taking an example from the Northwind database in Appendix A, in a document instance with a <Customer> element with a missing City attribute, the default value ("Seattle") will be assumed and the document made valid. For example:

```
<Customer CustomerID="ALFKI" ContactName="Maria Anders" City="London" />
<Customer CustomerID="ANATR" ContactName="Ana Trujillo" />
```

The customer "ALFKI" has an explicitly stated City attribute ("London"), so the default value is ignored. On the other hand, the customer "ANATR" has no City attribute specified, so the default value ("Seattle") is supplied.

If the schema specifies both a default attribute and a required attribute, as in the following example, there is a slightly different behavior. Look at the following fragment, in which the <AttributeType> specifies the City attribute as required with a default value of "Seattle".

```
<AttributeType name="City" default="Seattle" required="yes" />
```

The Customer element is now required to have a City attribute, and it must have "Seattle" as its value.

Data Types

Data type specification is a necessary part of schemas. In fact, it was one of the major driving forces behind their creation. The W3C XML 1.0 Recommendation defines enumerated types and a set of tokenized types. These types are referred to as *primitive types* in Microsoft's XML documentation.

The primitive types listed in Table 5.3 include the following, defined in Section 3.3.1 of the W3C XML 1.0 Recommendation.

Table 5.3 **Microsoft's Primitive Data Types**

Primitive Data Type	Description
entity	Represents the XML ENTITY type.
entities	Represents the XML ENTITIES type.
enumeration	Represents an enumerated type (supported on attributes only).
id	Represents the XML ID type.
idref	Represents the XML IDREF type.
idrefs	Represents the XML IDREFS type.
nmtoken	Represents the XML NMTOKEN type.
nmtokens	Represents the XML NMTOKENS type.
notation	Represents a NOTATION type.
string	Represents a string type.

In addition to the primitive types, Microsoft's schema specification enumerates many other different types. These data types are listed in Table 5.4. Later in this chapter, in the "Data Type Coercions" section, we'll see how these entities map to SQL Server data types and what SQL Server conversion functions are used to translate XML data types.

Table 5.4 **Microsoft Supported XML Nonprimitive Data Types**

Data Type	Description
bin.base64	MIME-style, Base64-encoded binary large object (BLOB).
bin.hex	Hexadecimal digits representing octets.
boolean	0 or 1, where 0 = "false" and 1 = "true".
char	String, one character long.
date	Date in a subset ISO 8601 format, without the time data (for example, "1994-11-05"). The date itself is not validated. (For example, 2-31-99 will pass validation.)
dateTime	Date in a subset of ISO 8601 format, with optional time and no optional zone. Fractional seconds can be as precise as nanoseconds (for example, "1988-04-07T18:39:09").
dateTime.tz	Date in a subset ISO 8601 format, with optional time and optional zone. Fractional seconds can be as precise as nanoseconds (for example, "1988-04-07T18:39:09-08:00").
fixed.14.4	Same as number, but no more than 14 digits to the left of the decimal point and no more than 4 to the right.
float	Real number with no limits on digits; can potentially have a leading sign, fractional digits, and optionally, an exponent. Punctuation as in U.S. English. Values range from 1.7976931348623157E+308 to 2.2250738585072014E-308.
int	Number with optional sign, no fractions, and no exponent.
number	Number with no limit on digits; can potentially have a leading sign, fractional digits, and optionally, an exponent. Punctuation as in U.S. English. (Values have the same range as the most significant number, R8: 1.7976931348623157E+308 to 2.2250738585072014E-308.)
time	Time in a subset ISO 8601 format, with no date and no time zone (for example, "08:15:27").
time.tz	Time in a subset ISO 8601 format, with no date but optional time zone (for example, "08:1527-05:00").
i1	Integer represented in one byte. A number with optional sign, no fractions, and no exponent (for example, "1, 127, -128").
i2	Integer represented in one word. A number with optional sign, no fractions, and no exponent (for example, "1, 703, -32768").

continues

Table 5.4 **Continued**

Data Type	Description
i4	Integer represented in four bytes. A number with optional sign, no fractions, and no exponent (for example, "1, 703, -32768, 148343, -1000000000").
i8	Integer represented in eight bytes. A number with optional sign, no fractions, no exponent, and 19-digit precision. Range is from -9,223,372,036,854,775,808 to 9,223,372,036,854,775,807.
r4	Real number with seven-digit precision; can potentially have a leading sign, fractional digits, and optionally, an exponent. Punctuation as in U.S. English. Values range from 3.40282347E+38F to 1.17549435E-38F.
r8	Same as float. Real number with 15-digit precision; can potentially have a leading sign, fractional digits, and optionally, an exponent. Punctuation as in U.S. English. Values range from 1.7976931348623157E+308 to 2.2250738585072014E-308.
ui1	Unsigned integer. A number, unsigned, no fractions, no exponent (for example, "1, 255").
ui2	Unsigned integer, two bytes. A number, unsigned, no fractions, no exponent (for example, "1, 255, 65535").
ui4	Unsigned integer, four bytes. A number, unsigned, no fractions, no exponent (for example, "1, 703, 3000000000").
ui8	Unsigned integer, eight bytes. A number, unsigned, no fractions, no exponent. Range is 0 to 18,446,744,073,709,551,615.
uri	Uniform resource identifier (for example, "urn:schemas-microsoft-com:Office9").
uuid	Hexadecimal digits representing octets, optional embedded hyphens that are ignored (for example, "333C7BC4-460F-11D0-BC04-0080C7055A83").

Now that we've looked at Microsoft's version of XML schema documents, let's start establishing the connection between them and SQL Server 2000 and discuss whatever else is needed to make them work together.

Mapping Schema

So how do we get relational data from a database into an XML document format? Well, we first start with an XML schema document. This alone isn't enough, though. The schema describes the structure of the document, but there is still no relation between the document and the data yet. What we need to tie these two objects together are referred to as *annotations* to the XDR schema. An annotated XDR schema is referred to as a *mapping schema* because it maps the schema to the relational database. This enables data to be retrieved in the form of an XML document (see Figure 5.1).

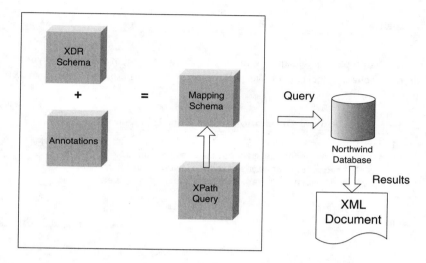

Figure 5.1 Schemas, annotations, and XPath.

Several schema annotations defined by Microsoft map the elements and attributes of XML data to database tables and columns. We will be examining each of these annotations in the remainder of this chapter.

Think of a mapping schema as a database view, which is created with the CREATE VIEW command. Queries against the mapping schema are carried out via XPath queries, much in the same way that SQL queries are used to extract data from a database view.

Namespaces

We'll be using two different namespaces in our mapping schema discussions, one for annotations and the other for data types.

Annotation namespace is declared with "urn:schemas-microsoft-com:xml-sql" inside the <schema> declaration. We will again be using sql as our namespace prefix, although the choice is completely arbitrary, as we've said previously. Listing 5.13 shows a sample declaration.

Listing 5.13 **A Sample Declaration of the Annotation Namespace**

```
<?xml version="1.0" ?>
<Schema xmlns="urn:schemas-microsoft-com:xml-data"
        xmlns:sql="urn:schemas-microsoft-com:xml-sql"
>
...
</Schema>
```

Data type namespace is declared with `"urn:schemas-microsoft-com:datatypes"`, again inside the `<schema>` declaration. We will use `dt` as our namespace prefix, as shown in Listing 5.14.

Listing 5.14 **A Sample Declaration of the Data Type Namespace**

```
<?xml version="1.0" ?>
<Schema xmlns="urn:schemas-microsoft-com:xml-data"
        xmlns:sql="urn:schemas-microsoft-com:xml-sql"
        xmlns:dt="urn:schemas-microsoft-com:datatypes"
>
...
</Schema>
```

Annotated Schema Example

Let's take what we've learned up to this point and tie it together with an example. First we'll look at an XDR schema of the Northwind database's Orders table, shown in Listing 5.15.

Listing 5.15 **XDR Schema for the Orders Table**

```
<?xml version="1.0" ?>
<Schema xmlns="urn:schemas-microsoft-com:xml-data"
        xmlns:dt="urn:schemas-microsoft-com:datatypes"
        xmlns:sql="urn:schemas-microsoft-com:xml-sql">

<ElementType name="Orders" >
    <AttributeType name="OrderID" />
    <AttributeType name="CustomerID" />
    <AttributeType name="ShipName" />

    <attribute type="OrderID"/>
    <attribute type="CustomerID" />
    <attribute type="ShipName" />
</ElementType>
</Schema>
```

Nothing is new here. Now let's map the schema to the Orders table by adding the appropriate annotations, as shown in Listing 5.16. Don't worry yet about exactly what the annotations themselves mean; I give a short explanation about what the annotations are doing. We'll be covering them in detail in the next several pages of this chapter.

Listing 5.16   **Mapping the Schema to the Orders Table**

```
<?xml version="1.0" ?>
<Schema xmlns="urn:schemas-microsoft-com:xml-data"
        xmlns:dt="urn:schemas-microsoft-com:datatypes"
        xmlns:sql="urn:schemas-microsoft-com:xml-sql">

<ElementType name="Order" sql:relation="Orders">
    <AttributeType name="OrdID" />
    <AttributeType name="CustID" />
    <AttributeType name="SName" />

    <attribute type="OrdID" sql:field="OrderID"/>
    <attribute type="CustID" sql:field="CustomerID"/>
    <attribute type="SName" sql:field="ShipName"/>
</ElementType>
</Schema>
```

In this example, we used two annotations, `sql:relation` and `sql:field`. The `sql:relation` annotation maps the `Order` element to the Orders table, and the `sql:field` annotation maps the `OrdID`, `CustID`, and `SName` attributes to the `OrderID`, `CustomerID`, and `ShipName` fields, respectively.

The relations specified by the annotations are case sensitive.

Default Mapping of XDR Elements and Attributes

The default behavior for an annotated XDR schema maps an element to the table or view with the same name. In the same manner, an attribute maps to the same-name column of the table or view.

It is possible to change this behavior if we want to. That is, we can map an element to a column. However, just like the supposed great deals on major airlines' fares, some restrictions apply.

- The elements to be mapped to columns cannot be of a complex type. (They cannot have child elements.)

- The elements must have the content attribute set to textOnly.

- If the content attribute is not specified, the `sql:field` annotation must explicitly specify the element to column mapping. (See the discussion of the `sql:field` annotation in this chapter.)

Now, to demonstrate the points we've made, let's execute these schema files on SQL Server and observe the results. First, save the schema file from Listing 5.16 to the template directory you specified during the virtual directory setup as `OrderSchema.xml`. Next, create the template file shown in Listing 5.17 and save it in the same template virtual directory as `OrderTemplate.xml`. Refer to Chapter 3, "Internet Information Server and Virtual Directories," if necessary to perform virtual names and directories setup. Refer to Chapter 4 for information on template files and their execution method.

Listing 5.17 **The Template File to Call the Order Schema File**

```
<ROOT xmlns:sql="urn:schemas-microsoft-com:xml-sql">
  <sql:Xpath-query mapping-schema="../OrderSchema.xml">
    /Orders
  </sql:xpath-query>
</ROOT>
```

Then execute `OrderTemplate.xml` with the following URL:

```
http://iisserver/Nwind/templates/OrderTemplate.xml
```

The first five returned records are displayed in Listing 5.18.

Listing 5.18 **Partial Results of Executing the Template File**

```
<ROOT xmlns:sql="urn:schemas-microsoft-com:xml-sql">
  <Orders OrderID="10248" CustomerID="VINET" ShipName="Vins et alcools
    Chevalier" />
  <Orders OrderID="10249" CustomerID="TOMSP" ShipName="Toms
    Spezialitäten" />
  <Orders OrderID="10250" CustomerID="HANAR" ShipName="Hanari Carnes" />
  <Orders OrderID="10251" CustomerID="VICTE" ShipName="Victuailles en
    stock" />
  <Orders OrderID="10252" CustomerID="SUPRD" ShipName="Suprêmes délices"
/>
  ...
</ROOT>
```

A couple of points here: First and foremost, the reason you saved the schema file into the template directory is because the template file specified the location of the schema file as being in the same directory. If you wanted to place the schema file in the schema directory, you would have had to specify the relative address of the schema file from the template directory. This means changing

```
<sql:xpath-query mapping-schema="OrderSchema.xml">
```

to

```
<sql:xpath-query mapping-schema="../schemas/OrderSchema.xml">
```

If your system administrators have allowed direct path access on servers (and I doubt they have), we could have specified an absolute path also, such as:

```
c:\inetpub\wwwroot\Nwind\schemas\OrderSchema.xml
```

This entire discussion assumes that the two directories are parallel to each other in the directory tree, just as we set up the structure in Chapter 3.

Second, the /Orders in the third line of Listing 5.15 is an XPath query that returns results for all orders found.

Before we dive into each of the individual annotations in detail, I'd like to take a small side trip and discuss Microsoft's proposed solution to several prominent distributed computing problems facing developers today. This solution utilizes XML and schemas as its language. This solution is what Microsoft calls BizTalk.

BizTalk

With every distributed object technology today that crosses application or business boundaries, new challenges associated with providing efficient, automated interaction seem to present themselves at every turn.

With the rapid growth of Internet e-business applications today, additional challenges in the areas of security and reliability must be addressed to communicate with other organizations.

These challenges, which evolve into requirements for interaction across business boundaries, interbusiness or departmental, include, at a minimum, the following:

- A flexible and extensible common language to specify, package, publish, and exchange both structured and unstructured information across application or business boundaries

- A flexible and extensible common language to convert information from one format to another as application and business boundaries are crossed

- Platform-independent, application-level communication protocols that enable interactions across application or business boundaries

- Platform-independent mechanisms to provide message security, integrity, and privacy

Microsoft's BizTalk specification is an attempt to provide a solution to these problems. It provides specifications for the design and development of XML-based messaging for communication between applications and organizations. The BizTalk Framework does not attempt to address all aspects of business-to-business (B-to-B) electronic commerce. It provides a set of basic mechanisms required for most B-to-B electronic exchanges. Microsoft is relying on other specifications and standards, consistent with the BizTalk Framework, being developed for the application- and domain-specific aspects. Currently, it functions in part as a repository for schemas developed by third-party organizations.

Now let's take a look at a representative BizTalk document.

BizTalk Schema Example

This discussion will not be an exhaustive, in-depth breakdown of BizTalk schema; rather, it will be an overview of the sections of a BizTalk document.

BizTalk relies on the *Simple Object Access Protocol (SOAP)* for messaging. More information on SOAP in the form of a W3C note can be found at `http://www.w3.org/TR/SOAP/`. An excellent white paper on SOAP, "Web Services and the Simple Object Access Protocol," is available on Microsoft's MSDN site at `http://msdn.microsoft.com/xml/general/soap_webserv.asp`.

In addition, BizTalk does not prescribe the content or structure (schema) of individual business documents. The details of the business document schema are defined and agreed on by the businesses involved. Think of BizTalk as a kind of wrapper for business documents.

Listing 5.19 shows a sample BizTalk document. This document consists of a standard SOAP 1.1 message containing the following:

- An application-specific business document (in this case, a book purchase order), with its own application-defined XML namespace, carried in the body of the message.

- BizTalk-specific `<endpoints>` and `<properties>` SOAP header tags, constructed using BizTags defined in standard BizTag namespaces. The schema is defined in the BizTalk specification.

Listing 5.19 **A Simple BizTalk Document**

```
<SOAP-ENV:Envelope
    xmlns:SOAP-ENV="http://schemas.xmlsoap.org/soap/envelope/"
    xmlns:xsi="http://www.w3.org/1999/XMLSchema-instance">
  <SOAP-ENV:Header>
    <eps:endpoints SOAP-ENV:mustUnderstand="1"
        xmlns:eps="http://schemas.biztalk.org/btf-2-0/endpoints"
        xmlns:agr="http://www.trading-agreements.org/types/">
      <eps:to>
        <eps:address xsi:type="agr:department">Book Orders</eps:address>
      </eps:to>
      <eps:from>
        <eps:address xsi:type="agr:organization">Book
Lovers</eps:address>
      </eps:from>
    </eps:endpoints>
    <prop:properties SOAP-ENV:mustUnderstand="1"
        xmlns:prop="http://schemas.biztalk.org/btf-2-0/properties">
      <prop:identity>uuid:74b9f5d0-33fb-4a81-b02b-
5b760641c1d6</prop:identity>
      <prop:sentAt>2000-05-14T03:00:00+08:00</prop:sentAt>
      <prop:expiresAt>2000-05-15T04:00:00+08:00</prop:expiresAt>
      <prop:topic>http://electrocommerce.org/purchase_order/</prop:topic>
```

```
        </prop:properties>
      </SOAP-ENV:Header>
      <SOAP-ENV:Body>
        <po:PurchaseOrder
   xmlns:po="http://electrocommerce.org/purchase_order/">
          <po:Title>Essential BizTalk</po:Title>
        </po:PurchaseOrder>
      </SOAP-ENV:Body>
    </SOAP-ENV:Envelope>
```

In general, the body of the BizTalk document contains several related business documents, and the header of the document contains several BizTalk-specific header entries. The SOAP-ENV:mustUnderstand attribute with a value of "1" implies that the destination point of this document must understand and correctly process the header entries so attributed, and if not, the processing of the document must be terminated with failure.

All BizTags are defined within standard BizTag namespaces with URIs derived by extension from the prefix http://schemas.biztalk.org/btf-2-0/.

The <to> and <from> routing tags often use business-entity names for source and destination addressing rather than transport addresses such as HTTP URLs. The form and interpretation of the address content is indicated by the xsi:type attribute. The BizTalk document structure and function are independent of the transport over which the documents are carried. This *transport independence* was one of the major considerations in the design of the BizTalk Framework.

The Body element of the document contains the business documents being carried. In general, a BizTalk document can carry a set of related business documents (for instance, a purchase order, a shipper's name, and an address for shipping that order).

There are many more BizTalk tags than I have shown here, and I refer you to the BizTalk specification for detailed listings and explanations of those tags.

Hopefully, BizTalk will realize its expectations and make the development of distributed applications a much less painful process.

Annotations to the XDR Schema

There are several annotations to the XDR schema language that enable it to carry out its intended purpose, mapping an XML document to a relational database. These annotations specify XML-to-relational mappings, including mapping from elements and attributes in the XDR schema to tables/views and columns in the databases. Remember the following and you'll have half the battle won: *Element names in an annotated schema map to table (view) names in a database, and attribute names map to the columns.* These annotations also can specify the hierarchical relationships in XML (modeling database relationships).

Table 5.5 is a list of the annotations. Each of these will be covered in detail with examples in this chapter.

Table 5.5 **Schema Annotations**

Annotation	Description
sql:relation	Maps an XML item to a database table.
sql:field	Maps an XML item to a database column.
sql:is-constant	Creates an XML element that does not map to a table but appears in the query output.
sql:map-field	Allows for excluding schema items from the results.
<sql:relationship>	Specifies relationships between XML elements. The key, key-relation, foreign-key, and foreign-relation attributes establish the relationship.
sql:limit-field	Allows limiting the values returned
sql:limit-value	Based on a limit value.
sql:key-fields	Allows specification of a column(s) that uniquely identifies the rows in a table.
sql:target-namespace	Allows moving the elements and attributes from the default namespace into a different namespace for query results.
sql:id-prefix	Creates valid XML ID, IDREF, and IDREFS. Prefixes the values of ID, IDREF, and IDREFS with a string.
sql:use-cdata	Allows specifying CDATA sections to be used for certain elements in the XML document.
sql:url-encode	When an XML element/attribute is mapped to a SQL Server BLOB column, allows a reference (URI) to be returned that can be used later for BLOB data.
sql:overflow-field	Identifies the database column that contains overflow data.

As seen in the simple example given in the section "Default Mapping of XDR Elements and Attributes," XDR schemas use XPath expressions in their queries to select data. In Chapter 2, "XSLT Stylesheets," we discussed the abbreviated form of XPath query. To keep it simple for now, we will continue to use this abbreviated form until we discuss XPath expressions at length in Chapter 6, "Using XPath Queries."

Explicit Mapping of XDR Elements and Attributes to Tables and Columns

As I said previously, as long as the names of the elements and attributes are the same as the table (view) and column names, respectively, in the database, explicit mappings are not necessary. An element name in an annotated schema maps to the table (view) name in the specified database, and the attribute names map to the column names.

In practice, however, this is rarely the case. Changes to column names for reports and so on are regularly done.

If the names are not the same, however, two annotations are provided to specify the mapping between an element/attribute in an XML document and the table/column in a database. These annotations are as follows:

- `sql:relation`
- `sql:field`

We'll cover these two annotations in the following sections.

sql:relation

The `sql:relation` annotation explicitly maps an XML element to a database table or view and can be added to an `<ElementType>`, `<element>`, or `<attribute>` node in the schema. A common use of the annotation is to relate illegal identifiers from SQL Server to an XML node. For example, a table named PUB INFO in SQL Server is a valid table name, but it's an invalid XML element name. We can get around this by using `sql:relation` to explicitly remap the table name, like this:

```
<ElementType name="PI" sql:relation="[PUB INFO]">
```

Using `sql:relation` on an `<ElementType>` causes the relation to apply to all attributes and subelements on that `<ElementType>`. This annotation is ignored on `<AttributeType>`.

Let's look at an example in Listing 5.20. Here, the `sql:relation` annotation maps the schema `<Order>` element to the Orders table. Because the annotation was applied to the `<ElementType>`, all the attributes also map to the Orders table. Save this file in your schema virtual directory.

Listing 5.20 **An Example of the *sql:relation* Annotation**

```
<?xml version="1.0" ?>
<Schema xmlns="urn:schemas-microsoft-com:xml-data"
        xmlns:dt="urn:schemas-microsoft-com:datatypes"
        xmlns:sql="urn:schemas-microsoft-com:xml-sql">

<ElementType name="Order" sql:relation="Orders">
    <AttributeType name="OrderID" />
    <AttributeType name="CustomerID" />
    <AttributeType name="ShipName" />

    <attribute type="OrderID" />
    <attribute type="CustomerID" />
    <attribute type="ShipName" />
</ElementType>
</Schema>
```

Let's use the template in Listing 5.21 to query against this schema.

Listing 5.21   **Query Template**

```
<ROOT xmlns:sql="urn:schemas-microsoft-com:xml-sql">
  <sql:xpath-query mapping-schema="../schemas/OrderSchema.xml">
    /Order[@CustomerID="VINET"]
  </sql:xpath-query>
</ROOT>
```

Executing the template with the following URL

```
http://iisserver/Nwind/templates/OrderTemplate.xml
```

provides the results in Listing 5.22.

Listing 5.22   **Results of Using the *sql:relation* Annotation**

```
<ROOT xmlns:sql="urn:schemas-microsoft-com:xml-sql">
  <Order OrderID="10248" CustomerID="VINET" ShipName="Vins et alcools
    Chevalier" />
  <Order OrderID="10274" CustomerID="VINET" ShipName="Vins et alcools
    Chevalier" />
  <Order OrderID="10295" CustomerID="VINET" ShipName="Vins et alcools
    Chevalier" />
  <Order OrderID="10737" CustomerID="VINET" ShipName="Vins et alcools
    Chevalier" />
  <Order OrderID="10739" CustomerID="VINET" ShipName="Vins et alcools
    Chevalier" />
</ROOT>
```

Notice that what used to be the <Orders> element is now the <Order> element.

In the event that the schema has a subelement, some changes have to be made. Look at Listing 5.23, a variation of our OrderSchema.xml.

Listing 5.23   **An XDR Schema with a Subelement**

```
<?xml version="1.0" ?>
<Schema xmlns="urn:schemas-microsoft-com:xml-data"
        xmlns:dt="urn:schemas-microsoft-com:datatypes"
        xmlns:sql="urn:schemas-microsoft-com:xml-sql">

<ElementType name="ShipAddress" content="textOnly" />
<ElementType name="Order" sql:relation="Orders">
    <AttributeType name="OrderID" />
    <AttributeType name="CustomerID" />

    <attribute type="OrderID" />
    <attribute type="CustomerID" />
```

```
        <element type="ShipAddress" />
    </ElementType>
</Schema>
```

As we know, elements map to table names and not columns by default, so it's necessary to specify the `content` attribute in the `<ElementType>` declaration and set it equal to `textOnly`.

In the next section, we'll see that there is another way to assign an XDR schema element to a column name instead of a table name. This is the `sql:field` annotation.

sql:field

The `sql:field` annotation maps an attribute or a noncomplex subelement to a database column by specifying the column name in its declaration. `<AttributeType>` elements ignore this annotation.

Four-part column names such as database.owner.table.columnname are not allowed. They are not allowed in any annotation that takes a column name for a value. For example, `sql:field` specifically needs a column name to perform its mapping function, so `sql:field` cannot use the four-part name.

Listing 5.24 is a sample schema that we'll use to illustrate the `sql:field` annotation.

Listing 5.24 **An Example of the *sql:field* Annotation**

```
<?xml version="1.0" ?>
<Schema xmlns="urn:schemas-microsoft-com:xml-data"
        xmlns:dt="urn:schemas-microsoft-com:datatypes"
        xmlns:sql="urn:schemas-microsoft-com:xml-sql">

  <ElementType name="Order" sql:relation="Orders">
    <AttributeType name="OrderID" />
    <AttributeType name="CustomerID" />
    <AttributeType name="SName" />

    <attribute type="OrderID" />
    <attribute type="CustomerID" />
    <attribute type="SName" sql:field="ShipName"/>
  </ElementType>
</Schema>
```

Listing 5.25 shows the partial results.

Listing 5.25 **Results of the *sql:field* Annotation**

```
<ROOT xmlns:sql="urn:schemas-microsoft-com:xml-sql">
  <Order OID="10248" CustomerID="VINET" SName="Vins et alcools Chevalier" />
  <Order OID="10274" CustomerID="VINET" SName="Vins et alcools Chevalier" />
  <Order OID="10295" CustomerID="VINET" SName="Vins et alcools Chevalier" />
```

continues

Listing 5.25 **Continued**

```
    <Order OID="10737" CustomerID="VINET" SName="Vins et alcools Chevalier" />
    <Order OID="10739" CustomerID="VINET" SName="Vins et alcools Chevalier" />
</ROOT>
```

The results show that the `OrderID` column is now `OID`, and the `ShipName` column is now `SName`.

I did not modify the `CustomerID` element in the schema. Because this is the qualifying criterion for the search, changing it can cause problems.

If there is an element type in your schema, as in the partial Listing 5.26, then you must specify either `content=textOnly` or `sql:field="`*fieldname*`"` (elements map to relations, not columns).

Listing 5.26 **Partial Listing of an element with** *sql:field*

```
...
    <attribute type="OrderID" />
    <attribute type="CustomerID" />
    <element type="ShipName" sql:field="ShipName"/>
...
```

Relating Tables with *sql:relationship*

The `sql:relationship` annotation specifies foreign key relationships between tables in a database. For example, the Products table is related to the Suppliers table because the SupplierID column in the Products table is a foreign key referring to the SupplierID column in the Suppliers table. This relationship is equivalent to the hierarchical nesting of XML elements in which `<Suppliers>` would have the child element `<Products>`.

From the XDR schema perspective, `sql:relationship` nests the elements based on the primary and foreign key relationships between tables to which the elements map.

To generate the proper nesting of elements, `sql:relationship` has four attributes that must be specified. These attributes are listed in Table 5.6.

Table 5.6 **Required** *sql:relationship* **Attributes**

Attribute	Description
`key-relation`	Specifies the primary table.
`key`	Specifies the primary key of the `key-relation`. If there are multiple columns making up the primary key, then a space-delimited list of the columns is used.
`foreign-relation`	Specifies the foreign table.
`foreign-key`	Specifies the foreign key in the `foreign-relation` referring to key in `key-relation`. If there are multiple columns making up the primary key, then a space-delimited list of the columns is used.

Some restrictions are placed on the `sql:relationship` annotation, as follows:

- It can only be added to attribute or element tags.
- On an attribute, `sql:relation` or `sql:field` must be specified so that only a single value is returned.
- On an element, a single value or a multiple value can be returned.
- Multiple instances of `sql:relationship` can appear in the same attribute or element. In this case, the order in which they appear is significant.

Leaving out the `sql:key-fields` specification can cause problems with proper element nesting. I recommend that you provide the `sql:key-fields` attribute in all schemas. That way, you guarantee that element nesting turns out the way you expected.

In the case of an `<element>` containing a child element and a `sql:relationship` attribute that doesn't specify the primary key of the parent element, you *must* provide the `sql:key-fields` attribute, which we'll cover shortly.

Listing 5.27 is a sample schema expressing the relationship between the Suppliers table and the Products table. Figure 5.2 diagrams the relationship.

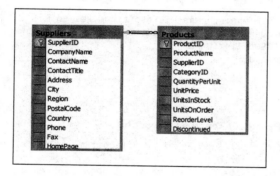

Figure 5.2   The Suppliers/Products relationship.

Listing 5.27   **A Schema with the *sql:relationship* Annotation**

```
<?xml version="1.0" ?>
<Schema xmlns="urn:schemas-microsoft-com:xml-data"
        xmlns:dt="urn:schemas-microsoft-com:datatypes"
        xmlns:sql="urn:schemas-microsoft-com:xml-sql">
  <ElementType name="Product" sql:relation="Products" >
    <AttributeType name="ProductID" />
    <AttributeType name="ProductName" />
    <AttributeType name="UnitPrice" />

    <attribute type="ProductID" />
    <attribute type="ProductName" />
```

continues

Listing 5.27 **Continued**

```
        <attribute type="UnitPrice" />
    </ElementType>
    <ElementType name="Supplier" sql:relation="Suppliers" >
        <AttributeType name="SupplierID" />
        <attribute type="SupplierID" />
        <element type="Product" >
                <sql:relationship
                    key-relation="Suppliers"
                    key="SupplierID"
                    foreign-key="SupplierID"
                    foreign-relation="Products" />
        </element>
    </ElementType>
</Schema>
```

Using the template file in Listing 5.28 produces the results in Listing 5.29.

Listing 5.28 **Template File for Schema Listing 5.27**

```
<ROOT xmlns:sql="urn:schemas-microsoft-com:xml-sql">
  <sql:xpath-query mapping-schema="../schemas/OrderSchema.xml">
    Supplier[@SupplierID="3"]
  </sql:xpath-query>
</ROOT>
```

Listing 5.29 **Results of Template Execution**

```
<ROOT xmlns:sql="urn:schemas-microsoft-com:xml-sql">
  <Supplier SupplierID="3">
    <Product ProductID="6" ProductName="Grandma's Boysenberry Spread"
     UnitPrice="25" />
    <Product ProductID="7" ProductName="Uncle Bob's Organic Dried Pears"
     UnitPrice="30" />
    <Product ProductID="8" ProductName="Northwoods Cranberry Sauce"
     UnitPrice="40" />
  </Supplier>
</ROOT>
```

Indirect Relationships

So far, we have talked about and examined examples in which tables were directly related via foreign keys. If I want to generate XML data from two tables that are related by an intermediate table but I don't want any of the intermediate table's data, I have an indirect relationship.

Let's look at the relationship between the three tables Customers, Orders, and Order Details. Let's say we want data from Customers and Order Details but not Orders. Customers make orders, which have details, so how do we present customer data and order detail data? Let's look at Listing 5.30.

Listing 5.30 **Eliminating the Middle Man**

```
<?xml version="1.0" ?>
<Schema xmlns="urn:schemas-microsoft-com:xml-data"
        xmlns:dt="urn:schemas-microsoft-com:datatypes"
        xmlns:sql="urn:schemas-microsoft-com:xml-sql">
  <ElementType name="OD" sql:relation="[Order Details]" >
    <AttributeType name="OrderID" />
    <AttributeType name="ProductID" />
    <AttributeType name="UnitPrice" />

    <attribute type="OrderID" />
    <attribute type="ProductID" />
    <attribute type="UnitPrice" />
  </ElementType>
  <ElementType name="Customer" sql:relation="Customers" >
    <AttributeType name="CustomerID" />
    <attribute type="CustomerID" />
    <element type="OD" >
            <sql:relationship
                    key-relation="Customers"
                    key="CustomerID"
                    foreign-relation="Orders"
                    foreign-key="CustomerID"/>
            <sql:relationship
                    key-relation="Orders"
                    key="OrderID"
                    foreign-relation="[Order Details]"
                    foreign-key="OrderID" />
    </element>
  </ElementType>
</Schema>
```

In this XDR schema, there is no mention of the Orders element, even though this is the table that relates Customers to Order Details. To accomplish this, we specify two relationships, the first between the Customers table and the Orders tables and the second between the Orders table and the Order Details table. Listing 5.31 shows the template file we will execute. It applies the OrderSchema.xml mapping schema and queries for all customers who have a CustomerID of "ALFKI." Listing 5.32 shows the results obtained. Figure 5.3 diagrams the relationship.

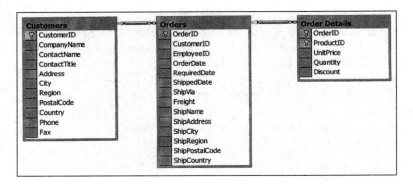

Figure 5.3   The Customers/Orders/Order Details relationship.

Listing 5.31   **Template for the Schema in Listing 5.30**

```
<ROOT xmlns:sql="urn:schemas-microsoft-com:xml-sql" >
  <sql:xpath-query mapping-schema="../schemas/OrderSchema.xml" >
    /Customer[@CustomerID="ALFKI"]
  </sql:xpath-query>
</ROOT>
```

Listing 5.32   **Results of the Indirect Relation**

```
<ROOT xmlns:sql="urn:schemas-microsoft-com:xml-sql">
  <Customer CustomerID="ALFKI">
  <OD OrderID="10643" ProductID="28" UnitPrice="45.6" />
  <OD OrderID="10643" ProductID="39" UnitPrice="18" />
  <OD OrderID="10643" ProductID="46" UnitPrice="12" />
  <OD OrderID="10692" ProductID="63" UnitPrice="43.9" />
  <OD OrderID="10702" ProductID="3" UnitPrice="10" />
...
</ROOT>
```

Next we'll look at adding our own elements to resulting documents.

Including Schema Elements in XML Documents with *sql:is-constant*

The sql:is-constant annotation enables us to specify an element that does not map to a table/view or a data column. These types of elements are called *constant elements*. They are specified on <ElementType> elements and require a Boolean value assignment (0 = false, 1 = true). The <ElementType> to which it is assigned does not map to any database table.

This annotation can be used to do the following:

- Add a top-level (root) element to the generated XML document.
- Create a container element that wraps other elements, such as a `Products` element that wraps multiple `Product` elements.

Listing 5.33 is the schema for our `sql:is-constant` example. This is followed by the template in Listing 5.34 and the partial results Listing 5.35. In this example, we generate the `ProductList` element to act as a container element for our list of products.

Listing 5.33 **Schema for *sql:is-constant***

```xml
<?xml version="1.0" ?>
<Schema xmlns="urn:schemas-microsoft-com:xml-data"
        xmlns:dt="urn:schemas-microsoft-com:datatypes"
        xmlns:sql="urn:schemas-microsoft-com:xml-sql">
  <ElementType name="Products" >
    <AttributeType name="ProductID" />
    <AttributeType name="ProductName" />
    <AttributeType name="UnitPrice" />

    <attribute type="ProductID" />
    <attribute type="ProductName" />
    <attribute type="UnitPrice" />
  </ElementType>
  <ElementType name="ProductList" sql:is-constant="1">
    <element type="Products">
            <sql:relationship
                    key-relation="Suppliers"
                    key="SupplierID"
                    foreign-key="SupplierID"
                    foreign-relation="Products" />
    </element>
  </ElementType>
  <ElementType name="Suppliers">
    <AttributeType name="SupplierID" />
    <attribute type="SupplierID" />
    <element type="ProductList" />
  </ElementType>
</Schema>
```

Listing 5.34 **Template for *sql:is-constant***

```xml
<ROOT xmlns:sql="urn:schemas-microsoft-com:xml-sql">
  <sql:xpath-query mapping-schema="../schemas/OrderSchema.xml">
    /Suppliers
  </sql:xpath-query>
</ROOT>
```

Listing 5.35 **Partial Results for the** *sql:is-constant* **Example**

```
<ROOT xmlns:sql="urn:schemas-microsoft-com:xml-sql">
  <Suppliers SupplierID="1">
    <ProductList>
      <Products ProductID="1" ProductName="Chai" UnitPrice="18" />
      <Products ProductID="2" ProductName="Chang" UnitPrice="19" />
      <Products ProductID="3" ProductName="Aniseed Syrup" UnitPrice="10"
/>
    </ProductList>
  </Suppliers>
...
<ROOT>
```

Excluding Schema Elements from XML Documents with *sql:map-field*

The previous annotation, `sql:is-constant`, provided us with a mechanism to generate elements that did not map to a database table or column, yet they appeared in the XML document. The `sql:map-field` annotation does the opposite. It prevents schema elements from appearing in the XML output. This is useful if you want to use third-party XDR schemas, and one or more of the elements in these schemas contains elements that don't map to your data. See the example in Listing 5.36 in which the attribute `short-desc` (this is a third-party schema) is prevented from appearing in our output because we don't have that data in our database.

Just like `sql:is-constant`, `sql:map-field` takes a Boolean value (true = 1, false = 0). It can be used on `<attribute>`, `<element>`, or `<ElementType>` with the `content=textOnly` setting. If an `<element>` or `<ElementType>` maps to a table, this annotation is not valid.

Listing 5.36 **An Example of** *sql:map-field* **Use**

```
<?xml version="1.0" ?>
<Schema xmlns="urn:schemas-microsoft-com:xml-data"
        xmlns:dt="urn:schemas-microsoft-com:datatypes"
        xmlns:sql="urn:schemas-microsoft-com:xml-sql">

<ElementType name="Products" >
  <AttributeType name="ProductName" />
  <AttributeType name="SupplierID" />
  <AttributeType name="QuantityPerUnit" />
  <AttributeType name="Short-desc" />

  <attribute type="ProductName" />
  <attribute type="SupplierID" />
  <attribute type="QuantityPerUnit" />
```

```
    <attribute type="Short-desc" sql:map-field="0" />
  </ElementType>
</Schema>
```

Listing 5.37 shows the template file to execute.

Listing 5.37   **The *sql:map-field* Template File**

```
<ROOT xmlns:sql="urn:schemas-microsoft-com:xml-sql">
  <sql:xpath-query mapping-schema="../schemas/OrderSchema1.xml">
    /Products[@SupplierID="1"]
  </sql:xpath-query>
</ROOT>
```

The results are shown in Listing 5.38.

Listing 5.38   **Results**

```
<ROOT xmlns:sql="urn:schemas-microsoft-com:xml-sql">
  <Products ProductName="Chai" SupplierID="1" QuantityPerUnit="10 boxes x
    20 bags" />
  <Products ProductName="Chang" SupplierID="1" QuantityPerUnit="24 - 12
    oz bottles" />
  <Products ProductName="Aniseed Syrup" SupplierID="1"
    QuantityPerUnit="12 - 550 ml bottles" />
</ROOT>
```

Notice that the Short-desc attribute did not appear in our output. That was on purpose.

Identifying Key Columns with *sql:key-fields*

The sql:key-fields annotation's purpose is to ensure the proper nesting of elements and to maintain their hierarchy.

I recommend that this annotation be used in all your schemas. It guarantees that proper nesting will occur.

The sql:key-fields annotation can be added to <element> and <ElementType> entities. This will identify columns that uniquely identify rows (keys). Placing spaces between the column values specifies multicolumn keys.

One last point: sql:key-fields must be specified in an element containing a child element and a <sql:relationship>, which is defined between the element and the child, that does not provide the primary key of the table specified in the parent element. Listing 5.39 starts another example for you by providing a schema file that is utilized by the template in Listing 5.40. The results are given in Listing 5.41.

Listing 5.39 **Schema Utilizing** *sql:key-fields*

```xml
<?xml version="1.0" ?>
<Schema xmlns="urn:schemas-microsoft-com:xml-data"
        xmlns:dt="urn:schemas-microsoft-com:datatypes"
        xmlns:sql="urn:schemas-microsoft-com:xml-sql">
  <ElementType name="Product" sql:relation="Products" >
    <AttributeType name="ProductID" />
    <AttributeType name="ProductName" />
    <AttributeType name="UnitPrice" />

    <attribute type="ProductID" />
    <attribute type="ProductName" />
    <attribute type="UnitPrice" />
  </ElementType>
  <ElementType name="Supplier" sql:relation="Suppliers"
                              sql:key-fields="SupplierID" >
    <AttributeType name="SupplierID" />
    <attribute type="SupplierID" />
    <element type="Product" >
            <sql:relationship
                    key-relation="Suppliers"
                    key="SupplierID"
                    foreign-key="SupplierID"
                    foreign-relation="Products" />
    </element>
  </ElementType>
</Schema>
```

Listing 5.40 **The Template to Execute the** *sql:key-fields* **Schema**

```xml
<ROOT xmlns:sql="urn:schemas-microsoft-com:xml-sql">
  <sql:xpath-query mapping-schema="../schemas/OrderSchema.xml">
    Supplier
  </sql:xpath-query>
</ROOT>
```

Listing 5.41 **The Results of Using** *sql:key-fields*

```xml
<ROOT xmlns:sql="urn:schemas-microsoft-com:xml-sql">
  <Supplier SupplierID="1">
    <Product ProductID="1" ProductName="Chai" UnitPrice="18" />
    <Product ProductID="2" ProductName="Chang" UnitPrice="19" />
    <Product ProductID="3" ProductName="Aniseed Syrup" UnitPrice="10" />
  </Supplier>
  <Supplier SupplierID="2">
    <Product ProductID="4" ProductName="Chef Anton's Cajun Seasoning"
UnitPrice="22" />
```

```
      <Product ProductID="5" ProductName="Chef Anton's Gumbo Mix"
        UnitPrice="21.35" />
      <Product ProductID="65" ProductName="Louisiana Fiery Hot Pepper
        Sauce" UnitPrice="21.05" />
      <Product ProductID="66" ProductName="Louisiana Hot Spiced Okra"
        UnitPrice="17" />
    </Supplier>
  ...
  <ROOT>
```

Specifying a Target Namespace with *sql:target-namespace*

The sql:target-namespace annotation places elements and attributes from the default namespace into another specified namespace. This prevents having to add a namespace prefix to the elements of a previously generated document when you want to assign that document to a namespace. This annotation can only appear as an attribute of the <schema> element.

sql:target-namespace utilizes a namespace URI to generate mapping schema elements and attributes. This URI is applied to all elements and attributes in the default namespace. Query documents contain *xmlns:prefix="uri"* declarations and prefixes. The URI comes from the value of the sql:target-namespace annotation. The prefix is generated arbitrarily and does not correspond to any values in the schema. Listing 5.42 shows how the target namespace is specified.

Listing 5.42   **Schema Utilizing *sql:target-namespace***

```
<?xml version="1.0" ?>
<Schema xmlns="urn:schemas-microsoft-com:xml-data"
        xmlns:dt="urn:schemas-microsoft-com:datatypes"
        xmlns:sql="urn:schemas-microsoft-com:xml-sql"
        sql:target-namespace="urn:SchemaNamespace">
  <ElementType name="Product" sql:relation="Products" >
    <AttributeType name="ProductID" />
    <AttributeType name="ProductName" />
    <AttributeType name="UnitPrice" />

    <attribute type="ProductID" />
    <attribute type="ProductName" />
    <attribute type="UnitPrice" />
  </ElementType>
  <ElementType name="Suppliers">
    <AttributeType name="SupplierID" />
    <attribute type="SupplierID" />
    <element type="Product" >
            <sql:relationship
                    key-relation="Suppliers"
                    key="SupplierID"
```

continues

Listing 5.42   Continued

```
                            foreign-key="SupplierID"
                            foreign-relation="Products" />
      </element>
    </ElementType>
  </Schema>
```

The template file in Listing 5.43 can be used to test the schema in Listing 5.42.

Listing 5.43   The Template to Test the *sql:target-namespace* **Annotation**

```
<ROOT xmlns:sql="urn:schemas-microsoft-com:xml-sql">
  <sql:xpath-query mapping-schema="../schemas/OrderSchema.xml"
                   xmlns:x="urn:SchemaNamespace" >
    x:Suppliers[@SupplierID="3"]
  </sql:xpath-query>
</ROOT>
```

Looking at this template, you can see that we assigned an arbitrary prefix to the XPath query to request all the Suppliers elements from the namespace SchemaNamespace. The results are shown in Listing 5.44. Notice that our xmlns was returned in the second line with the value we specified for a namespace. Also, notice that the returned prefix is entirely arbitrary.

Listing 5.44   Results of the *sql:target-namespace* **Query**

```
<ROOT xmlns:sql="urn:schemas-microsoft-com:xml-sql">
  <y0:Suppliers xmlns:y0="urn:SchemaNamespace" SupplierID="3">
  <y0:Product ProductID="6" ProductName="Grandma's Boysenberry Spread"
   UnitPrice="25" />
  <y0:Product ProductID="7" ProductName="Uncle Bob's Organic Dried Pears"
   UnitPrice="30" />
  <y0:Product ProductID="8" ProductName="Northwoods Cranberry Sauce"
   UnitPrice="40" />
  </y0:Suppliers>
</ROOT>
```

sql:id-prefix and Valid *ID, IDREF,* and *IDREFS* Type Attributes

The sql:id-prefix annotation ensures that if a document contains multiple IDs, they will be unique. Attributes can be made an ID type attribute, and intradocument links can then be created by specifying IDREF or IDREFS to refer to the ID type attributes.

`ID`, `IDREF`, and `IDREFS` relate directly to database primary key/foreign key relationships (differences are minimal). By definition, `ID` attributes must be distinct in XML documents; therefore, `CustomerID` and `OrderID` must also be distinct in XML documents if they exist. A problem occurs in a database, however, because it is possible for `CustomerID` and `OrderID` to both be equal to "1" or "2" or whatever.

Validity of `ID`, `IDREF`, and `IDREFS` in a document requires the following:

- An `ID`'s value must be unique.

- Every `IDREF` and `IDREFS` must have a referenced `ID` value in the XML document.

- The `ID`, `IDREF`, and `IDREFS` values must be a named token. (An integer cannot be an `ID` value.)

- The `ID`, `IDREF`, and `IDREFS` columns must not be mapped to text, ntext, image, or any other binary data type such as timestamp.

Essentially, `sql:id_prefix` prepends a string to `ID`, `IDREF`, and `IDREFS` to make it unique.

Prefix validity and value uniqueness of ID, IDREF, and IDREFS are not checked. Also, the value of the attributes is limited to 4,000 characters, including the prefix, if present.

Listing 5.45 is a schema document illustrating `sql:id-prefix`. This is followed by the template in Listing 5.46 to test it and results in Listing 5.47.

Listing 5.45 *sql:id_prefix* **Schema Document**

```
<?xml version="1.0" ?>
<Schema xmlns="urn:schemas-microsoft-com:xml-data"
        xmlns:dt="urn:schemas-microsoft-com:datatypes"
        xmlns:sql="urn:schemas-microsoft-com:xml-sql">

  <ElementType name="Product" sql:relation="Products" sql:key-
  fields="ProductID" >
    <AttributeType name="ProductID" dt:type="id" sql:id-prefix="Prod-"/>
    <AttributeType name="ProductName" />
    <AttributeType name="UnitPrice" />

    <attribute type="ProductID" />
    <attribute type="ProductName" />
    <attribute type="UnitPrice" />
  </ElementType>
  <ElementType name="Supplier" sql:relation="Suppliers" >
    <AttributeType name="SupplierID" dt:type="id"/>
    <attribute type="SupplierID" />

    <AttributeType name="ProductList" dt:type="idrefs"
    sql:id-prefix="Prod-"/>
    <attribute type="ProductList" sql:relation="Products"
```

continues

Listing 5.45 **Continued**

```
sql:field="ProductID">
                <sql:relationship
                        key-relation="Suppliers"
                        key="SupplierID"
                        foreign-key="SupplierID"
                        foreign-relation="Products" />
        </attribute>
        <element type="Product" >
                <sql:relationship
                        key-relation="Suppliers"
                        key="SupplierID"
                        foreign-key="SupplierID"
                        foreign-relation="Products" />
        </element>
    </ElementType>
</Schema>
```

Listing 5.46 **The *sql:id_prefix* Template to Test the Schema**

```
<ROOT xmlns:sql="urn:schemas-microsoft-com:xml-sql">
  <sql:xpath-query mapping-schema="../schemas/OrderSchema.xml">
    Supplier[@SupplierID="1"]
  </sql:xpath-query>
</ROOT>
```

Listing 5.47 *sql:id_prefix* **Results**

```
<ROOT xmlns:sql="urn:schemas-microsoft-com:xml-sql">
  <Supplier SupplierID="1" ProductList="Prod-1 Prod-2 Prod-3">
    <Product ProductID="Prod-1" ProductName="Chai" UnitPrice="18" />
    <Product ProductID="Prod-2" ProductName="Chang" UnitPrice="19" />
    <Product ProductID="Prod-3" ProductName="Aniseed Syrup"
      UnitPrice="10" />
  </Supplier>
</ROOT>
```

Why all the fuss? In this schema, we declared the Suppliers element to be an ID type. We also declared the Products element to be an ID type and to have a prefix of *Prod-*. If we had not declared this prefix, and both a SupplierID and ProductID of, say, 1 had come up (look at the results, it did!), then the document would not have been valid because duplicate ID values are illegal. sql:id-prefix prevented this.

Before you start yelling about changing the data value retrieved from the database and therefore invalidating the data, remember that XSLT has a function that can change the data back to the way it was at any time—problem solved.

Creating *CDATA* Sections with *sql:use-cdata*

As we saw in the section "Entities in XML" in Chapter 4, there are certain characters—such as <, >, &, and so on—that are treated as markup characters by XML. If it were necessary to prevent this behavior and output the characters as is, you would surround these characters with a CDATA section. You can do the equivalent in XDR schemas by utilizing the sql:use-cdata annotation.

The sql:use-cdata annotation is used as an attribute on <ElementType> or <element> entities and requires a boolean value (0 = false, 1 = true). Listing 5.48 presents a schema that applies CDATA sections to the ShipName column of the Orders table to ensure that any special characters are not interpreted as markup. Listing 5.49 shows the template, and the partial result list is shown in Listing 5.50.

sql:use-cdata cannot be used with sql:url-encode, which we talk about in the next section, or the attribute types ID, IDREFS, NMTOKEN, or NMTOKENS.

Listing 5.48 **Schema Utilizing** *sql:use-cdata*

```
<?xml version="1.0" ?>
<Schema xmlns="urn:schemas-microsoft-com:xml-data"
   xmlns:dt="urn:schemas-microsoft-com:datatypes"
   xmlns:sql="urn:schemas-microsoft-com:xml-sql">
   <ElementType name="ShipName" content="textOnly" />
   <ElementType name="Orders" >
      <element type="ShipName" sql:use-cdata="1"  />
   </ElementType>
</Schema>
```

Listing 5.49 **The Template to Test** *sql:use-cdata*

```
<ROOT xmlns:sql="urn:schemas-microsoft-com:xml-sql">
  <sql:xpath-query mapping-schema="../schemas/OrderSchema1.xml">
    /Orders
  </sql:xpath-query>
</ROOT>
```

Listing 5.50 **The Results of Specifying** *sql:use-cdata*

```
<ROOT xmlns:sql="urn:schemas-microsoft-com:xml-sql">
  <Orders>
    <ShipName>
      <![CDATA[Vins et alcools Chevalier]]>
    </ShipName>
  </Orders>
  <Orders>
    <ShipName>
```

continues

Listing 5.50   **Continued**

```
        <![CDATA[Toms Spezialitäten]]>
      </ShipName>
    </Orders>
  ...
  </ROOT>
```

Requesting URL References to BLOB data with *sql:url-encode*

BLOB data is stored in SQL Server columns in base 64–encoded format. The
sql:url-encode annotation returns a reference (URI) to this data instead of the value
of the field. You can then use this URI to access the data.

sql:url-encode is dependent on the primary key field to generate a unique select.
Use the sql:key-fields annotation for this purpose. sql:url-encode also is one of
the annotations that takes a Boolean value attribute (0 = false, 1 = true).

sql:url-encode cannot be used with the sql:use-cdata annotation or on ID,
IDREF, IDREFS, NMTOKEN, or NMTOKENS.

In Listing 5.51, we specify sql:url-encode on the Photo attribute to have a URI
reference returned instead of the filed value. We can then use the URI to retrieve the
data later. The template file is given in Listing 5.52.

Listing 5.51   *sql:url-encode* **Example**

```
<?xml version="1.0" ?>
<Schema xmlns="urn:schemas-microsoft-com:xml-data"
    xmlns:dt="urn:schemas-microsoft-com:datatypes"
    xmlns:sql="urn:schemas-microsoft-com:xml-sql">
    <ElementType name="Employee" sql:relation="Employees"
                 sql:key-fields="EmployeeID" >
        <AttributeType name="EmployeeID" />
        <AttributeType name="Photo" />

        <attribute type="EmployeeID" />
        <attribute type="Photo"  sql:url-encode="1" />
    </ElementType>
</Schema>
```

Listing 5.52   **The Template to Execute the *sql:url-encode* Example**

```
<ROOT xmlns:sql="urn:schemas-microsoft-com:xml-sql">
  <sql:xpath-query mapping-schema="../schemas/ProductSchema.xml">
    /Employee[@EmployeeID=1]
  </sql:xpath-query>
</ROOT>
```

The result of specifying `sql:url-encode` is as follows:

```
<ROOT xmlns:sql="urn:schemas-microsoft-com:xml-sql">
  <Employee EmployeeID="1"
Photo="dbobject/Employees[@EmployeeID="1"]/@Photo" />
</ROOT>
```

Retrieving Unconsumed Data with *sql:overflow-field*

This annotation applies to the use of the OPENXML extension, which we'll cover in Chapter 8, "OPENXML." I'll defer discussion of this annotation until then, where it will make more sense.

Filtering Records with *sql:limit-field* and *sql:limit-value*

The `sql:limit-field` and `sql:limit-value` annotations specify the database column and limiting value, respectively, that are used to restrict the rows returned from a query. The `sql:limit-field` actually further qualifies the relation specified in `sql:relationship`.

Data Type Coercions

Using an XDR schema, we can control the type of data that is output when data is obtained from a database. The `dt:type` and `sql:datatype` annotations control the mapping between SQL Server data types and XML data types.

The *dt:type* Data Type

`dt:type` can be an attribute on `<AttributeType>` or `<ElementType>`. It specifies the XML data type of the element or attribute that maps to a column. Not only does `dt:type` affect the document returned from a query, it also affects the query itself. Specifying a `dt:type` of int (integer) causes the query to be executed expecting a column of integer data.

Because all data returned in an XML document is strings, some conversions to other data types will be required for proper data manipulation. Table 5.7 enumerates the conversion function required for different `dt:types`.

Keep in mind that there are always some conversions that are impossible. Examples include trying to convert a float to an i2 (tinyint) or an "ABC" to a numeric form.

Table 5.7 **SQL Conversion Functions for XML Data Types**

XML Data Type	SQL Server Conversion
bit	CONVERT(bit, COLUMN)
date	LEFT(CONVERT(nvarchar(4000), COLUMN, 126), 10)
fixed.14.4	CONVERT(money, COLUMN)
id/idref/idrefs	id-prefix + CONVERT(nvarchar(4000), COLUMN, 126)
nmtoken/nmtokens	id-prefix + CONVERT(nvarchar(4000), COLUMN, 126)
time/time.tz	SUBSTRING(CONVERT(nvarchar(4000), COLUMN, 126), 1+CHARINDEX(N'T', CONVERT(nvarchar(4000), COLUMN, 126)), 24)
All others types	No additional conversion needed

Table 5.8 shows default data type mappings between SQL Server and XML.

Table 5.8 **Data Type Mappings Between SQL Server and XML**

SQL Server Data Type	XML Data Type
bigint	i8
binary	bin.base64
bit	boolean
char	char
datetime	datetime
decimal	r8
float	r8
image	bin.base64
int	int
money	r8
nchar	string
ntext	string
nvarchar	string
numeric	r8
real	r4
smalldatetime	datetime
smallint	i2
smallmoney	fixed.14.4
sysname	string

SQL Server Data Type	XML Data Type
text	string
timestamp	ui8
tinyint	ui1
varbinary	bin.base64
varchar	string
uniqueidentifier	uuid

The *sql:datatype* Data Type

The SQL Server data types binary, image, and varbinary all use bin.base64 encoding. The sql:datatype annotation specifies exactly which of the data types an XDR schema bin.base64 attribute maps to in a database. When inserting data into a database, the sql:datatype will specify the type of data to store. Valid values are text, ntext, image, and binary.

First let's work with an example of dt:type on an attribute in a schema. Listing 5.53 shows a schema in which we've used dt:type in two different places: one on OrdDate and the other on Shipdate. This is followed by the template file in Listing 5.54 and the results in Listing 5.55.

Listing 5.53 **The Schema Utilizing** *dt:type*

```
<?xml version="1.0" ?>
<Schema xmlns="urn:schemas-microsoft-com:xml-data"
        xmlns:dt="urn:schemas-microsoft-com:datatypes"
        xmlns:sql="urn:schemas-microsoft-com:xml-sql">

<ElementType name="Order" sql:relation="Orders">
    <AttributeType name="OID" />
    <AttributeType name="CustID"  />
    <AttributeType name="OrdDate" dt:type="date" />
    <AttributeType name="ReqDate" />
    <AttributeType name="ShipDate" dt:type="time" />

    <attribute type="OID" sql:field="OrderID" />
    <attribute type="CustID" sql:field="CustomerID" />
    <attribute type="OrdDate" sql:field="OrderDate" />
    <attribute type="ReqDate" sql:field="RequiredDate" />
    <attribute type="ShipDate" sql:field="ShippedDate" />
</ElementType>
</Schema>
```

Listing 5.54 **The Template File to Test the *dt:type* Schema**

```
<ROOT xmlns:sql="urn:schemas-microsoft-com:xml-sql">
  <sql:xpath-query mapping-schema="../schemas/OrderSchema.xml">
    /Order
  </sql:xpath-query>
</ROOT>
```

Listing 5.55 **Partial Results of Testing *dt:type***

```
- <ROOT xmlns:sql="urn:schemas-microsoft-com:xml-sql">
<Order OID="10248" CustID="VINET" OrdDate="1996-07-04" ReqDate="1996-08-
01T00:00:00"
        ShipDate="00:00:00" />
<Order OID="10249" CustID="TOMSP" OrdDate="1996-07-05" ReqDate="1996-08-
16T00:00:00"
        ShipDate="00:00:00" />
<Order OID="10250" CustID="HANAR" OrdDate="1996-07-08" ReqDate="1996-08-
05T00:00:00"
        ShipDate="00:00:00" />
...
</ROOT>
```

In this example, dt:type was not applied to the ReqDate, so the full value of the data was returned (both date and time). The OrdDate attribute had the date data type applied, so only the date portion of the data was returned. Finally, ShipDate has the time data type applied, so only the time portion of the data was returned.

In the example in Listing 5.56, we use the sql:datatype annotation on the Photo attribute to identify the data type of the Picture column in the Categories table.

Listing 5.56 **Schema Utilizing *sql:datatype***

```
<?xml version="1.0" ?>
<Schema xmlns="urn:schemas-microsoft-com:xml-data"
        xmlns:dt="urn:schemas-microsoft-com:datatypes"
        xmlns:sql="urn:schemas-microsoft-com:xml-sql">

<ElementType name="Category" sql:relation="Categories">
    <AttributeType name="ID" />
    <AttributeType name="Name" />
    <AttributeType name="Desc" />
    <AttributeType name="Photo"  />

    <attribute type="ID" sql:field="CategoryID" />
    <attribute type="Name" sql:field="CategoryName" />
    <attribute type="Desc" sql:field="Description" />
    <attribute type="Photo" sql:field="Picture" sql:datatype="image" />
</ElementType>
</Schema>
```

Listing 5.57 illustrates a template file that utilizes the schema in Listing 5.56.

Listing 5.57 **The Template to Test the** *sql:datatype* **Schema**

```
<ROOT xmlns:sql="urn:schemas-microsoft-com:xml-sql">
  <sql:xpath-query mapping-schema="../schemas/CategoriesSchema.xml">
    /Category[@ID="1"]
  </sql:xpath-query>
</ROOT>
```

The result of testing `sql:datatype` is as follows:

```
<ROOT xmlns:sql="urn:schemas-microsoft-com:xml-sql">
  <Category ID="1" Name="Beverages" Desc="Soft drinks, coffees, teas,
beers, and ales"
            Photo="Base 64 encoded image here"/>
</ROOT>
```

Default Values for Schema Attributes

In XDR, schema elements cannot be assigned a default value. It is possible, however, to assign default values to attributes. Default values are allowed on the `<AttributeType>` entity. If a table column that is referenced by an attribute in a schema contains a null value, nothing will be returned in a query that canvasses this column. On the other hand, if a default attribute is specified, then that default value will be returned. An important point to remember here is that the returned value might still not appear in the document. The parser uses it to validate the document.

If you are using the MSXML Parser, you must ensure that the `resolveExternals` flag is set to `TRUE` (the default value). The Document Object Model (DOM) will now supply the default value. A discussion of this property is located at `http://msdn.microsoft.com/library/psdk/xmlsdk/xmld1vg3.htm`.

Listing 5.58 gives an example utilizing the Orders table that supplies the `"Not Known"` default value for any returned record that has a null value in the ShipRegion column. The accompanying template file is given in Listing 5.59, and the results are shown in Listing 5.60.

Listing 5.58 **Schema Demonstrating the Default Attribute**

```
<?xml version="1.0" ?>
<Schema xmlns="urn:schemas-microsoft-com:xml-data"
        xmlns:dt="urn:schemas-microsoft-com:datatypes"
        xmlns:sql="urn:schemas-microsoft-com:xml-sql">

  <ElementType name="Orders">
    <AttributeType name="Name" />
    <AttributeType name="Address" />
```

continues

Listing 5.58 **Continued**

```
    <AttributeType name="City" />
    <AttributeType name="Region" default="Not Known" />

    <attribute type="Name" sql:field="ShipName" />
    <attribute type="Address" sql:field="ShipAddress" />
    <attribute type="City" sql:field="ShipCity" />
    <attribute type="Region" sql:field="ShipRegion" />
  </ElementType>
</Schema>
```

Listing 5.59 **The Template to Test the Schema**

```
<ROOT xmlns:sql="urn:schemas-microsoft-com:xml-sql">
  <sql:xpath-query mapping-schema="../schemas/DefaultSchema.xml">
    /Orders
  </sql:xpath-query>
</ROOT>
```

Listing 5.60 **Partial Results of Testing the Default Attribute**

```
<ROOT xmlns:sql="urn:schemas-microsoft-com:xml-sql">
  <Orders Name="Vins et alcools Chevalier" Address="59 rue de l'Abbaye"
  City="Reims" />
  <Orders Name="Toms Spezialitäten" Address="Luisenstr. 48"
  City="Münster" />
  <Orders Name="Hanari Carnes" Address="Rua do Paço, 67" City="Rio de
  Janeiro" Region="RJ" />
...
</ROOT>
```

Notice that, just as was previously mentioned, even though you specify a default value, it might not appear in the document. The parser to validate the document uses the value.

Microsoft has released a visual drag-and-drop schema-generation utility called the *SQL SERVER XML View Mapper*. This is a very easy tool to use and is freely downloadable from the Microsoft Web site at www.microsoft.com. Search on "view mapper" in the search utility. Appendix G of this book provides its basic operation and an explanation of the time this utility can save you.

Using Annotated XDR Schemas in Queries

There are three ways to query annotated XDR schemas to generate XML documents. One we've used already, and the other two we haven't dealt with until now. We'll talk first about the method we've already used.

Template Files Utilizing XPath Queries

This is the method we've been using up to this point. We specify a `<sql:xpath-query>` element in a template file that enables us to use XPath queries and post them against the view created by an XDR schema. Within the `<sql:xpath-query>` element, we utilize the `mapping-schema` attribute to specify the XDR schema that the XPath query is posted against. XPath queries and the FOR XML extension return document fragments to the template. The template enables us to apply a `ROOT` element to the returned fragment and thereby make the fragment a valid XML document.

Inline Mapping Schemas

Now, for a slightly new way of doing things, let's put the XDR schema and the template together in the same file. That's right, together in the same file. There's really nothing difficult here, just a slightly different syntax (famous last words, right?). We add the `sql:is-mapping-schema` annotation to the `<SCHEMA>` portion of the file. This annotation takes a Boolean value (0 = false, 1 = true). Also specified within the `<SCHEMA>` element is the ID type attribute annotation `sql:id`. The value assigned to the `sql:id` annotation references the matching mapping-schema value of the `sql:xpath-query` element and executes the XPath query there.

Listing 5.61 shows an example of what is called an *inline mapping schema*. Listing 5.62 shows the partial results. All we need to execute it is a URL, which is `http://iisserver/Nwind/templates/InlineMappingTemplate.xml`.

Be sure to place the inline mapping schema file in the template's virtual directory. By default, that's where the file is looked for. Putting the file in the schema's virtual directory results in a Page Not Found error.

Listing 5.61 **An Inline Mapping Schema**

```
<ROOT    xmlns:sql="urn:schemas-microsoft-com:xml-sql">
  <Schema xmlns="urn:schemas-microsoft-com:xml-data"

    sql:id="MappingSchema"
    sql:is-mapping-schema="1">

    <ElementType name="Orders" >
      <AttributeType name="OrderID" />
      <AttributeType name="CustomerID" />
      <AttributeType name="OrderDate" />
```

continues

Listing 5.61 **Continued**

```
        <attribute type="OrderID" />
        <attribute type="CustomerID" />
        <attribute type="OrderDate" />
      </ElementType>
    </Schema>

<sql:xpath-query mapping-schema="#MappingSchema">
  Orders
</sql:xpath-query>
</ROOT>
```

Listing 5.62 **Partial Results From the Inline Mapping Schema**

```
<ROOT xmlns:sql="urn:schemas-microsoft-com:xml-sql">
  <Orders OrderID="10248" CustomerID="VINET" OrderDate="1996-07-
    04T00:00:00" />
  <Orders OrderID="10249" CustomerID="TOMSP" OrderDate="1996-07-
    05T00:00:00" />
  <Orders OrderID="10250" CustomerID="HANAR" OrderDate="1996-07-
    08T00:00:00" />
...
</ROOT>
```

Mapping Schema in the URL

The third and final method of querying XDR annotated schema is placing the XPath query directly in the URL. To accomplish this, create a schema file and place it in the *schema virtual directory*. Then, in the calling URL, specify the schema file name and the XPath query used. Listing 5.63 gives you a simple schema for this example.

The following is the calling URL we'll use:

```
http://iisserver/Nwind/schemas/URLSchema.xml/Orders[@OrderID="10250"].
```

This dictates that the file name is URLSchema.xml and that it exists in the schema's virtual directory.

Listing 5.63 **A Schema to Test Querying Via a URL**

```
<?xml version="1.0" ?>
<Schema xmlns="urn:schemas-microsoft-com:xml-data"
        xmlns:dt="urn:schemas-microsoft-com:datatypes"
        xmlns:sql="urn:schemas-microsoft-com:xml-sql">

  <ElementType name="Orders">
    <AttributeType name="CustomerID" />
```

```
        <AttributeType name="Name" />
        <AttributeType name="Address" />
        <AttributeType name="City" />

        <attribute type="CustomerID" />
        <attribute type="Name" sql:field="ShipName" />
        <attribute type="Address" sql:field="ShipAddress" />
        <attribute type="City" sql:field="ShipCity" />
      </ElementType>
    </Schema>
```

This is the result of our mapping schema in a URL:

```
<Orders OrderID="10250" Name="Hanari Carnes" Address="Rua do Paço, 67"
City="Rio de Janeiro" />
```

Be sure to place the mapping schema file in the schema's virtual directory. By default, that's where the file is looked for. Putting the file in the template's virtual directory results in a Page Not Found error.

Schema Caching and Performance

This short topic is a discussion of performance issues. When annotated XDR schemas are queried via an XPath expression, the schema is stored in memory. Being able to cache schemas greatly improves system performance by reducing the amount of direct disk access.

A Registry setting that you can change controls schema cache size. Here's the Registry entry:

```
HKEY_LOCAL_MACHINE\SOFTWARE\Microsoft\MSSQLServer\Client\SQLXMLX\SchemaCa
cheSize
```

If you don't know what you're doing with the Registry, find someone who does!

If you do something wrong, you could very easily trash the box. Microsoft always issues a disclaimer when it gives out Registry changes, stating that the company will not support calls dealing with changes made to the Registry. You're on your own. Many times, the only recourse is to rebuild the box.

The default value for SchemaCacheSize is 31, and you adjust this setting based on the number of schemas you have and the amount of available memory in the server. If you have the memory, adjust the SchemaCacheSize to be slightly higher than the number of your schemas. If you don't have the memory, you'll have to reduce the size. *This will degrade performance, so buy more RAM.*

Remember that in production environments, you should enable caching by *unchecking* the Cache Control box on the Advanced tab of the IIS Virtual Directory Management utility. We talked about this in Chapter 3.

Recap of What Was Discussed in This Chapter

- Microsoft's version of XML schemas differs from the schemas documented in the W3C specification. This came about from Microsoft taking the initial specification, immediately adopting it, modifying it accordingly, and not paralleling the W3C specification. In this chapter, you saw just how different the two specifications are.

- Microsoft's BizTalk specification is an attempt to provide a solution to the problems of an extensible universal conversion language, platform independence and message security integrity, and privacy, among other things. It provides specifications for the design and development of XML-based messaging for communication between applications and organizations. The BizTalk Framework does not attempt to address all aspects of B-to-B electronic commerce. It provides a set of basic mechanisms required for most B-to-B electronic exchanges.

- XDR schema annotations specify XML-to-relational mappings, including mapping from elements and attributes in the XDR schema to tables/views and columns in the databases. Remember the following and you'll have half the battle won: *Element names in an annotated schema map to table (view) names in a database, and attribute names map to the columns.* These annotations also can specify the hierarchical relationships in XML (modeling database relationships).

- Using an XDR schema, we can control the type of data that is output when data is obtained from a database. The `dt:type` and `sql:datatype` annotations control the mapping between SQL Server data types and XML data types.

6

Using XPath Queries

THROUGHOUT THIS BOOK, WHENEVER WE MENTION or implement XPath expressions, we use what is called the *abbreviated* form. In this chapter, we will learn the parts that Microsoft supports of an enhanced syntax, called the *verbose* form of XPath. Yes, that's right. Microsoft has implemented only a subset of the query language. Also, there are some differences between Microsoft's implementation and the original W3C specification. We'll cover these topics first thing.

We'll be discussing things like *selection predicates*, *node tests*, and *axes* and how these are combined to form *location paths*. You'll have plenty of examples, as usual, along the way to verify your understanding of the subject matter.

Let's first look at implementation limitations and then at the differences between Microsoft's implementation and the W3C standard.

This chapter will cover the following topics:

- Microsoft's adaptation of the W3C XPath requirements and its limitations

- XPath data types and processes, such as conversion of these data types and mapping between XDR schema and XPath data types

- The SQL Server 2000 CONVERT function and its use in implicit conversions

- Location paths and their components: node tests, axes, and predicates

- Boolean, arithmetic, relational, and equality operators and how they are used in selection predicates

- Accessing database objects and the limited functionality this process provides

Implementation Limitations

XPath is used to perform tree navigation and to select node sets from an XML document. Each XPath operator selects a node set based on a previously selected node set. For example, with an `<Order>` node set, XPath can select all `<OrderDetails>` nodes with the `Discount` attribute value greater than 0.15. The resulting node set contains all the orders with a `Discount` attribute value greater than 0.15.

Table 6.1 shows the subset of axes, functions, and operators that Microsoft supports in its implementation. Quite a bit of functionality has been left out; exactly what has been left out is enumerated in Table 6.2.

Table 6.1 **What Microsoft Supports**

Feature	Item
Axes	Attribute, child, parent, and self axes.
	Boolean-valued predicates including successive and nested predicates –this will be shown in the "Working with Boolean Predicates" section later in this chapter
All relational operators	=, !=, <, <=, >, >=
Arithmetic operators	+, -, *, div
Explicit conversion functions	number(), string(), Boolean()
Boolean operators	AND, OR
Boolean functions	true(), false(), not()
XPath variables	This will be shown in the examples section later in this chapter.

Table 6.2 **What Microsoft Does Not Support**

Feature	Item
Axes	Ancestor, ancestor-or-self, descendant, descendant-or-self (//), following, following-sibling, namespace, preceding, preceding-sibling
Numeric-valued predicates	n/a
Arithmetic operators	mod
Node functions	Ancestor, ancestor-or-self, descendant, descendant-or-self (//), following, following-sibling, namespace, preceding, preceding-sibling
String functions	string(), concat(), starts-with(), contains(), substring-before(), substring-after(), substring(), string-length(), normalize(), translate()
Boolean functions	lang()
Numeric functions	sum(), floor(), ceiling(), round()
Union operator		

Refer to Chapter 4, "Accessing SQL 2000 via HTTP," to the two sections "Entities in XML" and "Entities in URLs." Remember that depending on where an XPath expression is used, you might have to encode special characters so that they are correctly interpreted.

The following URL

```
http://iisserver/VirtualRoot/SchemaVirtualName/Schema File/Orders/..
```

will be transformed to

```
http://iisserver/VirtualRoot/SchemaVirtualName/Schema File/
```

because the ".." in the first URL is interpreted to mean "parent," and the parent of Orders is Schema File.

Differences from W3C Specification

The Microsoft implementation of XPath differs from the W3C specification in the following ways:

- **Root queries.** The root query (/) is not supported in SQL Server 2000 XPath queries. Every XPath query must begin at a top-level <ElementType> in the schema. The slash mark can, however, be explicitly placed in front of the beginning <ElementType>.

- **Reporting errors.** The W3C XPath specification has no provisions to cover error conditions. The only thing returned from an invalid XPath query or another error condition is an empty node set. In SQL Server 2000, a query might return many different types of error messages. I'm sure that in your experimentation with queries up to this point, you've come across an error or two.

- **Document order.** Document order in SQL Server 2000 is not always deterministic, so document order specifications are not implemented.

  This shortcoming also means that the string value of a node can be evaluated only when that node maps to a single column in a single row. An element with subelements or an IDREFS or NMTOKENS node cannot be converted to a string.

- **Data types.** Microsoft's implementation of the string, number, and Boolean data types is limited. These limitations are discussed in the section "XPath Data Types" later in this chapter.

- **Cross-product queries.** Cross-product XPath queries are not supported. An example of this is Customer[Order/@OrderDate=Order/@ShippedDate]. This produces a node set of all customers with any order for which the OrderDate equals the ShippedDate of any order.

  However, this type of query is supported: Customer[Order[@OrderDate= @ShippedDate]]. This selects customers with any order for which the OrderDate equals its ShippedDate.

That summarizes the differences. Now let's examine XPath data types and various conversions along with how XDR data types map to XPath data types. Then we'll start working with the syntax.

XPath Data Types

It isn't always possible to map one data type to another when you're talking about XDR schema, XPath, and SQL Server 2000. Each of these entities has its own data types, and many of these data types have no counterpart in the other entities. A very important example of this is that XPath has no integer data type, while SQL Server has several different kinds. XPath has only number, string, and Boolean data types, but even then, its number data type doesn't map to SQL Server's closest match, float(53). Float(53) does not completely follow the IEEE 754 double-precision floating-point specification, whereas the XPath number data type does.

I refer you to the section "Data Type Coercions" in Chapter 5, "Creating XML Views with XDR Schemas," to see how XDR data types map to SQL Server data types. We'll see how XDR schema data types map to XPath data types in just a minute.

XPath Conversions

Explicit conversions are conversions that a developer writes that utilize functions or other methods to change one entity to another of a different type. The important point is that the developer explicitly states what he wants to occur. *Implicit* conversions are those that occur when an application changes an entity from one data type to another with little or no input from the developer. These conversions of data types can often change a query meaning in ways we are not expecting. So it is of utmost importance that we understand exactly how XPath data types change under different circumstances.

Some discussions of XPath data types include the equality operators equal (=) and not equal (!=) with relational operators such as greater than (>). XPath operators are split into four different categories:

- Arithmetic operators (+, -, $\star$, div)
- Equality operators (=, !=)
- Relational operators (>, <, <=, >=)
- Boolean operators (AND, OR)

All four of these categories convert operands in their own way. The arithmetic operators convert their operands to numbers and provide a number result. Boolean operators convert their operands to Boolean values and provide a Boolean result. However, relational and equality operator results depend heavily on the original data type of their operands even though they result eventually in a Boolean value. Table 6.3 shows how relational and equality operators are interpreted to provide their respective Boolean results based on the type of operands compared.

Table 6.3 **Conversion Rules for Relational and Equality Operators**

Operand	Relational Operator	Equality Operator
Both operands are node sets	TRUE if and only if there is a node in one set and a node in the second set such that the comparison of their string values is TRUE.	Same
One is a node set, the other a string	TRUE if and only if there is a node in the node set such that when converted to number, the comparison of it with the string converted to number is TRUE.	TRUE if and only if there is a node in the node set such that when converted to string, the comparison of it with the string is TRUE.
One is a node set, the other a number	TRUE if and only if there is a node in the node set such that when converted to number, the comparison of it with the number is TRUE.	Same
One is a node set, the other a Boolean	TRUE if and only if there is a node in the node set such that when converted with the Boolean is TRUE.	TRUE if and only if there is a node in the node set such that when converted to Boolean, the comparison of to Boolean and then to number, the comparison of it with the Boolean converted to number is TRUE.
Neither is a node set	Convert both operands to number and then compare.	Convert both operands to a common type and then compare. Convert to Boolean if either is Boolean, number if either is number; otherwise, convert to a string

If you examine Table 6.3 closely, you'll see that XPath string comparisons are not possible. Operands are always converted to the number data type. SQL Server bends the rules a little bit for date comparisons. In these cases, a string comparison is done.

Node Set Conversions

Converting node sets is not exactly the most instinctive process we'll come across. They don't quite work the way you would expect.

To convert a node set to a string, take the first node's string value. To convert to a number, first convert to a string and then convert that string to a number. When one of these conversions to a string or a number takes place, the annotated schema's XDR type determines the proper conversion to use.

To convert a node set to Boolean, just test for its existence. The general rule of thumb here is that an attribute or element that maps to a column exists as long as that column is not null in the database. Elements that map to rows exist if any of their children exist.

There are some peculiarities of Boolean conversions, however. An example is a test made on a *bit* (Boolean) field. The Products table (refer to Northwind example in Appendix A) is the only table with a bit field, so we'll use that as an example. The XPath query `Products[@Discontinued=true()]` is the same thing as the SQL statement: `Discontinued is not null` instead of the SQL statement: `Discontinued = 1` as you would expect. If you wanted this last expression, first convert the node set to either a string or number like this: `Products[string(@Discontinued) = true()]`. Another thing to look out for is that most operators evaluate as false on empty node sets (a good way to test for an empty node set, don't you think?). This means that if X and Y are node sets and X is empty, then both X = Y and X != Y evaluate to false, and not(A = B) and not(A != B) both evaluate to true.

SQL Server's *CONVERT* Function

The SQL Server `CONVERT` function is used extensively when mapping XDR data types to XPath data types. The syntax for the SQL Server `CONVERT` function is as follows:

```
CONVERT(data_type[(length)], expression[, style]).
```

The various parts of this function in order are as follows:

- **data_type.** The target system-supplied data type, including `bigint` and `sql_variant`. User-defined data types cannot be used.

- **length.** An optional parameter of `nchar`, `nvarchar`, `char`, `varchar`, `binary`, or `varbinary` data types.

- **expression.** Any valid Microsoft SQL Server expression.

- **style.** The style of date format used to convert `datetime` or `smalldatetime` data to character data (`nchar`, `nvarchar`, `char`, `varchar`, `nchar`, or `nvarchar` data types), or the string format when converting `float`, `real`, `money`, or `smallmoney` data to character data (`nchar`, `nvarchar`, `char`, `varchar`, `nchar`, or `nvarchar` data types). The style used is exclusively *style 126*.

Style 126 is designed for XML use. For conversion from datetime or smalldatetime to character data, the output format is as described in the table. For conversion from float, money, or smallmoney to character data, the output is equivalent to style 2. For conversion from real to character data, the output is equivalent to style 1.

Table 6.4 shows just how often the CONVERT function is used for data type mapping purposes.

For much more detailed information on the CONVERT function, refer to the *SQL Books* documentation that accompanies SQL Server 2000. Search for the topic "CAST and CONVERT."

Mapping XDR Data Types to XPath Data Types

Table 6.4 shows that a node's XDR schema data type determines its data type.

Table 6.4 **Converting XDR Data Types to XPath Data Types**

XDR Data Type	Equivalent XPath Data Type	SQL Server Conversion Used
None bin.base64 bin.hex	N/A	None CustomerID
Boolean	Boolean	CONVERT(bit, CustomerID)
number, int, float, i1, i2, i4, i8, r4, r8, ui1, ui2, ui4, ui8	number	CONVERT(float(53), CustomerID)
id, idref, idrefs, entity, entities, enumeration, notation, nmtoken, nmtokens, char, dateTime, dateTime.tz, string, uri, uuid	string	CONVERT(nvarchar(4000), CustomerID, 126)
fixed14.4	N/A (there is no data type in XPath that is equivalent to the fixed14.4 XDR data type)	CONVERT(money, CustomerID)
date	string	LEFT(CONVERT(nvarchar(4000), CustomerID, 126), 10)
time, time.tz	string	SUBSTRING(CONVERT(nvarchar(4000), CustomerID, 126), 1 + CHARINDEX(N'T', CONVERT(nvarchar(4000), CustomerID, 126)), 24)

Let's look at the following example of how we can use Table 6.4 to understand exactly what conversions actually take place in XPath queries:

From a developer's point of view, it doesn't get any easier than a simple assignment statement, or so it appears. With an XPath expression of @Quantity = 14, where Quantity is of data type fixed14.4 and 14 is of data type int, a couple of conversions must take place before the expression can be evaluated.

First, according to Table 6.4, the Quantity entity is converted to type money with the conversion CONVERT(money, Quantity). Second, according to Table 6.4, the int data type 14 is converted to data type float with the conversion CONVERT(float(53), 14). Done yet? Nope. We still have two different data types, a money and a float. The last step, then, is to explicitly convert the money data type to a float data type using the float conversion function supplied by SQL Server 2000. The final conversion performed is as follows:

```
CONVERT(float(53), (CONVERT(money, Quantity))) + CONVERT(float(53), 14)
```

Table 6.5 shows additional conversions performed.

Table 6.5   **Explicit Conversion Functions**

	X is unknown	X is string	X is number	X is Boolean
string(X)	CONVERT (nvarchar , (4000) X, 126)	n/a	CONVERT (nvarchar (4000), X, 126)	CASE WHEN X THEN true ELSE false END
number(X)	CONVERT (float(53), X)	CONVERT (float(53), X)	n/a	CASE WHEN X THEN 1 ELSE 0 END
Boolean(X)	n/a	LEN(X) > 0	X != 0	n/a

Let's do one more example. This time we'll evaluate the XPath expression @UnitPrice * @Quantity > 65. Here, UnitPrice is again of data type fixed14.4, 65 is of data type int, and Quantity is of data type smallint.

UnitPrice is converted to type money via CONVERT(money, UnitPrice). Quantity is converted to type float via CONVERT(float(53), Quantity), and the smallint 65 is converted to type float with CONVERT(float(53), 65). UnitPrice needs one additional conversion with CONVERT(float(53), (CONVERT(money, Quantity))). This last conversion is to match data type float to float. The full conversion is then:

```
CONVERT(float(53), (CONVERT(money, UnitPrice))) * CONVERT(float(53),
Quantity) > CONVERT(float(53), 65).
```

As far as date and time conversions go, they are designed to work whether the value is stored in the database using the SQL Server datetime data type or a string. Note that the SQL Server datetime data type does not use timezone and has a smaller precision than the XML time data type. To include the timezone data type or additional precision, store the data in SQL Server 2000 using a string type.

Location Paths

A *location path* is an expression that selects a node set relative to the context node. You've already used these entities when you specified an XPath query inside of a template file or placed a query directly into an URL. This is just a formal name that we'll use from this point on.

A location path can be broken down into one or more *location steps* separated by forward slashes. In multiple location step paths, the location steps are interpreted left to right. Each location step identifies a node set in the XML document tree model relative to the preceding location step. The node set produced by the last location step is the final result of the overall XPath expression.

Location paths are composed of three different parts:

- A node test
- An axis identifier
- Zero or more predicates

The general form of a location step is as follows:

```
axis-identifier::node-test[predicate1][predicate2].
```

The axis identifier is separated from the node test with two colons (::), and each predicate, if any, is enclosed within square brackets ([]). Figure 6.1 illustrates the breakdown of an XPath expression into its component parts.

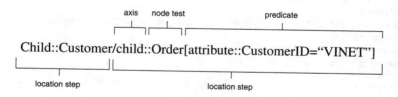

Figure 6.1   The parts of an XPath expression.

The following discussion might leave you wondering about the old "What came first, the chicken or the egg?" argument. That's really unavoidable because each of these three entities depends on each other to function and is somewhat defined in terms of each other.

Let's look at each of these individual parts and include examples. We'll start with node tests.

Specifying a Node Test

The node test is the main part of the XPath expression. This doesn't mean the other parts of the expression are not important. All I'm saying here is that the node test specifies the node type selected by the location step. It identifies the element or attribute that is the endpoint of the query.

A node type is associated with each of the four axes (child, parent, attribute, and self), as shown in Table 6.6.

Table 6.6 **Principal Node Types for Each Axis**

Axis	Principal Node Type
Child	`<element>`
Parent	`<element>`
Attribute	`<attribute>`
Self	`<element>`

The wildcard node test (`parent::*`, for example) is not supported.

Using Listing 6.1 to illustrate, if the location path specifies `child::Orders`, the `<Orders>` element children of the context node are selected. If the current context is `ROOT`, then the query results in a node set of three orders. This is shown graphically in Figure 6.2.

Listing 6.1 **XML Document for Use in Node Test Examples**

```
<ROOT xmlns:sql="urn:schemas-microsoft-com:xml-sql">
  <Orders OrderID="10248" CustomerID="VINET" OrderDate="1996-07-
04T00:00:00" />
  <Orders OrderID="10249" CustomerID="TOMSP" OrderDate="1996-07-
05T00:00:00" />
  <Orders OrderID="10250" CustomerID="HANAR" OrderDate="1996-07-
08T00:00:00" />
</ROOT>
```

Here's another example. Assume the context node is the third `Orders` element in the sample code in Listing 6.1. If we use the XPath query `attribute::OrderDate`, the resulting node set is composed of the attribute node `OrderDate` (has the value 1996-07-08T00:00:00). This is shown graphically in Figure 6.3.

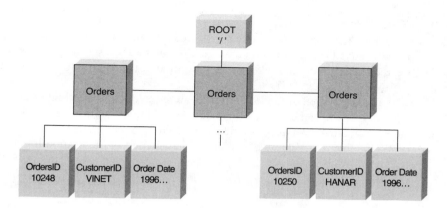

Figure 6.2   Results of the *child::Orders* XPath expression.

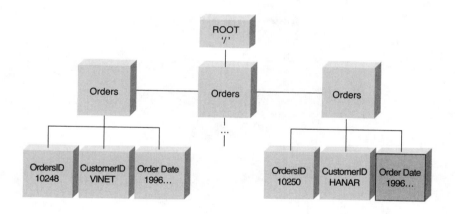

Figure 6.3   Results of the `attribute::OrderDate` XPath expression.

Because the child axis has `<element>` as its principal node type, the node test, `Orders`, is TRUE if `Orders` is an `<element>` node. Because the principal node type of the `attribute` axis is `<attribute>`, the node test is TRUE if `CustomerID` is an `<attribute>` node. If the context node doesn't have a `CustomerID` attribute, you'll get back an empty node set.

In Microsoft's implementation of XPath, every XPath query begins from the `ROOT` context. As an example, a query beginning with `Order` is treated as `/Order`. In the query `Order[Order Details]`, `Order` begins at the root context, but `Order Details` begins at the `Order` context.

Specifying Axes

Whereas the node test specifies the node type selected by the location step, axes specify the *tree relationship* between the nodes selected by the location step and the context node. Parent, child, attribute, and self axes are supported in the Microsoft implementation.

If a child axis is specified in the location path, all selected nodes are children of the context node. If a parent axis is specified, the selected node is the parent of the context node. If an attribute axis is specified, the selected nodes are attributes of the context node. Figure 6.4 shows a graphical representation of the relationships.

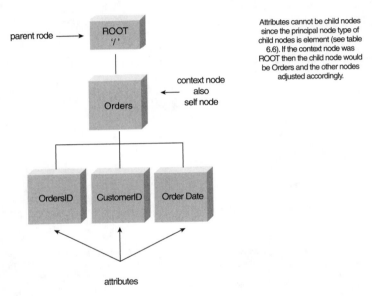

Figure 6.4 Axes relationships in XPath expressions.

The next four sections present examples of axis relationships in XPath queries. For these examples, we'll be using the XDR schema file shown in Listing 6.2. It relates the Customer, Order, Order Detail, and Employee tables of the Northwind database provided in Appendix A. We'll call this schema SampleSchema.xml and place it in our SchemaVirtualName directory.

Listing 6.2 **Sample XDR Schema File for Our Examples**

```
<?xml version="1.0" ?>
<Schema xmlns="urn:schemas-microsoft-com:xml-data"
        xmlns:dt="urn:schemas-microsoft-com:datatypes"
        xmlns:sql="urn:schemas-microsoft-com:xml-sql">
```

```
<ElementType name="Customer" sql:relation="Customers">
  <AttributeType name="CustomerID" dt:type="id" />
  <AttributeType name="CompanyName" />
  <AttributeType name="ContactName" />
  <AttributeType name="City" />
  <AttributeType name="Fax" />
  <AttributeType name="Orders" dt:type="idrefs"  sql:id-prefix="Ord-" />

  <attribute type="CustomerID" />
  <attribute type="CompanyName" />
  <attribute type="ContactName" />
  <attribute type="City" />
  <attribute type="Fax" />
  <attribute type="Orders" sql:relation="Orders" sql:field="OrderID">
    <sql:relationship
              key-relation="Customers"
              key="CustomerID"
              foreign-relation="Orders"
              foreign-key="CustomerID" />
  </attribute>

  <element type="Order">
    <sql:relationship
              key-relation="Customers"
              key="CustomerID"
              foreign-relation="Orders"
              foreign-key="CustomerID" />
  </element>
</ElementType>

<ElementType name="Order" sql:relation="Orders">
  <AttributeType name="OrderID" dt:type="id" sql:id-prefix="Ord-" />
  <AttributeType name="EmployeeID" />
  <AttributeType name="CustomerID" />
  <AttributeType name="OrderDate" />
  <AttributeType name="RequiredDate" />
  <AttributeType name="ShippedDate" />

  <attribute type="OrderID" />
  <attribute type="EmployeeID" />
  <attribute type="CustomerID" />
  <attribute type="OrderDate" />
  <attribute type="RequiredDate" />
  <attribute type="ShippedDate" />

  <element type="OrderDetail">
    <sql:relationship
              key-relation="Orders"
              key="OrderID"
              foreign-relation="[Order Details]"
              foreign-key="OrderID" />
```

continues

Listing 6.2 **Continued**

```
    </element>
  </ElementType>

  <ElementType name="OrderDetail" sql:relation="[Order Details]"
                           sql:key-fields="OrderID ProductID">
    <AttributeType name="ProductID" dt:type="idref"
                                sql:id-prefix="Prod-" />
    <AttributeType name="UnitPrice"/>
    <AttributeType name="Quantity" />

    <attribute type="ProductID" />
    <attribute type="UnitPrice" sql:field="UnitPrice" />
    <attribute type="Quantity" />

    <element type="Discount"  sql:field="Discount"/>
  </ElementType>

  <ElementType name="Discount" dt:type="string"
                           sql:relation="[Order Details]"/>

<ElementType name="Employee" sql:relation="Employees">
    <AttributeType name="EmployeeID" />
    <AttributeType name="LastName" />
    <AttributeType name="FirstName" />
    <AttributeType name="Title" />

    <attribute type="EmployeeID" />
    <attribute type="LastName" />
    <attribute type="FirstName" />
    <attribute type="Title" />
  </ElementType>
  </Schema>
```

Child Elements

This XPath query selects all the child <Customer> elements of the current context node:

```
Child::Customer
```

Listing 6.3 is a template file we'll use to test this expression. Place this file in the TemplateVirtualName directory.

Listing 6.3   **Template File to Test** *Child::Customer*

```
<ROOT xmlns:sql="urn:schemas-microsoft-com:xml-sql">
  <sql:xpath-query mapping-schema="../schemas/SampleSchema.xml">
    /child::Customer
  </sql:xpath-query>
</ROOT>
```

This template produces a rather large XML result file, a portion of which is given in Listing 6.4.

Listing 6.4   **Partial Result of** *Child::Customer*

```
<ROOT xmlns:sql="urn:schemas-microsoft-com:xml-sql">
  <Customer CustomerID="ALFKI" CompanyName="Alfreds Futterkiste"
ContactName="Maria Anders"
            City="Berlin" Fax="030-0076545" Orders="Ord-10643 Ord-10692
Ord-10702 Ord-10835
            Ord-10952 Ord-11011">
    <Order OrderID="Ord-10643" EmployeeID="6" OrderDate="1997-08-
25T00:00:00" CustomerID="ALFKI"
            RequiredDate="1997-09-22T00:00:00" ShippedDate="1997-09-
02T00:00:00">
      <OrderDetail ProductID="Prod-28" UnitPrice="45.6" Quantity="15">
        <Discount>0.25</Discount>
      </OrderDetail>
      <OrderDetail ProductID="Prod-39" UnitPrice="18" Quantity="21">
        <Discount>0.25</Discount>
      </OrderDetail>
      <OrderDetail ProductID="Prod-46" UnitPrice="12" Quantity="2">
        <Discount>0.25</Discount>
      </OrderDetail>
    </Order>
    <Order OrderID="Ord-10692" EmployeeID="4" OrderDate="1997-10-
03T00:00:00" CustomerID="ALFKI"
            RequiredDate="1997-10-31T00:00:00" ShippedDate="1997-10-
13T00:00:00">
      <OrderDetail ProductID="Prod-63" UnitPrice="43.9" Quantity="20">
        <Discount>0</Discount>
      </OrderDetail>
    </Order>
...
```

We could have placed the query directly in the URL, like this:

```
http://iisserver/Nwind/schema/SampleSchema.xml/child::Customer?root=root.
```

This would have produced the same result as Listing 6.4.

Grandchildren

Let's take the query one level lower and look for grandchildren elements. The XPath query will be `child::order/child::OrderDetail`. Listing 6.5 shows the template file, and Listing 6.6 shows the results.

Listing 6.5 **Template File for** *child::Order/child::OrderDetail*

```
<ROOT xmlns:sql="urn:schemas-microsoft-com:xml-sql">
  <sql:xpath-query mapping-schema="../schemas/SampleSchema.xml">
    /child::Order/child::OrderDetail
  </sql:xpath-query>
</ROOT>
```

Listing 6.6 **Partial Result of** *child::Order/child::OrderDetail*

```
<ROOT xmlns:sql="urn:schemas-microsoft-com:xml-sql">
  <OrderDetail ProductID="Prod-11" UnitPrice="14" Quantity="12">
    <Discount>0</Discount>
  </OrderDetail>
  <OrderDetail ProductID="Prod-42" UnitPrice="9.8" Quantity="10">
    <Discount>0</Discount>
  </OrderDetail>
  <OrderDetail ProductID="Prod-72" UnitPrice="34.8" Quantity="5">
    <Discount>0</Discount>
  </OrderDetail>
  <OrderDetail ProductID="Prod-14" UnitPrice="18.6" Quantity="9">
    <Discount>0</Discount>
  </OrderDetail>
...
```

Notice that only the grandchildren elements of the context node (root) are returned along with their subelements. No Order information is included. That's exactly what we said we wanted in our query.

Parent ".."

We can use the parent axis in any manner similar to the following XPath query:

```
/child::Customer/child::Order/child::OrderDetail[../@CustomerID="VINET"]
```

This query should return the `OrderDetail` elements for all orders that have a `CustomerID` of `"VINET"`. Listing 6.7 shows the template file, and Listing 6.8 shows the results.

Listing 6.7 **Template File for the @CustomerID="VINET" XPath Query**

```
<ROOT xmlns:sql="urn:schemas-microsoft-com:xml-sql">
  <sql:xpath-query mapping-schema="../schemas/SampleSchema.xml">
/child::Customer/child::Order/child::OrderDetail[../@CustomerID="VINET"]
  </sql:xpath-query>
</ROOT>
```

Listing 6.8 **Results of the @CustomerID="VINET" XPath Query**

```
<ROOT xmlns:sql="urn:schemas-microsoft-com:xml-sql">
  <OrderDetail ProductID="Prod-11" UnitPrice="14" Quantity="12">
    <Discount>0</Discount>
  </OrderDetail>
  <OrderDetail ProductID="Prod-42" UnitPrice="9.8" Quantity="10">
    <Discount>0</Discount>
  </OrderDetail>
  <OrderDetail ProductID="Prod-72" UnitPrice="34.8" Quantity="5">
    <Discount>0</Discount>
  </OrderDetail>
  <OrderDetail ProductID="Prod-71" UnitPrice="17.2" Quantity="20">
    <Discount>0</Discount>
  </OrderDetail>
  <OrderDetail ProductID="Prod-72" UnitPrice="27.8" Quantity="7">
    <Discount>0</Discount>
  </OrderDetail>
  <OrderDetail ProductID="Prod-56" UnitPrice="30.4" Quantity="4">
    <Discount>0</Discount>
  </OrderDetail>
  <OrderDetail ProductID="Prod-13" UnitPrice="6" Quantity="4">
    <Discount>0</Discount>
  </OrderDetail>
  <OrderDetail ProductID="Prod-41" UnitPrice="9.65" Quantity="12">
    <Discount>0</Discount>
  </OrderDetail>
  <OrderDetail ProductID="Prod-36" UnitPrice="19" Quantity="6">
    <Discount>0</Discount>
  </OrderDetail>
  <OrderDetail ProductID="Prod-52" UnitPrice="7" Quantity="18">
    <Discount>0</Discount>
  </OrderDetail>
</ROOT>
```

Attributes

Our last example of axis declarations deals with *attribute*. Here's our XPath query:

`/child::Customer/child::Order[attribute::CustomerID="VICTE"].`

This query will return all `Orders` elements that have a `CustomerID` attribute of `"VICTE"`. Listing 6.9 shows the testing template, and partial results are in Listing 6.10.

Listing 6.9   **Template File for the** *@CustomerID="VICTE"* **XPath Query**

```
<ROOT xmlns:sql="urn:schemas-microsoft-com:xml-sql">
  <sql:xpath-query mapping-schema="../schemas/SampleSchema.xml">
    /child::Customer/child::Order[attribute::CustomerID="VICTE"]
  </sql:xpath-query>
</ROOT>
```

Listing 6.10   **Partial Results of the** *@CustomerID="VICTE"* **XPath Query**

```
<ROOT xmlns:sql="urn:schemas-microsoft-com:xml-sql">
  <Order OrderID="Ord-10251" EmployeeID="3" OrderDate="1996-07-
08T00:00:00" CustomerID="VICTE"
        RequiredDate="1996-08-05T00:00:00" ShippedDate="1996-07-
15T00:00:00">
    <OrderDetail ProductID="Prod-22" UnitPrice="16.8" Quantity="6">
      <Discount>5.0000001E-2</Discount>
    </OrderDetail>
    <OrderDetail ProductID="Prod-57" UnitPrice="15.6" Quantity="15">
      <Discount>5.0000001E-2</Discount>
    </OrderDetail>
    <OrderDetail ProductID="Prod-65" UnitPrice="16.8" Quantity="20">
        <Discount>0</Discount>
    </OrderDetail>
  </Order>
  <Order OrderID="Ord-10334" EmployeeID="8" OrderDate="1996-10-
21T00:00:00" CustomerID="VICTE"
        RequiredDate="1996-11-18T00:00:00" ShippedDate="1996-10-
28T00:00:00">
    <OrderDetail ProductID="Prod-52" UnitPrice="5.6" Quantity="8">
      <Discount>0</Discount>
    </OrderDetail>
    <OrderDetail ProductID="Prod-68" UnitPrice="10" Quantity="10">
        <Discount>0</Discount>
    </OrderDetail>
  </Order>
  ...
```

Specifying Selection Predicates

If you haven't already noticed, a *selection* predicate acts similarly to the WHERE clause in an SQL statement. It narrows down or filters a node set with respect to an axis. It is placed between brackets. For each node in the node set to which the selection predicate is applied, the selection predicate is evaluated with that node as the context node. If the selection predicate expression evaluates to TRUE for that node, the node is included in the resulting node set.

To illustrate this filtering effect, we'll discuss the XPath expression (location path) `child::Customer/child::Order[attribute::CustomerID="VICTE"]`.

First, all of the <Order> element children of the context node are selected and produce a node set. Second, the selection predicate test is applied to this node set, and all Order elements that do not have a CustomerID attribute with the value of "VICTE" are eliminated from the node set. So this XPath query returns only the <Order> element nodes having the attribute value "VICTE" for its CustomerID attribute.

This discussion was illustrated in Listings 6.9 and 6.10.

Working with Boolean Predicates

There are selection pr times when multiple predicates will
be necessary to obtain the result you want. After you start using more than one predicate, you enter the realm of Boolean filtering. This filtering effect can be implemented both implicitly and explicitly. The next three sections discuss how to implement these Boolean predicates.

Implicit Boolean Predicates

Let's say I want an XPath query that returns all orders placed by Bottom-Dollar Markets that were handled by Janet Leverling. The following query would accomplish this:

```
/child::Customer[attribute::CustomerID="BOTTM"]/child::Order
[attribute::EmployeeID="3"].
```

We can test this by using the template file in Listing 6.11. Four orders will be returned. The first two are given in Listing 6.12.

Listing 6.11 **Template File for the *CustomerID="BOTTM"* XPath Query**

```
<ROOT xmlns:sql="urn:schemas-microsoft-com:xml-sql">
  <sql:xpath-query mapping-schema="../schemas/SampleSchema.xml">
    /child::Customer[attribute::CustomerID="BOTTM"]/child::Order
[attribute::EmployeeID="3"]
  </sql:xpath-query>
</ROOT>
```

Listing 6.12 **Partial Results of *CustomerID="BOTTM"***

```
<ROOT xmlns:sql="urn:schemas-microsoft-com:xml-sql">
  <Order OrderID="Ord-10410" EmployeeID="3" OrderDate="1997-01-
10T00:00:00" CustomerID="BOTTM"
        RequiredDate="1997-02-07T00:00:00" ShippedDate="1997-01-
15T00:00:00">
    <OrderDetail ProductID="Prod-33" UnitPrice="2" Quantity="49">
      <Discount>0</Discount>
    </OrderDetail>
    <OrderDetail ProductID="Prod-59" UnitPrice="44" Quantity="16">
      <Discount>0</Discount>
    </OrderDetail>
  </Order>
  <Order OrderID="Ord-10492" EmployeeID="3" OrderDate="1997-04-
01T00:00:00" CustomerID="BOTTM"
        RequiredDate="1997-04-29T00:00:00" ShippedDate="1997-04-
11T00:00:00">
    <OrderDetail ProductID="Prod-25" UnitPrice="11.2" Quantity="60">
      <Discount>5.0000001E-2</Discount>
    </OrderDetail>
    <OrderDetail ProductID="Prod-42" UnitPrice="11.2" Quantity="20">
      <Discount>5.0000001E-2</Discount>
    </OrderDetail>
  </Order>
...
```

This combination of predicates is one way of implicitly defining the Boolean *and* operator.

Multiple attributes can also be used in a couple of other ways. They can be specified as successive predicates (one right after the other) and also as nested predicates (one inside the other).

Here is an example of successive predicates:

```
/child::Customer/child::Order[attribute::CustomerID="ERNSH"]
[attribute::ShippedDate]
```

This query, which returns a node set of all orders placed by the Ernst Handel company that have been shipped (read that as *have a ShippedDate element*), should return 28 records. A test template file for this query is in Listing 6.13. A more logical query might be for all those orders that have *not* been shipped. We'll have an example of that in the "Boolean Functions" section later in this chapter. Partial results showing the first returned order are given in Listing 6.14.

Listing 6.13 **Template File for the** *CustomerID="ERNSH"* **XPath Query**

```
<ROOT xmlns:sql="urn:schemas-microsoft-com:xml-sql">
  <sql:xpath-query mapping-schema="../schemas/SampleSchema.xml">
    /child::Customer/child::Order[attribute::CustomerID="ERNSH"]
[attribute::ShippedDate]
  </sql:xpath-query>
</ROOT>
```

Listing 6.14 **Partial Results of the** *CustomerID="ERNSH"* **XPath Query**

```
<ROOT xmlns:sql="urn:schemas-microsoft-com:xml-sql">
  <Order OrderID="Ord-10258" EmployeeID="1" OrderDate="1996-07-
17T00:00:00" CustomerID="ERNSH"
         RequiredDate="1996-08-14T00:00:00" ShippedDate="1996-07-
23T00:00:00">
    <OrderDetail ProductID="Prod-2" UnitPrice="15.2" Quantity="50">
      <Discount>0.2</Discount>
    </OrderDetail>
    <OrderDetail ProductID="Prod-32" UnitPrice="25.6" Quantity="6">
      <Discount>0.2</Discount>
    </OrderDetail>
    <OrderDetail ProductID="Prod-5" UnitPrice="17" Quantity="65">
      <Discount>0.2</Discount>
    </OrderDetail>
  </Order>
...
```

Here is an example of nested predicates:

```
child::Customer[child::Order[attribute::EmployeeID=3]]
```

This produces a node set that contains any `Orders` elements with an `EmployeeID` attribute of 3.

Explicit Boolean Predicates Using Operators

In the preceding section, we saw the myriad of ways that exist to emulate the Boolean `AND` operator implicitly. This section discusses the use of *explicit* operator specification of both `AND` and `OR`. We'll stick with *or* because we haven't had examples of it so far.

Because explicit specification is so straightforward, employing the *or* operator is a very simple process. We'll use the following query, which generates a node set of all orders placed by either the Vins et alcools Chevalier or the Toms Spezialitaüten company.

```
/child::Customer/child::Order[attribute::CustomerID="VINET" or
attribute::CustomerID="TOMSP"]
```

Listing 6.15 shows the template that tests our XPath query, and Listing 6.16 shows the results. There should be 11 records returned.

Listing 6.15   **Template File for the** *CustomerID="VINET"* **XPath Query**

```
<ROOT xmlns:sql="urn:schemas-microsoft-com:xml-sql">
  <sql:xpath-query mapping-schema="../schemas/SampleSchema.xml">
    /child::Customer/child::Order[attribute::CustomerID="VINET" or
attribute::CustomerID="TOMSP"]
  </sql:xpath-query>
</ROOT>
```

Listing 6.16   **Partial Results of the** *CustomerID="VINET"* **XPath Query**

```
<ROOT xmlns:sql="urn:schemas-microsoft-com:xml-sql">
  <Order OrderID="Ord-10249" EmployeeID="6" OrderDate="1996-07-
05T00:00:00" CustomerID="TOMSP"
        RequiredDate="1996-08-16T00:00:00" ShippedDate="1996-07-
10T00:00:00">
    <OrderDetail ProductID="Prod-14" UnitPrice="18.6" Quantity="9">
      <Discount>0</Discount>
    </OrderDetail>
    <OrderDetail ProductID="Prod-51" UnitPrice="42.4" Quantity="40">
      <Discount>0</Discount>
    </OrderDetail>
  </Order>
  <Order OrderID="Ord-10438" EmployeeID="3" OrderDate="1997-02-
06T00:00:00" CustomerID="TOMSP"
        RequiredDate="1997-03-06T00:00:00" ShippedDate="1997-02-
14T00:00:00">
    <OrderDetail ProductID="Prod-19" UnitPrice="7.3" Quantity="15">
      <Discount>0.2</Discount>
    </OrderDetail>
    <OrderDetail ProductID="Prod-34" UnitPrice="11.2" Quantity="20">
      <Discount>0.2</Discount>
    </OrderDetail>
    <OrderDetail ProductID="Prod-57" UnitPrice="15.6" Quantity="15">
      <Discount>0.2</Discount>
    </OrderDetail>
  </Order>
...
```

Boolean Functions

This section covers the Boolean functions `not()`, `true()`, and `false()`. The `not()` function enables you to reverse the conditions of the predicate test. Two sections ago in "Implicit Boolean Predicates," we used the following XPath query:

```
/child::Customer/child::Order[attribute::CustomerID="ERNSH"]
[attribute::ShippedDate]
```

This query generated a node set composed of all Orders placed by the Ernst Handel company that have a `ShippedDate` element. I also told you that it would be more logical to search for orders that have not been shipped (keyword *not*). To accomplish this, we would reverse the `attribute::shipped` predicate. The query would then become:

```
/child::Customer/child::Order[attribute::CustomerID="ERNSH"]
[not(attribute::ShippedDate)]
```

This query produces two Order nodes, and the results are given in Listing 6.17. The template file doesn't change and is the same as the template given in Listing 6.13.

Listing 6.17 **Results of the *CustomerID="ERNSH"* XPath Query**

```
<ROOT xmlns:sql="urn:schemas-microsoft-com:xml-sql">
  <Order OrderID="Ord-11008" EmployeeID="7" CustomerID="ERNSH"
OrderDate="1998-04-08T00:00:00"
         RequiredDate="1998-05-06T00:00:00">
    <OrderDetail ProductID="Prod-28" UnitPrice="45.6" Quantity="70">
      <Discount>5.0000001E-2</Discount>
    </OrderDetail>
    <OrderDetail ProductID="Prod-34" UnitPrice="14" Quantity="90">
      <Discount>5.0000001E-2</Discount>
    </OrderDetail>
    <OrderDetail ProductID="Prod-71" UnitPrice="21.5" Quantity="21">
      <Discount>0</Discount>
    </OrderDetail>
  </Order>
  <Order OrderID="Ord-11072" EmployeeID="4" CustomerID="ERNSH"
OrderDate="1998-05-05T00:00:00"
         RequiredDate="1998-06-02T00:00:00">
    <OrderDetail ProductID="Prod-2" UnitPrice="19" Quantity="8">
      <Discount>0</Discount>
    </OrderDetail>
    <OrderDetail ProductID="Prod-41" UnitPrice="9.65" Quantity="40">
      <Discount>0</Discount>
    </OrderDetail>
    <OrderDetail ProductID="Prod-50" UnitPrice="16.25" Quantity="22">
      <Discount>0</Discount>
    </OrderDetail>
    <OrderDetail ProductID="Prod-64" UnitPrice="33.25" Quantity="130">
      <Discount>0</Discount>
    </OrderDetail>
  </Order>
</ROOT>
```

The `true()` and `false()` Boolean functions can be used to form queries that we've written previously. For example, the query that produced the results in Listing 6.17 could have been written as follows:

```
/child::Customer/child::Order[attribute::CustomerID="ERNSH"]
[attribute::ShippedDate = false()]
```

The use of the Boolean `true()` function in the following query generates a node set of all customers that have placed at least one order:

```
/child::Customer[child::Order = true()]
```

Relational Operators

So far, we've written queries that test for an entity being equal to something, an entity that satisfies multiple equalities (Boolean *and*), and several other types of predicate tests, but we haven't used the relational operators in any way. Just as a reminder, the relational operators are =, !=, <, <=, >, >=. In the following query, we use the greater than (>) relational operator to demonstrate their use. From there, it is simple substitution to utilize the other operators.

This XPath query generates a node set of all `OrderDetail` records that have a `Quantity` attribute greater than 2:

```
/child::Customer/child::Order/child::OrderDetail[attribute::Quantity > 2]
```

The template containing this query is Listing 6.18, and partial results are given in Listing 6.19.

Listing 6.18   **The Template File for the** *Quantity > 2* **XPath Query**

```
<ROOT xmlns:sql="urn:schemas-microsoft-com:xml-sql">
  <sql:xpath-query mapping-schema="../schemas/SampleSchema.xml">
    /child::Customer/child::Order/child::OrderDetail
    [attribute::Quantity > 2]
  </sql:xpath-query>
</ROOT>
```

Listing 6.19   **Partial Results of the** *Quantity > 2* **XPath Query**

```
<ROOT xmlns:sql="urn:schemas-microsoft-com:xml-sql">
  <OrderDetail ProductID="Prod-28" UnitPrice="45.6" Quantity="15">
    <Discount>0.25</Discount>
  </OrderDetail>
  <OrderDetail ProductID="Prod-39" UnitPrice="18" Quantity="21">
    <Discount>0.25</Discount>
  </OrderDetail>
  <OrderDetail ProductID="Prod-63" UnitPrice="43.9" Quantity="20">
    <Discount>0</Discount>
```

```
  </OrderDetail>
  <OrderDetail ProductID="Prod-3" UnitPrice="10" Quantity="6">
    <Discount>0</Discount>
  </OrderDetail>
  ...
```

The relational operators < and <= will not work as written. You must substitute the entity encoding expression < for the < symbol in each instance. For example, you would rewrite the <= operator to <= (ugly but necessary).

For some reason, I never seem to remember this little tidbit, and it's cost me development time. All you get for an error message is something like, "Sorry, I can't display that page," (wonderfully explanatory, don't you think?). Hopefully, it won't cost you.

Arithmetic Operators

Utilizing arithmetic operators in XPath expressions is just as straightforward as using the relational operators we discussed in the preceding section without the hiccup of the < operator. Listing 6.20 shows a sample query for determining when a customer spends more than $15,000 on an item. Listing 6.21 shows the result of Listing 6.20.

```
/child::Customer/child::Order/child::OrderDetail[attribute:: Quantity *
attribute::UnitPrice > 15000]
```

Listing 6.20　**Template File for the *UnitPrice* > 15000 XPath Query**

```
<ROOT xmlns:sql="urn:schemas-microsoft-com:xml-sql">
  <sql:xpath-query mapping-schema="../schemas/SampleSchema.xml">
    /child::Customer/child::Order/child::OrderDetail[attribute::Quantity *
          attribute::UnitPrice > 15000]]  </sql:xpath-query>
</ROOT>
```

Listing 6.21　**Results of the *UnitPrice* > 15000 XPath Query**

```
<ROOT xmlns:sql="urn:schemas-microsoft-com:xml-sql">
  <OrderDetail ProductID="Prod-38" UnitPrice="263.5" Quantity="60">
    <Discount>0</Discount>
  </OrderDetail>
  <OrderDetail ProductID="Prod-38" UnitPrice="263.5" Quantity="60">
    <Discount>5.0000001E-2</Discount>
  </OrderDetail>
</ROOT>
```

Specifying Explicit Conversion Functions

It's time to talk about the explicit conversion functions `string()` and `number()`. We'll discuss the latter first.

The `number()` function is used to convert a nonnumeric value to a numeric one. If the database you're using was originally designed correctly, then generally these functions are rarely used. By designed correctly, I mean that if a column will not be used in some type of math calculation, define it as a string value. If it will be used in a math calculation, define it as one of the numeric data types.

Here's an example utilizing the `string()` function. The XPath query

```
/Customer/Order[string(@EmployeeID)="6"]
```

selects all Orders belonging to the employee with `EmployeeID` equal to 6. The `EmployeeID` value is an integer, so to compare it to a string, it must first be converted before the comparison is made. The template file is given in Listing 6.22, with the partial results given in Listing 6.23.

Listing 6.22 **Template file for** *string(@OrderID)="Ord-10248"*

```
<ROOT xmlns:sql="urn:schemas-microsoft-com:xml-sql">
  <sql:xpath-query mapping-schema="../schemas/SampleSchema.xml">
    /child::Customer/child::Order[string(@OrderID)="Ord-10248"]
  </sql:xpath-query>
</ROOT>
```

Listing 6.23 **Partial Results of** *string(@OrderID)="Ord-10248"*

```
<ROOT xmlns:sql="urn:schemas-microsoft-com:xml-sql">
  <Order OrderID="Ord-10248" EmployeeID="5" CustomerID="VINET"
OrderDate="1996-07-04T00:00:00" RequiredDate="1996-08-01T00:00:00"
ShippedDate="1996-07-16T00:00:00">
    <OrderDetail ProductID="Prod-11" UnitPrice="14" Quantity="12">
      <Discount>0</Discount>
    </OrderDetail>
    <OrderDetail ProductID="Prod-42" UnitPrice="9.8" Quantity="10">
      <Discount>0</Discount>
    </OrderDetail>
    <OrderDetail ProductID="Prod-72" UnitPrice="34.8" Quantity="5">
      <Discount>0</Discount>
    </OrderDetail>
  </Order>
</ROOT>
```

Specifying XPath Variables

In the section "Using XML Templates" in Chapter 4, I briefly showed the structure of a template file that utilized an XPath query to determine the resulting node set. Because we had not talked about XPath queries at that time, I wanted to hold off on discussing their use in template files. We will now discuss using XPath queries in template files.

XPath variables and setting default values for them is very similar to what we discussed previously when we talked about parameter passing to template files. Listing 6.24 shows a template file with two variable values, one for `EmployeeID` and the other for `CustomerID`. The `EmployeeID` has a default value of 5 supplied, and `VINET` is supplied as the default value for the `CustomerID`. Listing 6.25 shows the results of executing this query without specifying values for the two quantities, thereby employing the default values.

Listing 6.24 **Template File with XPath Variables**

```
<ROOT xmlns:sql="urn:schemas-microsoft-com:xml-sql">
  <sql:header>
    <sql:param name='EmployeeID'>5</sql:param>
    <sql:param name='CustomerID'>VINET</sql:param>
  </sql:header>
  <sql:xpath-query mapping-schema="../schemas/SampleSchema.xml">
    /child::Customer/child::Order[attribute::CustomerID=$CustomerID and
      attribute::EmployeeID=$EmployeeID]
  </sql:xpath-query >
</ROOT>
```

Listing 6.25 **Default Results of Template Execution**

```
<ROOT xmlns:sql="urn:schemas-microsoft-com:xml-sql">
  <Order OrderID="Ord-10248" EmployeeID="5" OrderDate="1996-07-
04T00:00:00" CustomerID="VINET"
          RequiredDate="1996-08-01T00:00:00" ShippedDate="1996-07-
16T00:00:00">
    <OrderDetail ProductID="Prod-11" UnitPrice="14" Quantity="12">
      <Discount>0</Discount>
    </OrderDetail>
    <OrderDetail ProductID="Prod-42" UnitPrice="9.8" Quantity="10">
      <Discount>0</Discount>
    </OrderDetail>
    <OrderDetail ProductID="Prod-72" UnitPrice="34.8" Quantity="5">
      <Discount>0</Discount>
     </OrderDetail>
  </Order>
</ROOT>
```

Listing 6.26 shows the results after specifying the value of 6 for the EmployeeID and TOMSP for the CustomerID in the following URL:

```
http://iisserver/Nwind/templates/template.xml?EmployeeID=6&CustomerID=TOMSP
```

Listing 6.26 **Default Results of Template Execution**

```
<ROOT xmlns:sql="urn:schemas-microsoft-com:xml-sql">
  <Order OrderID="Ord-10249" EmployeeID="6" OrderDate="1996-07-05T00:00:00"
CustomerID="TOMSP"
         RequiredDate="1996-08-16T00:00:00" ShippedDate="1996-07-
10T00:00:00">
    <OrderDetail ProductID="Prod-14" UnitPrice="18.6" Quantity="9">
      <Discount>0</Discount>
    </OrderDetail>
    <OrderDetail ProductID="Prod-51" UnitPrice="42.4" Quantity="40">
      <Discount>0</Discount>
    </OrderDetail>
  </Order>
  <Order OrderID="Ord-10446" EmployeeID="6" OrderDate="1997-02-14T00:00:00"
CustomerID="TOMSP"
         RequiredDate="1997-03-14T00:00:00" ShippedDate="1997-02-
19T00:00:00">
    <OrderDetail ProductID="Prod-19" UnitPrice="7.3" Quantity="12">
      <Discount>0.1</Discount>
    </OrderDetail>
    <OrderDetail ProductID="Prod-24" UnitPrice="3.6" Quantity="20">
      <Discount>0.1</Discount>
    </OrderDetail>
    <OrderDetail ProductID="Prod-31" UnitPrice="10" Quantity="3">
      <Discount>0.1</Discount>
    </OrderDetail>
    <OrderDetail ProductID="Prod-52" UnitPrice="5.6" Quantity="15">
      <Discount>0.1</Discount>
    </OrderDetail>
  </Order>
</ROOT>
```

Accessing Database Objects via HTTP

We've covered template files and schema files extensively up to this point but haven't mentioned dbobject at all. There is a reason for this. We know that dbobject allows direct access to database tables and views. That much we have mentioned. What we didn't know was that its use is almost exclusive to binary data database columns. This isn't nearly as prevalent as the type of usage we've gotten from templates and schemas. We have a couple of examples of this usage, first in a short discussion of URL usage and then in Listing 6.27.

We'll first retrieve an employee's photo from the Employees table via this URL:

```
http://IISServer/Nwind/dbobjects/Employees[@EmployeeID='6']/@Photo
```

Employees specifies the Employees table, @EmployeeID is the predicate that identifies the requested information as belonging to employee 6, and @Photo identifies the column to access to obtain the data.

In this case, the XPath query must refer to a single row and single column. Listing 6.27 shows another way to get at the binary data utilizing a template file, and Listing 6.28 shows the result.

Listing 6.27 **Retrieving Binary Data from a Template File**

```
<?xml version ='1.0' encoding='UTF-8'?>
<root xmlns:sql='urn:schemas-microsoft-com:xml-sql'>
  <sql:query >
     SELECT EmployeeID, Photo FROM Employees FOR XML AUTO
  </sql:query>
</root>
```

Listing 6.28 **Binary Data Results**

```
<?xml version="1.0" encoding="UTF-8" ?>
<root xmlns:sql="urn:schemas-microsoft-com:xml-sql">
  <Employees EmployeeID="1"
Photo="dbobject/Employees[@EmployeeID='1']/@Photo" />
  <Employees EmployeeID="2"
Photo="dbobject/Employees[@EmployeeID='2']/@Photo" />
  <Employees EmployeeID="3"
Photo="dbobject/Employees[@EmployeeID='3']/@Photo" />
  <Employees EmployeeID="4"
Photo="dbobject/Employees[@EmployeeID='4']/@Photo" />
  <Employees EmployeeID="5"
Photo="dbobject/Employees[@EmployeeID='5']/@Photo" />
  <Employees EmployeeID="6"
Photo="dbobject/Employees[@EmployeeID='6']/@Photo" />
  <Employees EmployeeID="7"
Photo="dbobject/Employees[@EmployeeID='7']/@Photo" />
  <Employees EmployeeID="8"
Photo="dbobject/Employees[@EmployeeID='8']/@Photo" />
  <Employees EmployeeID="9"
Photo="dbobject/Employees[@EmployeeID='9']/@Photo" />
</root>
```

Hmmm, I don't think Listing 6.28 is quite the result we were looking for. What we need to do is send the results of the template file through an XSL stylesheet. This should give us what we were looking for. Add sql:xsl='photo.xsl' to the opening ROOT tag. The XSL stylesheet itself is given in Listing 6.29.

Listing 6.29 **XSL Stylesheet for Employees' Photos**

```
<?xml version='1.0' encoding='UTF-8'?>
 <xsl:stylesheet xmlns:xsl='http://www.w3.org/TR/WD-xsl' >
    <xsl:template match = '*'>
       <xsl:apply-templates />
    </xsl:template>
    <xsl:template match = 'Employees'>
      <TR>
        <TD><xsl:value-of select = '@EmployeeID' /></TD>
        <TD><B> <IMG><xsl:attribute name='src'>
                   <xsl:value-of select = '@Photo'/>
                   </xsl:attribute>
                </IMG>
        </B></TD>
      </TR>
    </xsl:template>
    <xsl:template match = '/'>
      <HTML>
        <HEAD>
          <STYLE>th { background-color: #CCCCCC }</STYLE>
          <BASE href='http://iisserver/Nwind/'></BASE>
        </HEAD>
        <BODY>
         <TABLE border='1' style='width:300;'>
           <TR><TH colspan='2'>Employees</TH></TR>
           <TR><TH >EmployeeID</TH><TH>Photo</TH></TR>
           <xsl:apply-templates select = 'root' />
         </TABLE>
        </BODY>
      </HTML>
    </xsl:template>
 </xsl:stylesheet>
```

The <BASE> tag references the virtual server root that enables the page to properly present the photos. If you look at the generated source code of the HTML page given in Listing 6.30, you'll see how the photo references are generated.

Listing 6.30 **Partial Listing of Generated HTML Code**

```
<HTML>
  <HEAD>
    <STYLE>th { background-color: #CCCCCC }</STYLE>
    <BASE href="http://iisserver/Nwind/"></BASE>
  </HEAD>
  <BODY>
    <TABLE border="1" style="width:300;">
      <TR><TH colspan="2">Employees</TH></TR>
      <TR><TH>EmployeeID</TH><TH>Photo</TH></TR>
      <TR>
```

```
        <TD>1</TD>
        <TD><B>
          <IMG src="dbobject/Employees[@EmployeeID='1']/@Photo" />
        </B></TD>
      </TR>
      <TR>
        <TD>2</TD>
        <TD><B>
          <IMG src="dbobject/Employees[@EmployeeID='2']/@Photo" />
        </B></TD>
      </TR>
      <TR>
        <TD>3</TD>
        <TD><B>
          <IMG src="dbobject/Employees[@EmployeeID='3']/@Photo" />
          </B></TD>
      </TR>

    </BODY>
  </HTML>
```

Recap of What Was Discussed in This Chapter

- Microsoft supports a subset of axes, functions, and operators in its implementation. Quite a bit of functionality has been left out. An exact listing of what has been left out is shown in Table 6.2. The Microsoft implementation of XPath digresses from the W3C specification in root queries, reporting errors, document order, data types, and cross-product queries.

- It isn't always possible to map one data type to another when you're talking about XDR schema, XPath, and SQL Server 2000. Each of these entities has its own data types, and many of these data types have no counterpart in the other entities. Along with this, implicit and explicit conversions of data types can often change query meanings in ways we are not expecting.

- SQL Server provides the CONVERT function, which implicit conversions use to interchange data types.

- A location path is an expression that selects a node set relative to the context node. It can be broken down into one or more *location steps* separated by forward slashes. Location paths are composed of three different parts: a node test, an axis identifier, and zero or more predicates.

The general form of a location step follows:

```
axis-identifier::node-test[predicate1][predicate2].
```

- A predicate acts similarly to the WHERE clause in a SQL statement. It narrows down or filters a node with respect to an axis. For each node in the node set to which the predicate is applied, the predicate is evaluated with that node as the context node. If the predicate expression evaluates to TRUE for that node, the node is included in the resulting node set. Predicates are composed of node identifiers that have conditions placed on them via Boolean, arithmetic, relational, and equality operators.

- `dbobject` allows direct access to database tables and views. Its use is almost exclusive to binary data database columns, which aren't nearly as prevalent as the type of usage obtained from templates and schemas.

7

FOR XML

STARTING IN CHAPTER 4, "ACCESSING SQL 2000 via HTTP," we introduced the FOR XML extension to SQL Server 2000's Transact-SQL SELECT statement, showing how it could be used to generate XML documents from a relational database. We also went through numerous examples of how to accomplish this transformation. These examples ranged from placing the SQL query directly in an URL to writing a template file to contain the query to execute.

The FOR XML extension also has an XML mode category that we used by specifying FOR XML AUTO, which generated an *attribute-centric* XML document. I mentioned then that there are additional parameters to the FOR XML directive, and we'll talk about them now in this chapter.

One of the additional modes we'll cover in this chapter, the EXPLICIT mode, is one of the more difficult and complicated subjects we'll cover in this book.

Many of the examples in this chapter utilize the Query Analyzer. By default, the column size of returned results is limited to a 256-character width. This is too small for some of the XDR schema results that are returned in the examples. To enlarge the width, open the Query Analyzer, select Tools, and then select Options. Click the Results tab. Change Maximum Characters Per Column to a larger number (say, 2,000) and you should be okay (see Figure 7.1).

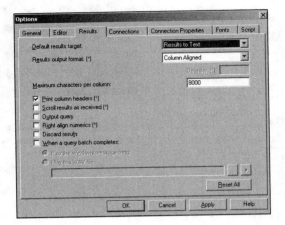

Figure 7.1   Changing the results column width.

This chapter will cover the following topics:

- The limitations of the FOR XML extension
- FOR XML RAW mode and what it accomplishes
- FOR XML AUTO mode and what it accomplishes
- FOR XML EXPLICIT mode and why it is the most complicated of the modes
- Overflow data fields and how to use and manipulate them

Syntax

Here is the syntax for the FOR XML mode expression:

```
FOR XML mode [, XMLDATA][, ELEMENTS][, BINARY BASE64]
```

The additional parameters are defined as follows:

- **mode.** Specifies the XML mode, which can be one of three possibilities
  - **RAW**. Transforms each row in the result set into an XML element with a generic identifier <row /> as the element tag.
  - **AUTO**. Returns results in a simple XML tree. Each table in the FROM clause, with at least one column listed in the SELECT clause, is represented as an XML element. The columns listed in the SELECT clause become element attributes.
  - **EXPLICIT**. Specifies that there is an explicit definition for the shape of the resulting XML. In this mode, queries must be written a specific way so that additional information about the desired nesting is explicitly specified.

- **XMLDATA.** A data schema should be returned and prepended to the document.
- **ELEMENTS.** This changes the returned document from being attribute-centric to element-centric. In other words, database columns are mapped to child elements instead of to attributes. This option can only be used in AUTO mode.
- **BINARY BASE64.** Specifies that all returned binary data must be in base64 encoding. In RAW and EXPLICIT modes, this parameter must be specified for binary data. In AUTO mode, a reference to the data is always returned.

  Binary base64 encoding applies to any data stored in SQL Server that must be treated as a data stream. In our situation (for this text), this is usually graphic data of some type such as the Photo column of the Employees table (refer to Appendix A), which contains a photo of the employee. JPEG and GIF images are other examples of binary data.

FOR XML Limitations

There is quite a long list of limitations associated with FOR XML. If you are having trouble getting FOR XML to work the way you think it should at any time, refer to this list of limitations and make sure what you're trying to accomplish is not listed here.

SELECT Statements

The following SELECT statements using FOR XML are invalid:

- The use of COMPUTE, COMPUTE BY, and FOR BROWSE is invalid in SELECT using FOR XML. For example, the following is invalid:

  ```
  SELECT OrderID, Freight FROM Orders ORDER BY OrderID COMPUTE
  AVG(Freight) for XML AUTO
  ```

- The use of GROUP BY and aggregate functions is invalid in SELECT using FOR XML. The following won't work:

  ```
  SELECT COUNT(*) FROM Employees FOR XML RAW
  ```

- FOR XML is not valid in compound SELECT statements, sub-selects, or SELECT INTO. The following sample code is invalid:

  ```
  SELECT * FROM Orders WHERE … (SELECT * FROM [Order Details] for XML
  ➥AUTO)
  ```

- You cannot use FOR XML in SELECT statement inside a stored procedure if the returned data requires further processing.

CREATE VIEW Statements that Return Rowsets

FOR XML AUTO is not allowed in CREATE VIEW statements or in user-defined functions that return rowsets. The following is not allowed:

```
CREATE VIEW SmallOrders AS SELECT * FROM Orders WHERE Quantity <= 10 FOR XML RAW
```

But you *can* do this:

```
SELECT * FROM SmallOrders FOR XML RAW
```

FOR XML Quirk

A little quirk of FOR XML is that if you specify the servername.databasename. owner.tablename four-part name in a SELECT statement on a local computer, the server name isn't returned in the tag name. When executed on a network computer, the server name *is* returned. For example

```
SELECT TOP 2 CustomerID FROM sqlserver.Northwind.dbo.Customers for XML AUTO
```

returns

```
<Northwind.dbo.Customers CustomerID ="ALFKI"/>
<Northwind.dbo.Customers CustomerID ="ANATR"/>
```

when the query is performed locally on a server.

If the SQL server is a network server, the query returns the following:

```
<sqlserver.Northwind.dbo.Customers CustomerID ="ALFKI"/>
<sqlserver.Northwind.dbo.Customers CustomerID ="ANATR"/>
```

A workaround for this is to use an *alias* for the four-part name as follows:

```
SELECT TOP 2 CustomerID FROM sqlserver.Northwind.dbo.Customers CustID for XML
    AUTO
```

The preceding query returns

```
<CustID ="ALFKI"/>
<CustID ="ANATR"/>
```

Derived Tables

FOR XML AUTO might not produce the exact nesting you want if you are using derived tables. See Listing 7.1 for the query utilizing a derived table. Listing 7.2 shows the partial results.

Listing 7.1 **SELECT Statement Using a Derived Table**

```
SELECT c.ContactName,
       o.OrderID,
       p.ProductName,            call quantities from the derived table 'p'
       p.UnitPrice,
       p.Quantity
FROM   Customers as c
```

```
      JOIN
      Orders as o
      ON
      c.CustomerID = o.CustomerID
      (
        SELECT od.OrderID,              create the derived table
               pr.ProductName,
               od.UnitPrice,
               od.Quantity
        FROM   Products as pr
               JOIN
               [Order Details] as od
               ON
               pr.ProductID = od.ProductID
      ) AS p
      ON
      o.OrderID = p.OrderID
FOR XML AUTO
```

Listing 7.2 **Partial Results of a Derived Table**

```
<?xml version="1.0" encoding="utf-8" ?>
<root>
  <c ContactName="Maria Anders">
    <o OrderID="10643">
      <pr ProductName="Rössle Sauerkraut">
        <od UnitPrice="45.6" Quantity="15"/>
      </pr>
      <pr ProductName="Chartreuse verte">
        <od UnitPrice="18" Quantity="21"/>
      </pr>
      <pr ProductName="Spegesild">
        <od UnitPrice="12" Quantity="2"/>
      </pr>
    </o>
    <o OrderID="10692">
      <pr ProductName="Vegie-spread">
        <od UnitPrice="43.9" Quantity="20"/>
      </pr>
    </o>
    <o OrderID="10702">
      <pr ProductName="Aniseed Syrup">
        <od UnitPrice="10" Quantity="6"/>
      </pr>
      <pr ProductName="Lakkalikööri">
        <od UnitPrice="18" Quantity="15"/>
      </pr>
    </o>
    <o OrderID="10835">
...
```

Notice that the <p> element is missing and that the <pr> and <od> elements are returned. The query optimizer did this. You would expect the <c>, <o>, and <p> elements. Now that you know how this works, a workaround to obtain the proper element nesting is to rewrite the query. First create a view and then use it in the XML query. Listings 7.3, 7.4, and 7.5 show the VIEW statement, the rewritten query, and the partial results, respectively.

Listing 7.3 **CREATE VIEW** Statement

```
CREATE VIEW p AS
        SELECT od.OrderID,
                pr.ProductName,
                od.UnitPrice,
                od.Quantity
        FROM    Products AS pr
                JOIN
                [Order Details] AS od
                ON
                pr.ProductID = od.ProductID
```

Listing 7.4 **Query Utilizing the VIEW**

```
SELECT c.ContactName,
        o.OrderID,
        p.ProductName,            call quantities from the view 'p'
        p.UnitPrice,
        p.Quantity
FROM Customers AS c
        JOIN
        Orders AS o
        ON
        c.CustomerID = o.CustomerID
        JOIN
        p
        ON
        o.OrderID = p.OrderID
```

Listing 7.5 **Partial Results of the Rewrite**

```
<?xml version="1.0" encoding="utf-8" ?>
<root>
  <c ContactName="Maria Anders">
    <o OrderID="10643">
      <p ProductName="Rössle Sauerkraut" UnitPrice="45.6" Quantity="15" />
      <p ProductName="Chartreuse verte" UnitPrice="18" Quantity="21" />
      <p ProductName="Spegesild" UnitPrice="12" Quantity="2" />
```

```
    </o>
    <o OrderID="10692">
      <p ProductName="Vegie-spread" UnitPrice="43.9" Quantity="20" />
    </o>
    <o OrderID="10702">
      <p ProductName="Aniseed Syrup" UnitPrice="10" Quantity="6" />
      <p ProductName="Lakkalikööri" UnitPrice="18" Quantity="15" />
    </o>
    <o OrderID="10835">
...
```

CAST Operator

Utilizing the CAST operator on a BLOB entity causes an error in AUTO mode. (The CAST causes the BLOB to lose its table and column name, so AUTO mode doesn't know where to put it.) To simulate this, first create a test table:

```
CREATE TABLE Test (One int PRIMARY KEY, Two binary)
INSERT INTO Test VALUES (100, 0xFF)
```

Then run the following query:

```
SELECT LastName,
       CAST(Photo AS image) as Photo
FROM   Employees
FOR XML AUTO
```

This creates the error in Listing 7.6.

Listing 7.6 **Error Generated Trying to CAST a BLOB**

```
<?xml version="1.0" encoding="utf-8" ?>
<root>
<?MSSQLError HResult="0x80040e14" Source="Microsoft OLE DB Provider for SQL
Server" Description="FOR XML AUTO could not find the table owning the following
column 'Two' to create a URL address for it. Remove the column, or use the BINARY
BASE64 mode, or create the URL directly using the
'dbobject/TABLE[@PK1="V1"]/@COLUMN' syntax."?>
</root>
```

To fix this, just take out the CAST operator. The result is as follows:

```
<?xml version="1.0" encoding="utf-8" ?>
<root>
  <Test One="100" Two="dbobject/Test[@One='100']/@Two" />
</root>
```

Other Limitations

FOR XML also has other limitations:

- FOR XML cannot be used with cursors.
- As a general rule, FOR XML can only be used in statements that produce direct output to the end user's presentation device (browser).
- You cannot use FOR XML in an INSERT statement inside of a stored procedure.

RAW Mode

The RAW mode of FOR XML is just that; it presents every row of a database query result with the simplistic identifier <ROW>. All columns of the result set's row are returned as attributes of the row, like this:

```
<row OrderID="10258" EmployeeID="1" ShipName="Ernst Handel" />
<row OrderID="10270" EmployeeID="1" ShipName="Wartian Herkku" />
```

Some people really like the simplicity of RAW mode, while others argue that the documents generated by this mode are just not rich enough XML documents. You'll have to decide.

The XMLDATA and BINARY BASE64 arguments to FOR XML are applicable in RAW mode. The XMLDATA argument causes the XML schema to be returned at the beginning of the document with the requested data as a declared namespace. The BINARY BASE64 argument must be specified so that binary data is returned in base64-encoded format; otherwise, the error shown in Listing 7.6 is generated.

Listing 7.7 is a template file utilizing a basic example of RAW mode; the results are given in Listing 7.8.

Listing 7.7 **FOR XML RAW**

```
<ROOT xmlns:sql='urn:schemas-microsoft-com:xml-sql'>
  <sql:query>
    SELECT TOP 4 OrderID,EmployeeID,ShipName
    FROM Orders
    WHERE EmployeeID=1
    FOR XML RAW
  </sql:query>
</ROOT>
```

As a reminder, execute this template with `http://iisserver/Nwind/templates/template.xml`.

Listing 7.8 **Results of the FOR XML RAW Example**

```
<ROOT xmlns:sql="urn:schemas-microsoft-com:xml-sql">
  <row OrderID="10258" EmployeeID="1" ShipName="Ernst Handel" />
  <row OrderID="10270" EmployeeID="1" ShipName="Wartian Herkku" />
  <row OrderID="10275" EmployeeID="1" ShipName="Magazzini Alimentari Riuniti" />
  <row OrderID="10285" EmployeeID="1" ShipName="QUICK-Stop" />
</ROOT>
```

AUTO Mode

With the exception of the previous section, all our dealings with the FOR XML extension have been related to AUTO mode. In this section, we'll talk about this mode some more and will introduce some new things, including some unexpected quirks.

XML AUTO returns result in documents with nested elements. We've never really discussed how the elements are nested with respect to the query used to generate the results. Here goes:

Each table in the FROM clause with at least one column is listed in the SELECT clause, and is represented as an XML element. Element nesting in the resulting document depends on the order in which the columns are listed in the SELECT clause; the leftmost table defines the first element, the next table defines the first nested element, and so on. The columns listed in the SELECT clause are mapped to the appropriate element as attributes. If the column name is from a table already identified by a previous column in the SELECT clause, it also becomes an attribute.

Consider the following SQL statement illustrating nesting rules:

```
SELECT Orders.CustomerID, [Order Details].UnitPrice,Orders.OrderDate
FROM   Orders, [Order Details]
WHERE  Orders.OrderID = [Order Details].OrderID
FOR XML AUTO
```

The results of the rules are illustrated in Listing 7.9. Notice that the Orders table was mentioned first, so it's the first element. The Order Details table is mentioned next, so it becomes the first nested element. Because the Orders table was already mentioned as the first quantity of the SELECT statement, the OrderDate becomes an attribute of the Orders element.

Listing 7.9 **Partial Results of Element Nesting Rules Example**

```
<ROOT xmlns:sql="urn:schemas-microsoft-com:xml-sql">
  <Orders CustomerID="VINET" OrderDate="1996-07-04T00:00:00">
    <Order_x0020_Details UnitPrice="14" />
    <Order_x0020_Details UnitPrice="9.8" />
    <Order_x0020_Details UnitPrice="34.8" />
  </Orders>
```

continues

Listing 7.9 **Continued**

```
<Orders CustomerID="TOMSP" OrderDate="1996-07-05T00:00:00">
  <Order_x0020_Details UnitPrice="18.6" />
  <Order_x0020_Details UnitPrice="42.4" />
</Orders>
...
```

Listing 7.9 demonstrates the attribute-centric form of FOR XML AUTO, in which all data entities are assigned to attributes of the related element. By specifying the ELEMENTS argument, the returned document can be made element-centric, which places data entities as nested elements of the related element. Which parameter you choose usually depends on the situation.

Listing 7.10 is a partial results listing of the SQL statement for nesting rules with the addition of the ELEMENTS argument as follows: FOR XML AUTO, ELEMENTS.

Listing 7.10 **Partial Results of Adding the *ELEMENTS* Argument**

```
<ROOT xmlns:sql="urn:schemas-microsoft-com:xml-sql">
<Orders>
  <CustomerID>VINET</CustomerID>
  <OrderDate>1996-07-04T00:00:00</OrderDate>
  <Order_x0020_Details>
    <UnitPrice>14</UnitPrice>
  </Order_x0020_Details>
  <Order_x0020_Details>
    <UnitPrice>9.8</UnitPrice>
  </Order_x0020_Details>
  <Order_x0020_Details>
    <UnitPrice>34.8</UnitPrice>
  /Order_x0020_Details>
</Orders>
  <CustomerID>TOMSP</CustomerID>
    <OrderDate>1996-07-05T00:00:00</OrderDate>
    <Order_x0020_Details>
...
```

Primary key fields play a role in the nesting of the resulting XML document also. There is a one-to-one correspondence between a change in the primary key field and a change in the new element. Consider the following SQL statement illustrating primary key usage:

```
SELECT Orders.OrderID, Orders.CustomerID, [Order
Details].UnitPrice,Orders.OrderDate
FROM    Orders, [Order Details]
WHERE   Orders.OrderID = [Order Details].OrderID
FOR XML AUTO
```

If the `OrderID` is the primary key, then the results returned are shown in Listing 7.11.

Listing 7.11   **Partial Results of *OrderID* Being the Primary Key**

```
<ROOT xmlns:sql="urn:schemas-microsoft-com:xml-sql">
<Orders OrderID="10248" CustomerID="VINET" OrderDate="1996-07-04T00:00:00">
  <Order_x0020_Details UnitPrice="14" />
  <Order_x0020_Details UnitPrice="9.8" />
  <Order_x0020_Details UnitPrice="34.8" />
</Orders>
<Orders OrderID="10249" CustomerID="TOMSP" OrderDate="1996-07-05T00:00:00">
  <Order_x0020_Details UnitPrice="18.6" />
  <Order_x0020_Details UnitPrice="42.4" />
  </Orders>
<Orders OrderID="10250" CustomerID="HANAR" OrderDate="1996-07-08T00:00:00">
...
```

Notice in Listing 7.11 that every new `OrderID` starts a new `Orders` element. This is due to `OrderID` being the primary key. Whenever it changes, a new element is created. Let's assume that `OrderID`, in this case, was not a primary key. The output would be totally different. In the absence of a primary key, every field is examined for changes. If any of the fields change, a new element is created.

Table Name Aliases

We worked earlier with a couple of examples of using aliases for table names. The following example shows our SQL query using aliases, and Listing 7.12 gives the results.

```
SELECT o.OrderID, o.CustomerID, od.UnitPrice,o.OrderDate
FROM   Orders o, [Order Details] od
WHERE  o.OrderID = od.OrderID
FOR XML AUTO
```

Listing 7.12   **Partial Results of Utilizing Aliases**

```
<ROOT xmlns:sql="urn:schemas-microsoft-com:xml-sql">
<o OrderID="10248" CustomerID="VINET" OrderDate="1996-07-04T00:00:00">
  <od UnitPrice="14" />
  <od UnitPrice="9.8" />
  <od UnitPrice="34.8" />
</o>
<o OrderID="10249" CustomerID="TOMSP" OrderDate="1996-07-05T00:00:00">
  <od UnitPrice="18.6" />
  <od UnitPrice="42.4" />
</o>
<o OrderID="10250" CustomerID="HANAR" OrderDate="1996-07-08T00:00:00">
...
```

Nothing is new here; the o is substituted for the Orders element, and od takes the place of Order Details. We're looking at this again for one reason: *nested queries*. The problem is that the query optimizer doesn't guarantee that aliases used in the inner query of nested queries will keep their alias. The following example shows the SQL statement giving partial results of using aliases; Listing 7.13 shows the resulting XML.

```
SELECT TOP 3 *
FROM    (SELECT * FROM Orders) as ORD
FOR XML AUTO
```

Listing 7.13 **Partial Results of the Nested Query**

```
<ROOT xmlns:sql="urn:schemas-microsoft-com:xml-sql">
  <Orders CustomerID="VINET" />
  <Orders CustomerID="TOMSP" />
  <Orders CustomerID="HANAR" />
</ROOT>
```

Notice how the element that we wanted to be called <ORD> was changed to <Orders>. There's no workaround for this. You just have to live with it.

GROUP BY and Aggregate Functions

In the "FOR XML Limitations" section at the beginning of this chapter, I mentioned that aggregate functions and the GROUP BY expression are not allowed with FOR XML. This is still true, but there is a workaround for these limitations, *nested queries* or *derived tables* as I called them earlier (here we go again). Basically, the inner query does the aggregate and grouping operations, creating a table that contains these different values, and then it passes them to the outer query. Listings 7.14 and 7.15 show a sample SQL statement and its results.

Listing 7.14 **SQL to Work Around Aggregate Limitations**

```
SELECT Emp.LastName, Emp.EmployeeID, TotalOrders, O.OrderID,
       O.CustomerID, OD.ProductID,   OD.Quantity
FROM (
     SELECT E.EmployeeID, E.LastName, count(*) as TotalOrders
     FROM Employees E left outer join
         Orders O ON E.EmployeeID = O.EmployeeID
     GROUP BY E.EmployeeID, E.LastName
     ) AS Emp
     left outer join Orders O on Emp.EmployeeID = O.EmployeeID
     left outer join [Order Details] OD on O.OrderID = OD.OrderID
FOR XML AUTO
```

Listing 7.15   **Partial Results of the Workaround**

```
<ROOT xmlns:sql="urn:schemas-microsoft-com:xml-sql">
  <Emp LastName="Davolio" EmployeeID="1" TotalOrders="123">
    <O OrderID="10258" CustomerID="ERNSH">
      <OD ProductID="2" Quantity="50" />
      <OD ProductID="5" Quantity="65" />
      <OD ProductID="32" Quantity="6" />
    </O>
    <O OrderID="10270" CustomerID="WARTH">
      <OD ProductID="36" Quantity="30" />
      <OD ProductID="43" Quantity="25" />
    </O>
    <O OrderID="10275" CustomerID="MAGAA">
      <OD ProductID="24" Quantity="12" />
      <OD ProductID="59" Quantity="6" />
    </O>
...
```

Computed Columns

Computed columns are another facet of the FOR XML extension that shouldn't present any surprises. Listing 7.16 shows an example and Listing 7.17 shows the results of a computed column, Contact. We combine ContactName, a space, and then ContactTitle.

Listing 7.16   **Computed Column SQL Query**

```
SELECT ContactName + ' ' + ContactTitle as Contact, Orders.OrderID
FROM Customers, Orders
WHERE Orders.CustomerID = Customers.CustomerID
ORDER BY Contact
FOR XML AUTO
```

Listing 7.17   **Partial Results of the Computed Column Query**

```
<ROOT xmlns:sql="urn:schemas-microsoft-com:xml-sql">
  <Orders Contact="Alejandra Camino Accounting Manager" OrderID="10281" />
  <Orders Contact="Alejandra Camino Accounting Manager" OrderID="10282" />
  <Orders Contact="Alejandra Camino Accounting Manager" OrderID="10306" />
  <Orders Contact="Alejandra Camino Accounting Manager" OrderID="10917" />
  <Orders Contact="Alejandra Camino Accounting Manager" OrderID="11013" />
  <Orders Contact="Alexander Feuer Marketing Assistant" OrderID="10277" />
  <Orders Contact="Alexander Feuer Marketing Assistant" OrderID="10575" />
...
```

If you want to make the `Contact` attribute its own element, you can rewrite the query to contain a subquery that generates a table called Contact containing the `Name` element, and then you can specify the name element of the Contact table first in the outer query. This is illustrated in Listings 7.18 and 7.19.

Listing 7.18   **Rearranging Elements via a Subquery**

```
SELECT Contact.Name, Orders.OrderID
FROM   (SELECT ContactName + ' ' + ContactTitle as Name, CustomerID
         FROM Customers) Contact
         LEFT OUTER JOIN Orders ON Contact.CustomerID = Orders.CustomerID
ORDER BY Contact.Name
FOR XML AUTO
```

Listing 7.19   **Partial Results of the Subquery**

```
<ROOT xmlns:sql="urn:schemas-microsoft-com:xml-sql">
  <Contact Name="Alejandra Camino Accounting Manager">
    <Orders OrderID="10281" />
    <Orders OrderID="10282" />
    <Orders OrderID="10306" />
    <Orders OrderID="10917" />
    <Orders OrderID="11013" />
  </Contact>
  <Contact Name="Alexander Feuer Marketing Assistant">
...
```

EXPLICIT Mode

The final mode we'll cover is EXPLICIT mode, which enables us to explicitly specify how we want the element nesting to appear in the XML output document. I mentioned in the beginning of this chapter that this mode is one of the more complicated and difficult subjects we will cover in this book. Now that you've heard that, are you wondering why we need *another* mode to generate XML documents? Look at it this way: RAW mode gives you absolutely no control over the layout or nesting of the XML elements in your documents. You get an element for every row in the rowset, and all data appears as attributes of those elements. AUTO mode gives you limited control over them, although it is much more than RAW mode. You can control whether the document is element-centric or attribute-centric and can adjust SQL queries somewhat to control results. Now we have EXPLICIT mode. This mode gives you total control over every facet of element layout in your documents, and that's the reason it exists.

The Universal Table

The EXPLICIT mode requires the that rowset returned from a query be in a special format. This format is called the *Universal table,* and it is used to produce the output document. Basically, a Universal table is a table created in memory by a series of SQL SELECT statements in a specific format that are combined via SQL UNION clauses.

One requirement on the rowset result is that it be ordered so that its children follow the parent element immediately. Also, it must associate the element names with the tag numbers (explained later) and provide attribute names (the default) as the column names of the Universal table. An example of a Universal table is given in Figure 7.2. This table shows the first two columns of metadata required for proper processing, Tag and Parent.

- **Tag.** An integer data type that stores the tag number of the current element. The column name must be Tag.

- **Parent.** An integer data type (or NULL) that stores the tag number of the element's parent element. The column name must be Parent.

These two columns are the most important in the table. They dictate the parent-child relationship in the resulting XML tree. This example shows how the `<Employee>`, `<Order>`, and `<OrderDetail>` elements are nested. The rest of the Universal table in Figure 7.2 describes the remaining parts of the XML document. This Universal table would generate the sample XML document in Listing 7.20.

Listing 7.20 **XML Document Generated from the Universal Table in Figure 7.2**

```
<Employee eid="5" name="Nancy">
   <Order id="60185" date="01/01/2001">
      <OrderDetail id="OD1" pid="P1"/>
      <OrderDetail id="OD2" pid="P2"/>
   </Order>
   <Order id="02" date="3/29/1997">   ...
</Employee>
```

Here are the key relationships within the table that define the hierarchy of the resulting XML tree that generates the proper nesting.

- If the parent column is 0 or NULL, the associated row is the top level of the XML tree.

- The columns in the Universal table define *groups*. Each of these groups becomes an XML element in the resulting document.

We'll be going over plenty of examples to help clarify these for you.

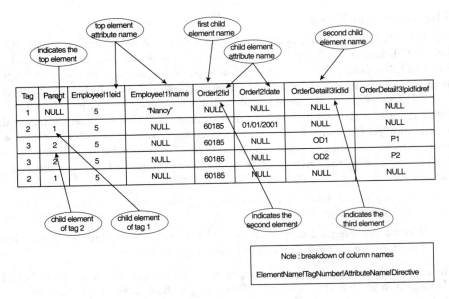

Figure 7.2 A sample Universal table specifying column names.

The column names in a Universal table *must* be specified in the query. These names follow the special format defined by the following arguments and shown in the legend in Figure 7.2

```
ElementName!TagNumber!AttributeName!Directive
```

These arguments are defined in Tables 7.1 and 7.2.

Table 7.1 **Column Name Argument Definitions**

Argument	Definition
ElementName	The identifying name of the element (if Employees is the ElementName, <Employees> is the element tag).
TagNumber	The tag number of the element. TagNumber is used to express the nesting of XML elements in the tree. Every TagNumber corresponds to exactly one ElementName.
AttributeName	The name of the XML attribute (with no Directive specified) or the name of the contained element (if Directive is either xml, CDATA, or element). With Directive specified, AttributeName can be empty. In this case, the value in the column is contained by the element with the specified ElementName.
Directive	Optional. With no Directive, AttributeName must be present. If AttributeName is not specified and Directive is not specified (for example, Employee!1), an element directive is implied (for example, Employes!1!!element) and data is contained.

Argument	Definition
	This option is used to encode ID, IDREF, and IDREFS by using the keywords ID, IDREF, and IDREFS. It is also used to indicate how to map the string data to XML using the keywords hide, element, xml, xmltext, and cdata. Combining directives between these two groups is allowed in most cases but not combining among themselves. There will be examples of these directives' uses in this chapter.

Table 7.2 **Directive Definitions**

Directive	Definition
ID	An element attribute can be specified to be an ID type attribute. Then IDREF and IDREFS attributes can be used to refer to them, enabling intradocument links. For this keyword to have an effect, the XMLDATA argument must be present.
IDREF	Attributes specified as IDREF can be used to refer to ID type attributes, enabling intradocument links. For this keyword to have an effect, the XMLDATA argument must be present.
IDREFS	Attributes specified as IDREFS can be used to refer to ID type attributes, enabling intradocument links. For this keyword to have an effect, the XMLDATA argument must be present.
hide	Prevents the attribute from being displayed. This is useful when an attribute is used to order a result, but you don't want to have it in the result.
ELEMENT	Generates a contained element with the specified name instead of an attribute (or it generates a contained element directly if no attribute name is specified). The contained data is encoded as an entity (for example, the & character becomes &). This keyword can be combined with ID, IDREF, or IDREFS.
xml	This is the same as an element directive except no entity encoding happens (the & character remains as &). This directive is only allowed with hide.
xmltext	The column content should be wrapped in a single tag that will be integrated with the rest of the document. If AttributeName is specified, the tag name is replaced by the specified name; otherwise, the attribute becomes one of the current list of attributes of the enclosing elements by putting the content at the beginning of the containment without entity encoding. The column with this directive must be a text type (varchar, nvarchar, char, nchar, text, ntext). This directive is only allowed with hide, and if the content is not a well-formed XML document, there's no telling what the behavior will be.
cdata	Wraps the data in a CDATA section with no entity encoding taking place. The original data type must be a text type (varchar, nvarchar, text, ntext). This directive is only allowed with hide, and when present, AttributeName cannot be specified.

Now let's get to those examples I told you about.

The approach I recommend when utilizing the EXPLICIT mode is to *reverse-engineer* the document you want to create. By this I mean you should sketch out the resulting document and then create the SQL query that will generate the document's Univesal table and then the document. Hmmm, two steps!?!? Not to worry!

Let's sketch out the document first and then break it down. Listing 7.21 shows it in its final form.

Listing 7.21   **The Document We Want to Create**

```
<Orders OrderID="10248">
  <OrderDetails ProductID="11" />
  <OrderDetails ProductID="42" />
  <OrderDetails ProductID="72" />
</Orders>
<Orders OrderID="10249">
  <OrderDetails ProductID="14" />
  <OrderDetails ProductID="51" />
</Orders>
<Orders OrderID="10250">
  <OrderDetails ProductID="41" />
  <OrderDetails ProductID="51" />
  <OrderDetails ProductID="65" />
</Orders>
...
```

Here's the breakdown of the first steps, which are illustrated in the SQL statement of Listing 7.22.

- Create the first two columns of the Universal table, Tag and Parent.
- `Orders` is the top element, so it gets a tag number of 1 and a NULL parent tag value.
- `OrderDetails` is the first subelement of `Orders`, so it gets a tag number of 2 and a parent tag value of 1.

Now that we have the document broken down, what do we do next? We write two separate SQL SELECT statements and combine their outputs with a UNION ALL statement.

When using multiple SELECT statements, all column names that are attributes of both top-level and child elements must be specified in the first SELECT statement. Any column names in successive queries are discarded.

Listing 7.22 shows the first SQL SELECT statement. Here we lay out the universal table by specifying the Tag and Parent columns and assigning the values 1 and NULL, respectively, to them. Next we assign `Orders` as the top-level element and give it the attribute of `OrderID`. Lastly, we assign the column name for the `ProductID` attribute to the table.

Listing 7.22   **The First Part of the SQL Query**

```
SELECT    1              as Tag,
          NULL           as Parent,
          Orders.OrderID as [Orders!1!OrderID],
          NULL           as [OrderDetails!2!ProductID]
FROM Orders
```

Listing 7.23 shows the second SQL SELECT statement. Here we grab the constants 2 and 1 (for the Tag and Parent columns) and the OrderID and ProductID attributes. Lastly, we compound sort the OrderID column and then the ProductID column. The UNION ALL statement combines the two queries. Table 7.3 shows a partial listing of the universal table generated during query execution. Listing 7.24 shows the combined queries.

Listing 7.23   **The Second Part of the SQL Query**

```
UNION ALL
SELECT    2,
          1,
          Orders.OrderID,
          [Order Details].ProductID
FROM   Orders, [Order Details]
WHERE Orders.OrderID = [Order Details].OrderID
ORDER BY [Orders!1!OrderID], [OrderDetails!2!ProductID]

FOR XML EXPLICIT
```

Table 7.3   **Partial Universal Table**

Tag	Parent	[Orders!1!OrderID]	[OrderDetails!2!ProductID]
1	NULL	10248	NULL
2	1	10248	11
2	1	10248	42
2	1	10248	72
1	NULL	10249	NULL
2	1	10249	14
2	1	10249	51

Listing 7.24   **The Entire SQL Query**

```
SELECT   1             as Tag,
         NULL          as Parent,
         Orders.OrderID  as [Orders!1!OrderID],
         NULL          as [OrderDetails!2!ProductID]
FROM Orders

UNION ALL
SELECT   2,
         1,
         Orders.OrderID,
         [Order Details].ProductID
FROM  Orders, [Order Details]
WHERE Orders.OrderID = [Order Details].OrderID
ORDER BY [Orders!1!OrderID], [OrderDetails!2!ProductID]
FOR XML EXPLICIT
```

ELEMENT Directive

Now that we've dissected the creation of an XML document utilizing the EXPLICIT mode, let's examine the various directives that were summarized in Table 7.2. We'll start with the ELEMENT directive.

Listing 7.25 shows a partial listing of the document we want to create. Notice that OrderID is a subelement of Order and not an attribute. Breaking this down as we did in the previous section, Employee is the top element, so it gets a tag number of 1 and a NULL parent tag value. Order is the first subelement of Employee, so it gets a tag number of 2 and a parent tag value of 1. As we stated previously, OrderID is a subelement of Order, so the ELEMENT directive must be used; otherwise, OrderID will show up as an attribute of Order. Again, we'll use multiple SQL queries and combine them with a UNION ALL statement. Listing 7.31 shows the first SQL SELECT statement.

Listing 7.25   **The Document to Create with the Element Directive**

```
<Employee LastName="Buchanan">
  <Order CustomerID="VINET">
    <OrderID>10248</OrderID>
  </Order>
  <Order CustomerID="CHOPS">
    <OrderID>10254</OrderID>
  </Order>
  <Order CustomerID="WHITC">
    <OrderID>10269</OrderID>
  </Order>
  ...
```

The interpretation of Listing 7.26 is identical to the interpretation given in the previous section, with one exception: The `ELEMENT` directive forces the `OrderID` to be a child element of `Order` and not an attribute.

Listing 7.26 **The First Part of the SQL Query**

```
SELECT   1                        as Tag,
         NULL                     as Parent,
         Employees.LastName       as [Employee!1!LastName],
         NULL                     as [Order!2!OrderID!element],
         NULL                     as [Order!2!CustomerID]
FROM Employees
```

Listing 7.27 gives the second SQL SELECT statement, and again, the only difference between this and the previous interpretation is the addition of the `ELEMENT` directive. A partial universal table generated by these queries is shown in Table 7.4.

Table 7.4 **Partial Listing of the Generated Univesal table**

Tag	Parent	[Employee! 1!LastName]	[Order! 2!OrderID! element]	[Order! 2!CustomerID]
1	NULL	Buchanan	NULL	NULL
2	1	Buchanan	10248	VINET
2	1	Buchanan	10254	CHOPS
2	1	Buchanan	10269	WHITC
1	NULL	Callahan	NULL	NULL
2	1	Callahan	10262	RATC
2	1	Callahan	10268	GROSR

Listing 7.27 **The Second Part of the SQL Query**

```
UNION ALL
SELECT   2,
         1,
         Employees.LastName,
         Orders.OrderID,
         Orders.CustomerID
FROM     Orders, Employees
WHERE    Orders.EmployeeID = Employees.EmployeeID
ORDER BY [Employee!1!LastName], [Order!2!OrderID!element]
FOR XML EXPLICIT
```

Hide **Directive**

As stated in Table 7.2, the `hide` directive is very useful when you want to order a result document by an attribute's value but don't want that attribute to appear in the result. Using the example from the previous section, let's say we want to order the document by `Employee LastName` and then `CustomerID` instead of `OrderID`. Listing 7.28 shows the resulting document. Notice how the OrderIDs have been rearranged.

Listing 7.28   **Partial Results of Using the** *hide* **Directive**

```
<Employee LastName="Buchanan">
<Order OrderID="10654" />
<Order OrderID="10866" />
<Order OrderID="10297" />
<Order OrderID="10730" />
<Order OrderID="10254" />
...
```

The query we utilize to accomplish this output is given in Listing 7.29. Here we've placed the `hide` directive with the `CustomerID` directive and changed the `ORDER BY` clause to do a secondary sort on this attribute. This prevents the `CustomerID` attribute from appearing in the output.

Listing 7.29   **Query Utilizing the** *hide* **Directive**

```
SELECT    1                    as Tag,
          NULL                 as Parent,
          Employees.LastName   as [Employee!1!LastName],
          NULL                 as [Order!2!OrderID],
          NULL                 as [Order!2!CustomerID!hide]
FROM Employees

UNION ALL
SELECT    2,
          1,
          Employees.LastName,
          Orders.OrderID,
          Orders.CustomerID
FROM      Orders, Employees
WHERE     Orders.EmployeeID = Employees.EmployeeID
ORDER BY [Employee!1!LastName], [Order!2!CustomerID!hide]
FOR XML EXPLICIT
```

CDATA Directive

The CDATA directive simply takes the entity you assign it to and encases its value in a CDATA section. Listing 7.30 shows a sample SQL query utilizing the CDATA directive followed by the resulting XML document in Listing 7.31. As far as breaking down the desired resulting document and generating the query, nothing has changed.

Listing 7.30 **Query Utilizing the CDATA Directive**

```
SELECT    1                 as Tag,
          NULL              as Parent,
          Employees.LastName  as [Employee!1!LastName],
          Employees.Address   as [Employee!1!!CDATA]
FROM Employees
ORDER BY [Employee!1!LastName]
FOR XML EXPLICIT
```

Listing 7.31 **Partial Results of the CDATA Directive**

```
<Employee LastName="Buchanan">
  <![CDATA[ 14 Garrett Hill ]]>
</Employee>
<Employee LastName="Callahan">
  <![CDATA[ 4726 - 11th Ave. N.E. ]]>
</Employee>
<Employee LastName="Davolio">
  <![CDATA[
          507 - 20th Ave. E.
          Apt. 2A
  ]]>
</Employee>
...
```

The ID, IDREF, and IDREFS Directives

As a brief review, ID, IDREF, and IDREFS are employed in XML documents to provide intradocument links. The ID type is applied to an element's attribute and distinguishes it from all other elements in the document. An IDREF attribute references an ID element in another part of the document (there's your intradocument link). An IDREFS attribute references multiple whitespace-separated IDs in the documents.

First let's look at an IDREF example. Listing 7.32 shows the XML document we want to generate. In this document, EmployeeID of the Employee element will be of type ID. EmployeeID of the Order element will be of type IDREF. In our SQL statement, we'll specify the XMLDATA argument to return the document's XDR schema. This will clearly show the ID and IDREF references.

Listing 7.32 **Partial Document Containing *ID* and *IDREF* Directives**

```
<Employee EmployeeID="1">
  <Order EmployeeID="1" CustomerID="ERNSH">
    <OrderID>10258</OrderID>
  </Order>
  <Order EmployeeID="1" CustomerID="WARTH">
    <OrderID>10270</OrderID>
  </Order>
  <Order EmployeeID="1" CustomerID="MAGAA">
    <OrderID>10275</OrderID>
  </Order>
...
```

In the SQL statement shown in Listing 7.33, you can see the `ID` and `IDREF` directives that will generate the proper data type in the XDR schema. Running this query in the Query Analyzer gives you Listing 7.34, which shows a partial listing of the results. The XDR schema is included. The data types of `ID` and `IDREF` can be seen there.

Listing 7.33 **The SQL Statement We Need**

```
SELECT    1                       as Tag,
          NULL                    as Parent,
          Employees.EmployeeID as [Employee!1!EmployeeID!id],
          NULL                    as [Employee!1!LastName],
          NULL                    as [Order!2!OrderID!element],
          NULL                    as [Order!2!EmployeeID!idref],
          NULL                    as [Order!2!CustomerID]
FROM Employees
UNION ALL
SELECT    2,
          1,
          Employees.EmployeeID,
          Employees.LastName,
          Orders.OrderID,
          Orders.EmployeeID,
          Orders.CustomerID
FROM      Orders, Employees
WHERE     Orders.EmployeeID = Employees.EmployeeID
ORDER BY [Employee!1!EmployeeID!id], [Order!2!OrderID!element]
FOR XML EXPLICIT, XMLDATA
```

Listing 7.34 **Partial Results Listing**

```
<Schema name="Schema2" xmlns="urn:schemas-microsoft-com:xml-data"
                       xmlns:dt="urn:schemas-microsoft-com:datatypes">
  <ElementType name="Employee" content="mixed" model="open">
    <AttributeType name="EmployeeID" dt:type="id"/>
    <AttributeType name="LastName" dt:type="string"/>
```

```
    <attribute type="EmployeeID"/>
    <attribute type="LastName"/>
  </ElementType>
  <ElementType name="Order" content="mixed" model="open">
    <AttributeType name="EmployeeID" dt:type="idref"/>
    <AttributeType name="CustomerID" dt:type="string"/>

    <element type="OrderID"/>
    <attribute type="EmployeeID"/>
    <attribute type="CustomerID"/>
  </ElementType>
  <ElementType name="OrderID" content="textOnly" model="closed" dt:type="i4"/>
</Schema>

<Employee xmlns="x-schema:#Schema2" EmployeeID="1">
  <Order EmployeeID="1" CustomerID="ERNSH">
    <OrderID>10258</OrderID>
  </Order>
  <Order EmployeeID="1" CustomerID="WARTH">
    <OrderID>10270</OrderID>
  </Order>
  <Order EmployeeID="1" CustomerID="MAGAA">
    <OrderID>10275</OrderID>
  </Order>
...
```

Now, for an IDREFS example, Listings 7.35, 7.36, and 7.37 show the document we want, the necessary SQL statement, and a very hacked-up partial result listing that includes the XDR schema. The slicing and dicing of the result was necessary because the result is a very large file. In this example, we declare the OrderID attribute of the Orders table to be of type ID. The Employee element contains an OrderList attribute of type IDREFS that lists all of the OrderIDs of the particular employee. Would this particular example be useful in some way? Probably not, but it does show a thorough example of the IDREFS type.

Listing 7.35   **Partial Document Containing ID and IDREF Directives**

```
<Employee xmlns="x-schema:#Schema3" EmployeeID="1" LastName="Davolio"
          OrderList="OID-10258 OID-10270 OID-10275...OID-11077">
  <Order OrderID="OID-10258"/>
  <Order OrderID="OID-10270"/>
  <Order OrderID="OID-10275"/>
  ...
  <Order OrderID="OID-11077"/>
</Employee>
<Employee xmlns="x-schema:#Schema3" EmployeeID="2" LastName="Fuller"
          OrderList="OID-10265 OID-10277 OID-10280...OID-11073">
...
```

Listing 7.36 **The SQL Statement We Need**

```
SELECT   1                      as Tag,
         NULL                   as Parent,
         Employees.EmployeeID as [Employee!1!EmployeeID],
         Employees.LastName     as [Employee!1!LastName],
         NULL                   as [Employee!1!OrderList!idrefs],
         NULL                   as [Order!2!OrderID!id]
FROM Employees

UNION ALL
SELECT   1                      as Tag,
         NULL                   as Parent,
         Employees.EmployeeID as [Employee!1!EmployeeID],
         Employees.LastName     as [Employee!1!LastName],
         'OID-' + CAST(Orders.OrderID as varchar(5)),
         NULL
FROM Employees join Orders on Employees.EmployeeID = Orders.EmployeeID

UNION ALL
SELECT   2,
         1,
         Employees.EmployeeID,
         Employees.LastName,
         NULL,
         'OID-' + CAST(Orders.OrderID as varchar(5))
FROM     Employees join Orders on Employees.EmployeeID = Orders.EmployeeID
WHERE    Orders.EmployeeID = Employees.EmployeeID
ORDER BY [Employee!1!EmployeeID],
[Order!2!OrderID!id],[Employee!1!OrderList!idrefs]

FOR XML EXPLICIT, XMLDATA
```

Listing 7.37 **Partial Results Listing with XDR Schema**

```
<Schema name="Schema3" xmlns="urn:schemas-microsoft-com:xml-data"
                        xmlns:dt="urn:schemas-microsoft-com:datatypes">
  <ElementType name="Employee" content="mixed" model="open">
    <AttributeType name="EmployeeID" dt:type="i4"/>
    <AttributeType name="LastName" dt:type="string"/>
    <AttributeType name="OrderList" dt:type="idrefs"/>

    <attribute type="EmployeeID"/>
    <attribute type="LastName"/>
    <attribute type="OrderList"/>
  </ElementType>
  <ElementType name="Order" content="mixed" model="open">
    <AttributeType name="OrderID" dt:type="id"/>
```

```
      <attribute type="OrderID"/>
    </ElementType>
  </Schema>

<Employee xmlns="x-schema:#Schema3" EmployeeID="1" LastName="Davolio"
          OrderList="OID-10258 OID-10270 OID-10275...OID-11077">
  <Order OrderID="OID-10258"/>
  <Order OrderID="OID-10270"/>
  <Order OrderID="OID-10275"/>
  ...
  <Order OrderID="OID-11077"/>
</Employee>
<Employee xmlns="x-schema:#Schema3" EmployeeID="2" LastName="Fuller"
          OrderList="OID-10265 OID-10277 OID-10280...OID-11073">
  <Order OrderID="OID-10265"/>
  <Order OrderID="OID-10277"/>
  <Order OrderID="OID-10280"/>
  ...
  <Order OrderID="OID-11073"/>
</Employee>
...
```

Retrieving Unconsumed Data with *sql:overflow-field*

In Chapter 5, "Creating XML Views with XDR Schemas," I said that I wanted to hold off on discussing *overflow data* until Chapter 7. Well, it's about time for that discussion now because the next section deals with this topic.

The OPENXML extension, which we'll discuss in detail in Chapter 8, "OPENXML," allows record insertion into a database from an XML document. Any data from that document that does not have a related column for storage can be stored in a column within that database known as the *unconsumed data* column. XDR schemas have the annotation `sql:overflow-field`, which identifies this column. This data can be recovered into an XML document in two ways:

- Attributes are added to the element with the `sql:overflow-field` annotation.
- Child elements and descendents are added to the XML document as child elements according to the schema (child element order is lost).

We'll have to change our normal sample methods for this exercise because none of the Northwind database's tables contain an overflow column. This isn't a big deal, though, because it's very simple to illustrate the principle. See Listing 7.38 for the SQL statement that creates our sample table. Listing 7.39 contains the schema file that will create an XML document including the overflow data. The results are given in Listing 7.41.

Listing 7.38 **SQL that Creates an Overflow Data Column**

```
CREATE TABLE Company (
    CompanyID    varchar(10),
    CompanyName  varchar(20),
    Employee     varchar(15),
    Overflow     nvarchar(100))
GO
INSERT INTO Company VALUES(
    '12345',
    'Fly By Night, Inc.',
    'Judith Griffin',
    N'<phone>555-1212</phone>')
GO
```

Listing 7.39 **Schema with the *sql:overflow-field* Annotation**

```
<?xml version="1.0" ?>
<Schema xmlns="urn:schemas-microsoft-com:xml-data"
        xmlns:dt="urn:schemas-microsoft-com:datatypes"
        xmlns:sql="urn:schemas-microsoft-com:xml-sql">
  <ElementType name="Company" sql:overflow-field="Overflow" >
    <AttributeType name="CompanyName" />
    <AttributeType name="Employee" />

    <attribute type="CompanyName" />
    <attribute type="Employee"/>
  </ElementType>
</Schema>
```

Save this schema as `schema.xml` in the *schema virtual directory*. Create the template file given in Listing 7.40 and execute it with the following:

```
http://iisserver/Nwind/schema/schema.xml
```

Listing 7.40 **Template File to Execute Listing 7.39's Schema**

```
<ROOT xmlns:sql="urn:schemas-microsoft-com:xml-sql">
  <sql:xpath-query mapping-schema="../schemas/Schema.xml">
    Company
  </sql:xpath-query>
</ROOT>
```

Listing 7.41   **Results from Our Table**

```
<ROOT xmlns:sql="urn:schemas-microsoft-com:xml-sql">
  <Company CompanyName="Fly By Night, Inc." Employee="Judith Griffin">
    <phone>555-1212</phone>
  </Company>
</ROOT>
```

Now that we've covered the basics of the overflow field, we can cover the last remaining directive of Table 7.2.

XMLTEXT Directive

Let's use the same table we used in the preceding section for examples here. First truncate the table to clear out remaining data and then issue these SQL statements to populate the table with fresh data, as shown in the following example. Listing 7.42 shows the SQL statement to create the Universal table.

```
INSERT INTO Company VALUES('C1','Fly by Night','Larry',N'<starttag
a1="attr1">safe</starttag>')
INSERT INTO Company VALUES('C2','Limo to Nowhere','Moe',N'<starttag
a2="attr2">sane</starttag>')
INSERT INTO Company VALUES('C3','Key Lime Pie Faces','Curly',N'<starttag
a3="attr3"
         CompanyID="C">clean</starttag>')
```

Listing 7.42   **SQL Statement to Create the Universal Table**

```
SELECT 1 as Tag, NULL as parent,
   CompanyID   as [Parent!1!CompanyID],
   CompanyName as [Parent!1!CompanyName],
   Employee    as [Parent!1!Employee],
   Overflow as [Parent!1!!xmltext] — No AttributeName; xmltext directive
FROM Company
FOR XML EXPLICIT
```

Listing 7.42 produces the output in the following example:

```
<Parent Companied="C1" CompanyName="Fly by Night" Employee="Larry"
a1="attr1">safe</Parent>
<Parent Companied="C2" CompanyName="Limo to Nowhere" Employee="Moe"
a2="attr2">sane</Parent>
<Parent CompanyID="C3" CompanyName="Key Lime Pie Faces" Employee="Curly"
a3="attr3">clean</Parent>
```

There are two things to take note of here. First, if `AttributeName` isn't specified and `XMLTEXT` is, then the overflow column attributes will be appended to the parent element's attributes list. Second, in the event that the overflow column has an attribute with the same name as an attribute belonging to the parent element, the parent element's attribute will take precedence.

In the event that `AttributeName` is specified with the `XMLTEXT` directive, the name given by `AttributeName` becomes a child element, and the overflow column's attributes become attributes of this child element. The following example shows the SQL used to populate the table.

```
INSERT INTO Company VALUES('C1','Fly by Night','Larry',N'<starttag
a1="attr1">safe</starttag>')
INSERT INTO Company VALUES('C2','Limo to Nowhere','Moe',N'<starttag
a2="attr2">sane</starttag>')
INSERT INTO Company VALUES('C3','Key Lime Pie Faces','Curly',N'<starttag
a3="attr3"
          CompanyID="C"><state>clean</state></starttag>')
```

Notice the differences between this listing and the sample SQL statements used to populate the table with fresh data earlier in this section. In the third `INSERT` statement, we add an additional element to the overflow column and specify `overflow` as the `AttributeName`. We'll use the SQL statements in Listing 7.43 to execute our query; the results are shown in Listing 7.44.

Listing 7.43 **The SQL Statement to Execute**

```
SELECT 1 as Tag, NULL as parent,
   CompanyID    as [Parent!1!CompanyID],
   CompanyName  as [Parent!1!CompanyName],
   Employee     as [Parent!1!Employee],
   Overflow as [Parent!1!overflow!xmltext] - overflow is the AttributeName;
                                    xmltext directive accompanies

FROM Company
FOR XML EXPLICIT
```

Listing 7.44 **Results of Executing the Listing 7.43 SQL Statement**

```
<Parent CompanyID="C1" CompanyName="Fly by Night" Employee="Larry">
  <overflow a1="attr1">safe</overflow>
</Parent>
<Parent CompanyID="C2" CompanyName="Limo to Nowhere" Employee="Moe">
  <overflow a2="attr2">sane</overflow>
</Parent>
<Parent CompanyID="C3" CompanyName="Key Lime Pie Faces" Employee="Curly">
  <overflow a3="attr3" CompanyID="C">
    <state>clean</state>
  </overflow>
</Parent>
```

Well, that completes Chapter 7. Next, in Chapter 8, we move on to writing data to tables utilizing XML documents along with additional methods of generating documents.

Recap of What Was Discussed in This Chapter

- There is quite a long list of limitations associated with the FOR XML extension. As a general rule, FOR XML can only be used in statements that produce direct output to the end user's presentation device (browser).

- The RAW mode of FOR XML is just that; it presents every row of a database query result with the simplistic identifier <ROW>. All columns of the result set's row are returned as attributes of the row.

- In previous chapters where we've generated XML documents, our dealings with the FOR XML extension have been related to AUTO mode. XML AUTO mode returns results in documents with nested elements, and strict rules are followed to accomplish this.

- This mode does exactly what its name leads you to believe. EXPLICIT mode allows you to explicitly specify exactly how you want the element nesting to appear in the XML output document. It requires the rowset that's returned from a query to be in a special format. This format is called the Univesal table, and it is used to produce the output document. One requirement on the rowset result is that it must be ordered so that its children follow the parent element immediately. Also, it must associate the element names with the tag numbers and provide attribute names (the default) as the column names of the Universal table.

- The OPENXML extension, which we'll discuss in detail in Chapter 8, allows record insertion into a database from an XML document. Any data from that document that does not have a related column for storage can be stored in a column within that database known as the unconsumed data column. XDR schemas have the annotation `sql:overflow-field`, which identifies this column.

8

OPENXML

THERE'S ONE MORE MICROSOFT EXTENSION TO SQL that we need to cover: OPENXML. Use of the OPENXML keyword causes an XML document to be presented as a data source similar to a view or a table. This is accomplished in memory by making the XML document appear as a relational rowset. Because the data now appears as a rowset, it can be stored into database tables.

This chapter will cover the following topics:

- The OPENXML keyword greatly enhances SQL Server's capabilities by utilizing XML documents to write data to database tables.

- The edge table format can offer several advantages when processing XML documents that you would not normally have.

- Metadata is data about data. Metaproperties enable us to obtain more information about a document than what is normally obtainable from just the textual representation of the XML document.

- OPENXML allows writing data to a database table from an XML document.

Using OPENXML

OPENXML can be utilized whenever a rowset provider is necessary, such as a table or view. This includes SELECT, SELECT INTO, and OPENROWSET.

A preliminary operation must be accomplished, however, before OPENXML can be used to write queries. `sp_xml_preparedocument` is a SQL Server internal stored procedure that takes an XML document and parses it into a memory representation of the XML document tree. I say that this is an *internal* stored procedure because you can't view it in the normal manner of viewing a stored procedure. If you try to view the procedure using SP_HELPTEXT, you'll see what is displayed in Figure 8.1.

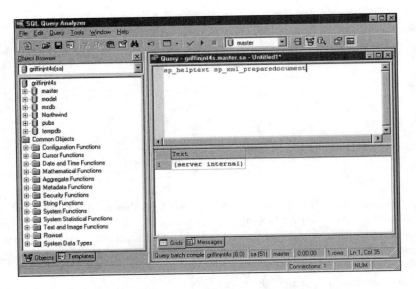

Figure 8.1 Attempting to view `sp_xml_preparedocument`.

`sp_xml_preparedocument` returns a file identifier (`handle`) after parsing it in memory. OPENXML takes this `handle` and, through a process known as *shredding*, provides a rowset representation of the data based on what is passed to it.

After processing is complete, another internal stored procedure must be called to flush the parsed document from memory. This procedure is `sp_xml_removedocument`. The entire process is diagrammed in Figure 8.2.

A parsed document is stored in internal cache. The MSXML parser uses one-eighth the total memory available for SQL Server. This means that if you have a SQL Server with 320MB of memory available, the MSXML parser will use 40MB of this memory. To avoid overutilization of RAM, run `sp_xml_removedocument` to free up the memory as soon as possible.

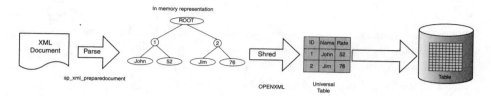

Figure 8.2   The OPENXML process.

OPENXML Syntax

A sample OPENXML statement looks similar to this:

```
FROM OPENXML (@idoc, '/ROOT/Employee',1)
     WITH (EmployeeID  varchar(4), LastName varchar(20), FirstName varchar(10))
```

We'll be examining this new keyword with detailed examples shortly, but for now, here is the syntax specification for OPENXML:

```
OPENXML ( handle, 'rowpattern', [flags] ) [WITH SchemaDeclaration]
```

The various arguments of this function are described in the following sections.

handle

This is the handle returned by `sp_xml_preparedocument` that points to the parsed XML document in SQL Server memory. It serves the identical function as a file handle in other programming languages.

This handle is valid for the duration of the connection to SQL Server, until the connection is reset, or until `sp_xml_removedocument` is executed, thereby dropping the handle and deleting the document from memory.

rowpattern

This is the familiar XPath expression that we've been using for the majority of this book. For every node identified by the XPath expression there is a row generated by OPENXML in the rowset. Because XPath can identify any type of node (attribute, text, or otherwise), if `rowpattern` ends in a text node, a row is generated for each text node identified by `rowpattern`.

SchemaDeclaration

OPENXML requires a custom schema created in the OPENXML statement to specify rowset structure. The WITH clause can be used to accomplish this, but there are a couple of ways of doing it. Here are our options:

- Use the WITH clause and specify the entire schema.

  If you specify the schema, you specify column names, their data types, and how they map to the XML document. Here is how ColPattern influences the schema declaration:

  With ColPattern in the schema declaration, a rowset column is mapped to the node identified by the XPath expression (rowpattern). If you specify ColPattern on a column, it overrides the flags parameter (explained in the next section), meaning the schema dictates how the nodes correspond to columns regardless of whether flags states element-centric or attribute-centric mode.

  Here's an example:

```
SELECT *
FROM OPENXML (@idoc, '/ROOT/Employee/Order/OrderDetail',2)
     WITH (OrderID     int          '../@OrderID',
           CustomerID nvarchar(10) '../@CustomerID',
           Lastname   nvarchar(10) './../@LastName',
...
```

  Without ColPattern in the schema declaration, mappings between rowset columns and XML nodes follow name correspondence based on the flags parameter setting.

  Here's an example:

```
...
SELECT *
FROM OPENXML (@idoc, '/ROOT/Employee',1)
     WITH (EmployeeID  varchar(4),
           LastName varchar(20),
           FirstName varchar(10))
...
```

  If you're still a little confused about this, examples will help clear it up. There are several complete examples in the section "OPENXML Examples" later in this chapter. There is one for each of the situations enumerated in the preceding.

  Remember, a schema is required to lay out the rowset structure when using the WITH clause.

- Use an existing table identified in the WITH clause.

  Simply specify an existing table with schema that OPENXML will utilize to generate the rowset.

Here's an example of this:

```
...
SELECT *
FROM OPENXML (@idoc, '/ROOT/Employee/Order',1)
     WITH Table1
```

- Leave the WITH clause out.

Without the WITH clause, the rowset is returned in the *edge table* format, so-called because every edge of the XML tree maps to a rowset row. The edge table format can offer several advantages that you would not normally have. It is possible to obtain the data type of an element/attribute, node types, namespaces, and other values, as listed in Table 8.1. In essence, wherever you would use an XML parser to obtain document information, you can use an edge table.

Here is an example:

```
...
SELECT *
FROM OPENXML (@idoc, '/ROOT/Employee')
...
```

Table 8.1 **The Structure of the Edge Table**

Column Name	Data Type	Description
id	Bigint	The unique ID of the document node. The ROOT element has an ID value of 0, and negative ID values are reserved.
parentid	Bigint	Identifies the node's parent. The parent identified by this ID is not necessarily an element because it depends on the nodetype of the node whose parent is identified by this ID. For example, if the node is a text node, its parent could be an attribute node. The top-level node has a parentid of NULL. (Sound familiar?)
nodetype	Int	An integer that corresponds to the XML DOM nodetype numbering system. (See DOM documentation for node information at http://www.w3.org/TR/2000/WD-DOM-Level-1-20000929/level-one-core.html). The DOM nodetypes are:

ELEMENT_NODE = 1	ATTRIBUTE_NODE = 2
TEXT_NODE = 3	CDATA_SECTION_NODE = 4
ENTITY_REFERENCE_NODE = 5	ENTITY_NODE = 6
PROCESSING_INSTRUCTION_NODE = 7	COMMENT_NODE = 8
DOCUMENT_NODE = 9	DOCUMENT_TYPE_NODE = 10
DOCUMENT_FRAGMENT_NODE = 11	NOTATION_NODE = 12

continues

Table 8.1 **The Structure of the Edge Table**

Column Name	Data Type	Description
localname	nvarchar	The local name of the element or attribute that is NULL if the DOM object does not have a name.
prefix	nvarchar	The namespace prefix of the node name.
namespaceuri	nvarchar	The namespace URI of the node. A NULL value indicates that no namespace is present.
datatype	nvarchar	The actual data type of the element or attribute row. It is NULL if otherwise specified. The data type is inferred from the inline DTD or from the inline schema.
prev	Bigint	The XML ID of the previous sibling element. It is NULL if there is no direct previous sibling.
text	Ntext	The attribute value or the element content in text form (or NULL if the edge table entry does not need a value).

flags

The `flags` argument specifies whether the mapping between the rowset columns and the XML document nodes will be *element-centric* (elements nested within other elements), *attribute-centric* (elements with data expressed as attribute values), or a mixture of both. `Flags` can have the following three values:

- 1, which specifies attribute-centric mapping
- 2, which specifies element-centric mapping
- 3, which specifies a combination of both attribute- and element-centric mapping

In addition to the `flags` argument, there is another way to define mappings. The `ColPattern` parameter, which is actually specified in the `SchemaDeclaration` through use of the WITH clause, also can be used. If it is used, it overrides the setting of the `flags` argument.

`ColPattern` is used under the following two circumstances:

- If the element/attribute name in the rowset has a different name than the column to which it is mapped, then `ColPattern` identified the correct column.
- When mapping metaproperty attributes to columns, `ColPattern` identifies the mapping between the metaproperty and the proper column. (Metaproperties are discussed in more detail later in this chapter.)

Both `flags` and `ColPattern` are optional parameters and, if missing, cause the default value of attribute-centric mapping to be used.

OPENXML Examples

This section contains a lot of examples demonstrating the uses of OPENXML. We'll be utilizing stored procedures here almost exclusively.

Let's start with a simple SELECT statement and OPENXML. Here we'll use the `<Employee>`, `<Order>`, and `<OrderDetail>` elements and return a rowset consisting of `EmployeeID`, `LastName`, and `FirstName`. We'll perform the following steps:

1. Declare our XML document.

2. Call the `sp_xml_preparedocument` stored procedure to parse the document into memory.

3. Specify the `flags` parameter, which in this case is `1` (attribute-centric), so that attributes map to rowset columns.

4. Specify the `rowpattern` (XPath expression) to identify the employee nodes to process.

Listing 8.1 contains the stored procedure we'll use in this example.

In this example, `ColPattern` need not be specified because the rowset column names correspond to the XML attribute names.

Listing 8.1 **Simple Select Stored Procedure**

```
DECLARE @idoc int
DECLARE @xmldoc varchar(1000)
SET @xmldoc ='
<ROOT>
<Employee EmployeeID="5" LastName="Buchanan" FirstName="Steven">
   <Order OrderID="10248" CustomerID="VINET" EmployeeID="5"
          OrderDate="1996-07-04T00:00:00">
     <OrderDetail ProductID="42" Quantity="10"/>
     <OrderDetail ProductID="72" Quantity="5"/>
   </Order>
</Employee>
<Employee EmployeeID="7" LastName="King" FirstName="Robert">
   <Order OrderID="10303" CustomerID="GODOS" EmployeeID="7"
          OrderDate="1996-09-11T00:00:00">
     <OrderDetail ProductID="40" Quantity="40"/>
   </Order>
</Employee>
</ROOT>'
-- Create an in memory representation of the document.
EXEC sp_xml_preparedocument @idoc OUTPUT, @xmldoc
SELECT *
FROM OPENXML (@idoc, '/ROOT/Employee',1)
      WITH (EmployeeID  varchar(4),
            LastName varchar(20),
            FirstName varchar(10))
EXEC sp_xml_removedocument @idoc
```

The following example shows the results of the simple select stored procedure in Listing 8.1.

```
EmployeeID LastName              FirstName
.......... ...................   ..........
5          Buchanan             Steven
7          King                 Robert
```

That was an easy one, but it represents the essence of this entire chapter. We've taken an XML document and turned it into a rowset data provider, which lets us use it in any situation that requires data (table or view, for example, remember?).

Let's modify the procedure slightly by changing the flags parameter to 2 (element-centric) and seeing what happens. The line and value to change is as follows:

```
FROM OPENXML (@idoc, '/ROOT/Employee',2)
```

Refer to the section "OPENXML Syntax" at the beginning of the chapter, if necessary, to understand the layout of the parameters.

The following example shows the results of changing flags to element-centric.

```
EmployeeID LastName              FirstName
.......... ...................   ..........
NULL       NULL                 NULL
NULL       NULL                 NULL
```

Not quite what you expected? EmployeeID, LastName, and FirstName are attributes, not child elements, so when you specified element-centric mapping, you were referring to nonexistent elements. That's why the NULLs came back.

To get the element-centric mapping to work (flags = 2), you'll need to define your elements similar to the XML document defined in the stored procedure in Listing 8.2. The results obtained from this procedure are identical to the results of the simple select stored procedure in Listing 8.1.

Listing 8.2 **Simple Select with Element Orientation**

```
DECLARE @idoc int
DECLARE @xmldoc varchar(1000)
SET @xmldoc ='
<ROOT>
<Employee>
   <EmployeeID>5</EmployeeID>
   <LastName>Buchanan</LastName>
   <FirstName>Steven</FirstName>
   <Order OrderID="10248" CustomerID="VINET" EmployeeID="5"
         OrderDate="1996-07-04T00:00:00">
      <OrderDetail ProductID="42" Quantity="10"/>
      <OrderDetail ProductID="72" Quantity="5"/>
   </Order>
</Employee>
<Employee>
   <EmployeeID>7</EmployeeID>
```

```
    <LastName>King</LastName>
    <FirstName>Robert</FirstName>
    <Order OrderID="10303" CustomerID="GODOS" EmployeeID="7"
           OrderDate="1996-09-11T00:00:00">
      <OrderDetail ProductID="40" Quantity="40"/>
    </Order>
  </Employee>
</ROOT>'
-- Create an in memory representation of the document.
EXEC sp_xml_preparedocument @idoc OUTPUT, @xmldoc
SELECT *
FROM OPENXML (@idoc, '/ROOT/Employee',2)
     WITH (EmployeeID  varchar(4),
           LastName varchar(20),
           FirstName varchar(10))
EXEC sp_xml_removedocument @idoc
```

Now let's see what the ColPattern specification in the WITH clause will do for us. Take a look at Listing 8.3. The results of this stored procedure are given in Listing 8.4.

Listing 8.3 **Stored Procedure Utilizing the *ColPattern* Parameter**

```
DECLARE @idoc int
DECLARE @xmldoc varchar(1000)
SET @xmldoc ='
<ROOT>
<Employee EmployeeID="5" LastName="Buchanan" FirstName="Steven">
  <Order OrderID="10248" CustomerID="VINET" EmployeeID="5"
         OrderDate="1996-07-04T00:00:00">
    <OrderDetail ProductID="42" Quantity="10"/>
    <OrderDetail ProductID="72" Quantity="5"/>
  </Order>
</Employee>
<Employee EmployeeID="7" LastName="King" FirstName="Robert">
  <Order OrderID="10303" CustomerID="GODOS" EmployeeID="7"
         OrderDate="1996-09-11T00:00:00">
    <OrderDetail ProductID="40" Quantity="40"/>
  </Order>
</Employee>
</ROOT>'
-- Create an in memory representation of the document.
EXEC sp_xml_preparedocument @idoc OUTPUT, @xmldoc
SELECT *
FROM OPENXML (@idoc, '/ROOT/Employee/Order/OrderDetail',2)
     WITH (OrderID      int           '../@OrderID',
           CustomerID nvarchar(10)    '../@CustomerID',
           Lastname   nvarchar(10)    '../../@LastName',
           FirstName  nvarchar(10)    '/Employee/@FirstName',
           ProductID  int             '@ProductID',
           Quant      int             '@Quantity')

EXEC sp_xml_removedocument @idoc
```

Listing 8.4　**Results of the *ColPattern* Parameter in a Stored Procedure**

OrderID	CustomerID	Lastname	FirstName	ProductID	Quant
10248	VINET	Buchanan	NULL	42	10
10248	VINET	Buchanan	NULL	72	5
10303	GODOS	King	NULL	40	40

Let's look at some of the important points of this procedure.

- First, the `flags` parameter is set to 2 (element-centric), but the elements in our XML document are not properly nested to accommodate this setting. This shouldn't have worked but it did. That's because, as stated in the "SchemaDeclaration" section, if you use `ColPattern` in the schema declaration, it will map a rowset column to the node identified by the XPath expression (rowPattern). In this case the `ColPattern` maps to attributes and overrides the `flags` setting.

- Second, `rowPattern` maps the query to the `OrderDetail` elements, so `ColPattern` maps the attributes to different elements in the XML document relative to this. `OrderID` and `CustomerID` are mapped to the `Order` element. `LastName` and `FirstName` are mapped to the `Employee` element in two different XPath expressions. Finally, `ProductID` and `Quantity` map to the `OrderDetail` element.

In the next example, we'll combine both attribute-centric and element-centric mappings.

Listing 8.5 is a stored procedure that has the `flags` parameter set to 3, indicating both attribute-centric and element-centric mappings. In this case, attribute-centric mapping is applied first, followed by element-centric mapping for columns not yet handled.

Listing 8.5　**A Stored Procedure with Both Types of Mappings**

```
DECLARE @idoc int
DECLARE @xmldoc varchar(1000)
SET @xmldoc ='
<ROOT>
<Employee EmployeeID="5">
   <LastName>Buchanan</LastName>
   <FirstName>Steven</FirstName>
   <Order OrderID="10248" CustomerID="VINET" EmployeeID="5"
        OrderDate="1996-07-04T00:00:00">
      <OrderDetail ProductID="42" Quantity="10"/>
      <OrderDetail ProductID="72" Quantity="5"/>
   </Order>
</Employee>
<Employee EmployeeID="7">
   <LastName>King</LastName>
```

```
      <FirstName>Robert</FirstName>
      <Order OrderID="10303" CustomerID="GODOS" EmployeeID="7"
              OrderDate="1996-09-11T00:00:00">
         <OrderDetail ProductID="40" Quantity="40"/>
      </Order>
   </Employee>
</ROOT>'
-- Create an in memory representation of the document.
EXEC sp_xml_preparedocument @idoc OUTPUT, @xmldoc
SELECT *
FROM OPENXML (@idoc, '/ROOT/Employee',3)
      WITH (EmployeeID int             ,
            LastName    nvarchar(10),
            FirstName   nvarchar(10))

EXEC sp_xml_removedocument @idoc
```

The results of the stored procedure in Listing 8.5 are as follows:

```
EmployeeID  LastName    FirstName
----------  ----------  ----------
5           Buchanan    Steven
7           King        Robert
```

Here, attribute-centric mapping is applied first for `EmployeeID`, and then element-centric mapping is applied because `LastName` and `FirstName` are left over.

Retrieving a text node is not much different from the types of data retrievals we've done so far. We'll utilize the XPath function `text()` in the `ColPattern` specification. Look at the stored procedure in Listing 8.6. We specify a column named `Remark` that extracts the text node associated with the `Order` element from the XML document.

Listing 8.6 **Stored Procedure Containing Text Nodes**

```
DECLARE @idoc int
DECLARE @xmldoc varchar(1000)
SET @xmldoc ='
<ROOT>
<Employee EmployeeID="5">
   <LastName>Buchanan</LastName>
   <FirstName>Steven</FirstName>
   <Order OrderID="10248" CustomerID="VINET" EmployeeID="5"
           OrderDate="1996-07-04T00:00:00">
      <OrderDetail ProductID="42" Quantity="10"/>
      <OrderDetail ProductID="72" Quantity="5"/>Customer returned merchandise
   </Order>
</Employee>
<Employee EmployeeID="7">
   <LastName>King</LastName>
   <FirstName>Robert</FirstName>
   <Order OrderID="10303" CustomerID="GODOS" EmployeeID="7"
```

continues

Listing 8.6 **Continued**

```
            OrderDate="1996-09-11T00:00:00" note="Almost out of inventory">
        <Priority>First Class</Priority>
        <OrderDetail ProductID="40" Quantity="40"/>Customer needs this ASAP
    </Order>
</Employee>
</ROOT>'

EXEC sp_xml_preparedocument @idoc OUTPUT, @xmldoc
SELECT *
FROM OPENXML (@idoc, '/ROOT/Employee/Order',1)
        WITH (OrderID      int          ,
              EmployeeID nvarchar(10),
              Remark       ntext 'text()')

EXEC sp_xml_removedocument @idoc
```

The following example shows the results of `ColPattern` and the `text()` function in Listing 8.6.

```
OrderID     EmployeeID Remark
..........  .......... ......
10248       5          Customer returned merchandise
10303       7          Customer needs this ASAP
```

Notice that only the text nodes of the `Order` element are retrieved and placed in the results. All other text comments are ignored.

In the section "SchemaDeclaration," I said that an existing table could be specified in the OPENXML clause that would dictate the schema of the result. Let's see how that works. Listing 8.7 illustrates a stored procedure that does exactly what we're talking about. Because we have to have a preexisting table, the first line in the procedure will create one for us to utilize in the OPENXML clause.

Listing 8.7 **Specifying a Table Name in the OPENXML Clause**

```
--create a test table
create table Table1(OrderID int, OrderDate datetime, EmployeeID int)

DECLARE @idoc int
DECLARE @xmldoc varchar(1000)
SET @xmldoc ='
<ROOT>
<Employee EmployeeID="5">
    <Order OrderID="10248" CustomerID="VINET" EmployeeID="5"
            OrderDate="1996-07-04T00:00:00">
        <OrderDetail ProductID="42" Quantity="10"/>
        <OrderDetail ProductID="72" Quantity="5"/>Customer returned merchandise
    </Order>
</Employee>
```

```
<Employee EmployeeID="7">
   <Order OrderID="10303" CustomerID="GODOS" EmployeeID="7"
          OrderDate="1996-09-11T00:00:00" note="Almost out of inventory">
      <Priority>First Class</Priority>
      <OrderDetail ProductID="40" Quantity="40"/>Customer needs this ASAP
   </Order>
</Employee>
</ROOT>'
-- Create an in memory representation of the document.
EXEC sp_xml_preparedocument @idoc OUTPUT, @xmldoc
SELECT *
FROM OPENXML (@idoc, '/ROOT/Employee/Order',1)
     WITH Table1

EXEC sp_xml_removedocument @idoc
```

The following example shows the results of using a table instead of a
`SchemaDescription` in Listing 8.7.

```
OrderID      OrderDate                                          EmployeeID
----------   -------------------------------------------------  ----------
10248        1996-07-04 00:00:00.000                                    5
10303        1996-09-11 00:00:00.000                                    7
```

One thing to remember here is that you can't utilize the `ColPattern` parameter in this
situation. You are limited to the structure of the table called by the OPENXML clause.

Let's take a look at the edge table format we talked about earlier. Remember that
an edge table format is produced when the WITH clause is left out of the
OPENXML clause. This example will be a little different than the examples to this
point. Listing 8.8 shows the procedure that illustrates the generation of an edge table.
This procedure includes two edge table queries toward the bottom of the procedure.
The results of the two queries are given in Listing 8.9.

Listing 8.8 **Generating an Edge Table**

```
DECLARE @idoc int
DECLARE @xmldoc varchar(1000)
SET @xmldoc ='
<ROOT>
<Employee EmployeeID="5">
   <Order OrderID="10248" CustomerID="VINET" EmployeeID="5"
          OrderDate="1996-07-04T00:00:00">
      <OrderDetail ProductID="42" Quantity="10"/>
      <OrderDetail ProductID="72" Quantity="5"/>
   </Order>
</Employee>
<Employee EmployeeID="7">
   <Order OrderID="10303" CustomerID="GODOS" EmployeeID="7"
          OrderDate="1996-09-11T00:00:00">
```

continues

Listing 8.8 **Continued**

```
        <OrderDetail ProductID="40" Quantity="40"/>
    </Order>
</Employee>
</ROOT>'
-- Create an in memory representation of the document.
EXEC sp_xml_preparedocument @idoc OUTPUT, @xmldoc
SELECT *
FROM OPENXML (@idoc, '/ROOT/Employee')

---------- query the edge table -------------------------------------------
SELECT count(*)          FROM OPENXML(@idoc, '/') where localname = 'EmployeeID'
SELECT DISTINCT localname FROM OPENXML(@idoc, '/') where nodetype  = 2
-----------------------------------------------------------------------------

EXEC sp_xml_removedocument @idoc
```

Listing 8.9 **Results of Querying an Edge Table**

```
4
(1 row(s) affected)

localname
----------------------------
CustomerID
EmployeeID
OrderDate
OrderID
ProductID
Quantity
(6 row(s) affected).
```

Notice the different way of querying an edge table. The OPENXML expression is specified directly in the WHERE clause.

Next up is a discussion of metaproperties, which enable us to obtain more information about a document than is normally obtainable from just the textual representation of the XML document.

Metaproperties

Anytime the term *meta* is used, you are usually talking about something that describes something else. If you have experience with the Java programming language and Java Database Connectivity (JDBC), the term *metadata* should be quite familiar to you. Metadata is data about data. For example, the title, subject, author, and size of a file constitute metadata about the file. *Metaproperties* associated with OPENXML, then, are attributes that describe the properties of an XML item, regardless of whether it is an element, an attribute, or any other node. These properties exist and are provided by OPENXML even though they are not present in the XML document text. The ColPattern parameter is used to map these metaproperties to the columns of a rowset created by an OPENXML statement. An edge table result has a column for each metaproperty attribute (excluding xmltext). XPath cannot be used to access any of these properties. Listing 8.10 shows an example of a metaproperty.

Listing 8.10   **A Sample Metaproperty**

```
...
SELECT *
FROM OPENXML (@idoc, '/ROOT/Employee/Order')
        WITH (id             int            @mp:id,
              OrderID        char(5),
              OrderDate      datetime,
              ParentID       int '@mp:parentid',
...
```

The @mp:parentid attribute provides an identifier for the ParentID element that is document wide.

To get at these metaproperties, a namespace specific to SQL Server 2000 is required. That namespace is urn:schemas-microsoft-com:xml-metaprop. Table 8.2 lists and describes the metaproperty attributes possessed by each XML element. Table 8.3 describes available parent properties that provide hierarchy information. The section following these tables will contain several examples of usage.

Table 8.2   **Metaproperty Attributes**

Attribute	Description
@mp:id	Provides a system-generated, document-wide identifier of the node for elements, attributes, and so on. It is guaranteed to refer to the same XML node as long as the document is not reparsed. An XML ID of 0 indicates that the element is a root element. Its parent XML ID is NULL. (Amazing, isn't it?)
@mp:localname	Stores the local part of the name of the node. It is used with prefix and namespace uniform resource identifiers (URIs) to name element or attribute nodes.
@mp:namespaceuri	Provides the current element's namespace URI. A value of NULL translates to no namespace present.
@mp:prefix	Stores the namespace prefix of the current element. A NULL value being present with a URI being given indicates the default namespace. If no URI is given, no namespace is attached.

continues

Table 8.2 **Continued**

Attribute	Description
@mp:prev	Stores a node's previous sibling to provide element ordering information of the document.
	@mp:prev contains the XML ID of the previous sibling that has the same parent element. A NULL value indicates that an element is at the beginning of the sibling list.
@mp:xmltext	This is used solely for processing purposes. It is the textual serialization of the element and its attributes and subelements as used in the overflow handling of OPENXML.

Table 8.3 **Parent Attributes**

Parent Metaproperty Attribute	Description
@mp:parentid	Corresponds to ../@mp:id
@mp:parentlocalname	Corresponds to ../@mp:localname
@mp:parentnamespacerui	Corresponds to ../@mp:namespaceuri
@mp:parentprefix	Corresponds to ../@mp:prefix

Examples of Metaproperties Usage

First let's see how the ColPattern parameter can map the metaproperties to rowset columns in an OPENXML statement. Listing 8.11 illustrates the use of several metaproperties.

Listing 8.11 **Stored Procedure with Selected Metaproperties**

```
DECLARE @idoc int
DECLARE @xmldoc varchar(1000)
SET @xmldoc ='
<ROOT>
<Employee EmployeeID="5">
   <LastName>Buchanan</LastName>
   <FirstName>Steven</FirstName>
   <Order OrderID="10248" CustomerID="VINET" EmployeeID="5"
        OrderDate="1996-07-04T00:00:00">
     <OrderDetail ProductID="42" Quantity="10"/>
     <OrderDetail ProductID="72" Quantity="5"/>Customer returned merchandise
   </Order>
</Employee>
```

```
<Employee EmployeeID="7">
    <LastName>King</LastName>
    <FirstName>Robert</FirstName>
    <Order OrderID="10303" CustomerID="GODOS" EmployeeID="7"
          OrderDate="1996-09-11T00:00:00" note="Almost out of inventory">
       <Priority>First Class</Priority>
        <OrderDetail ProductID="40" Quantity="40"/>Customer needs this ASAP
    </Order>
</Employee>
</ROOT>'
EXEC sp_xml_preparedocument @idoc OUTPUT, @xmldoc
SELECT *
FROM OPENXML (@idoc, '/ROOT/Employee/Order')
       WITH (id                  int          @mp:id,
             OrderID             char(5),
             OrderDate           datetime,
             ParentID            int '@mp:parentid',
             ParentLocalName varchar(20) '@mp:parentlocalname')

    EXEC sp_xml_removedocument @idoc
```

The following example shows the results of utilizing selected metaproperties in Listing 8.11.

id	OrderID	OrderDate	ParentID	ParentLocalName
6	10248	1996-07-04 00:00:00.000	2	Employee
22	10303	1996-09-11 00:00:00.000	18	Employee

The metaproperties in this example are as follows:

- `@mp:id`, which produces a column of guaranteed unique IDs generated by the system

- `@mp:parentid`, which produces a column containing the XML ID of the column's parent

- `@mp:parentlocalname`, which produces a column containing the parent element's local name

In our next example, we're going to go back again to the unconsumed (overflow) data column that we talked about in the section "Retrieving Unconsumed Data with `sql:overflow-field`" in Chapter 7, "FOR XML." Utilizing the `@mp:xmltext` metaproperty, which maps a column as an overflow column in the rowset, it is possible to retrieve the entire XML document. Listing 8.12 is the stored procedure that utilizes the `@mp:xmltext metaproperty`. I'll leave the results listing as an exercise for you to complete.

Listing 8.12 **Using the *@mp:xmltext* Metaproperty**

```
DECLARE @idoc int
DECLARE @xmldoc varchar(1000)
SET @xmldoc ='
<ROOT>
<Employee EmployeeID="5">
   <LastName>Buchanan</LastName>
   <FirstName>Steven</FirstName>
   <Order OrderID="10248" CustomerID="VINET" EmployeeID="5"
         OrderDate="1996-07-04T00:00:00">
     <OrderDetail ProductID="42" Quantity="10"/>
     <OrderDetail ProductID="72" Quantity="5"/>Customer returned merchandise
   </Order>
</Employee>
<Employee EmployeeID="7">
   <LastName>King</LastName>
   <FirstName>Robert</FirstName>
   <Order OrderID="10303" CustomerID="GODOS" EmployeeID="7"
         OrderDate="1996-09-11T00:00:00" note="Almost out of inventory">
     <Priority>First Class</Priority>
     <OrderDetail ProductID="40" Quantity="40"/>Customer needs this ASAP
   </Order>
</Employee>
</ROOT>'
-- Create an in memory representation of the document.
EXEC sp_xml_preparedocument @idoc OUTPUT, @xmldoc
SELECT *
FROM OPENXML (@idoc, '/')
     WITH (xmlcolumn  ntext  '@mp:xmltext')

EXEC sp_xml_removedocument @idoc
```

Here's another example of the @mp:xmltext metaproperty in which we only want selected data to be placed in the overflow column. We'll also see a new flags parameter value of 9. This value specifies two things: attribute-centric mapping, and that only the unconsumed data should be placed in the overflow column. Listing 8.13 shows the stored procedure that illustrates placing unconsumed data into an overflow column. Listing 8.14 shows the results.

Listing 8.13 **The *@mp:xmltext* Metaproperty and Overflow Columns**

```
DECLARE @idoc int
DECLARE @xmldoc varchar(1000)
SET @xmldoc ='
<ROOT>
<Employee EmployeeID="5">
   <LastName>Buchanan</LastName>
   <FirstName>Steven</FirstName>
```

```
    <Order OrderID="10248" CustomerID="VINET" EmployeeID="5"
           OrderDate="1996-07-04T00:00:00">
    </Order>
  </Employee>
  <Employee EmployeeID="7">
    <LastName>King</LastName>
    <FirstName>Robert</FirstName>
    <Order OrderID="10303" CustomerID="GODOS" EmployeeID="7"
           OrderDate="1996-09-11T00:00:00" note="Almost out of inventory">
       <Priority>First Class</Priority>
    </Order>
  </Employee>
</ROOT>'
-- Create an in memory representation of the document.
EXEC sp_xml_preparedocument @idoc OUTPUT, @xmldoc
SELECT *
FROM OPENXML (@idoc, '/ROOT/Employee/Order',9 )
        WITH (OrderID          char(5),
              ParentID         int       '@mp:parentid',
              ParentLocalName  varchar(20) '@mp:parentlocalname',
              Remarks          ntext      '@mp:xmltext')
```

Listing 8.14 **Results of Specifying an Overflow Column**

OrderID	ParentID	ParentLocalName	Remarks

10248	2	Employee	`<Order CustomerID="VINET" EmployeeID="5"`
			`           OrderDate="1996-07-04T00:00:00">`
			`</Order>`

10303	11	Employee	`<Order CustomerID="GODOS" EmployeeID="7"`
			`           OrderDate="1996-09-11T00:00:00"`
			`           note="Almost out`
			`           of inventory">`
			`           <Priority>First Class</Priority>`
			`</Order>`

Notice that the OrderID isn't included in the Remarks column. It was utilized in the OrderID column, so it was consumed.

Inserting Records via an HTML Form and OPENXML

At the beginning of this chapter, I made the point that OPENXML could be used to write data to a database, but then I spent the rest of this chapter showing you how to retrieve data. Well, now I'll show you how to do what I said could be done.

Let's take what we've learned to this point and apply it to an example that illustrates inserting data into a table. This example could very easily be expanded to real-world situations. You'll need to know a little about HTML and basic JavaScript.

The steps we'll perform in this example are as follows:

1. Create a simple table for the data.

2. Create a simple HTML form.

3. Create an XML document from the form data.

4. Pass the document to a template.

5. Use OPENXML to insert the record.

Let's create the table first with the following SQL statement:

```
CREATE TABLE Contact(ID int, LastName varchar(15), FirstName varchar(15))
```

Now let's create the HTML form, which is given in Listing 8.15 and illustrated in Figure 8.3. I want to emphasize the importance of the JavaScript portion of the HTML (the boldface type). This is the key function that takes the data entered in the form fields and then assembles and assigns the values to an XML element string. The string is assigned to the hidden field `contactdata`; from here it will be posted to the destination `Template.xml` and become the input parameter.

Those of you who are unfamiliar with JavaScript and posting data on the Web should contact one of your Web developers for an explanation of how this works. It is not a difficult concept.

Listing 8.15   **Our HTML Form**

```
<html>
<body>
  <form action="http://iisserver/Nwind/templates/Template.xml" method="post">
    <input type="hidden" id="cd" name="contactdata">
    <input type="hidden" name="contenttype" value="text/xml">
      ContactID: <input type=text id=cid value="1"><br>
      First Name: <input type=text id=firstname value="Harry"><br>
      Last Name: <input type=text id=lastname value="Smith"><br>
     <input type=submit onclick="Insert_Contact(cd, cid,
       lastname, firstname)" value="Insert Contact"><br><br>

  <script>
     function Insert_Contact(cd, cid, lastname, firstname)
       {
       cd.value = '<Contact ID="' + cid.value +
       '" LastName="' + lastname.value + '" FirstName="' +
       firstname.value + '"/>';
       }
  </script>
  </form>
  </body>
  </html>
```

Those of you who are familiar with the Java programming language will recognize the advantages it would offer here. Java servlets seem to have been made for this type of application. A disadvantage to this approach is the specialized knowledge required to develop servlets.

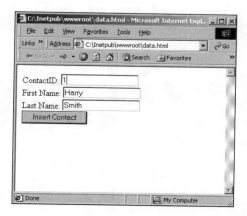

Figure 8.3 Our HTML form.

Listing 8.16 shows the stored procedure we need to execute, and Listing 8.17 shows the XML template file that executes the stored procedure.

Listing 8.16 **Our Stored Procedure**

```
CREATE PROC sp_insert_contact @contactdata ntext
AS
       DECLARE @hDoc int
    EXEC sp_xml_preparedocument @hDoc OUTPUT, @contactdata
    INSERT INTO Contact
      SELECT *
      FROM OPENXML(@hDoc, '/Contact')
           WITH Contact
     EXEC sp_xml_removedocument @hDoc
```

Listing 8.17 **Our XML Template**

```
<root xmlns:sql="urn:schemas-microsoft-com:xml-sql">
<sql:header>
  <sql:param name="contactdata"></sql:param>
</sql:header>
<sql:query>
  exec sp_insert_contact @contactdata
</sql:query>
</root>
```

Updating Records via an HTML Form and OPENXML

Our last example shows how to update data in a table utilizing an HTML form and OPENXML. We'll use the same `Contact` table that we utilized in the example in the preceding section. We'll load the table with preset data and then issue the `update` command. One new wrinkle is the use of a text area for the XML document. This illustrates the insertion of an XML document that might have been created by a third-party application.

Figure 8.4 shows the HTML form.

Figure 8.4 The HTML form utilizing a text area for input.

The following example shows the SQL statement to clear and preload table data:

```
TRUNCATE TABLE Contact
INSERT INTO Contact VALUES (501, 'Rick', 'Shelton')
INSERT INTO Contact VALUES (502, 'Corey', 'Tenney')
```

Listings 8.18, 8.19, and 8.20 show the stored procedure needed, the template file, and the HTML file that starts everything, respectively.

Listing 8.18 **The Stored Procedure**

```
DECLARE @hDoc int
exec sp_xml_preparedocument @hDoc OUTPUT,@contactdata
UPDATE Contact
SET
     Contact.FirstName = XMLContact.FirstName,
     Contact.LastName = XMLContact.LastName
FROM OPENXML(@hDoc, '/root/Contact')
          WITH Contact XMLContact
WHERE   Contact.ID = XMLContact.ID
EXEC sp_xml_removedocument @hDoc
SELECT    *
from      Contact
FOR XML AUTO
```

Listing 8.19   **The Template File**

```
<root xmlns:sql="urn:schemas-microsoft-com:xml-sql">
<sql:header>
<sql:param name="contactdata"></sql:param>
</sql:header>
<sql:query>exec sp_update_contact @contactdata
</sql:query>
</root>
```

Listing 8.20   **The HTML Page to Start Everything**

```
<html>
<body>
<form name="contact"
      action="http://iisserver/Nwind/Templates/template.xml"
      method="POST">
<h3>Data Update via OPENXML</h3><br>
<input type=hidden name="contenttype" value="text/xml">
<textarea name="contactdata" cols=50 rows=5>
   &lt;root&gt;
     &lt;Contact ID=&quot;502&quot; LastName=&quot;Griffin&quot;
FirstName=&quot;John&quot;/&gt;
   &lt;/root&gt;
</textarea>
<br><input type=Submit value="Submit">
</form>
</body>
</html>
```

The following example shows the updated table contents utilizing an XML document output.

```
<root xmlns:sql="urn:schemas-microsoft-com:xml-sql">
  <Contact ID="501" LastName="Rick" FirstName="Shelton" />
  <Contact ID="502" LastName="Griffin" FirstName="John" />
</root>
```

Recap of What Was Discussed in This Chapter

- OPENXML can be utilized whenever a rowset provider is necessary, such as a table or view. This includes SELECT, SELECT INTO, and OPENROWSET. This is accomplished in memory by making the XML document appear as a relational rowset. In doing so, the results become a data provider with the capability of writing XML data to database tables.

- Without the WITH clause in OPENXML, the rowset is returned in the edge table format, so-called because every edge of the XML tree maps to a rowset row. It is possible to obtain the data type of an element/attribute, node types, namespaces, and other values. In essence, wherever you would use an XML parser to obtain document information, you can use an edge table.

- Metaproperties associated with OPENXML are attributes that describe the properties of an XML item, regardless of whether it is an element, an attribute, or any other node. These properties exist and are provided by OPENXML even though they are not present in the XML document text.

A

Northwind Database Schema

THIS APPENDIX CONTAINS A COMPLETE LISTING OF TABLES contained in the
Northwind database. The details of each table, including indices, foreign keys, and the
details of the foreign key relationships are also included. Figure A.1 shows a diagram of
the tables to give you a visual table relationship.

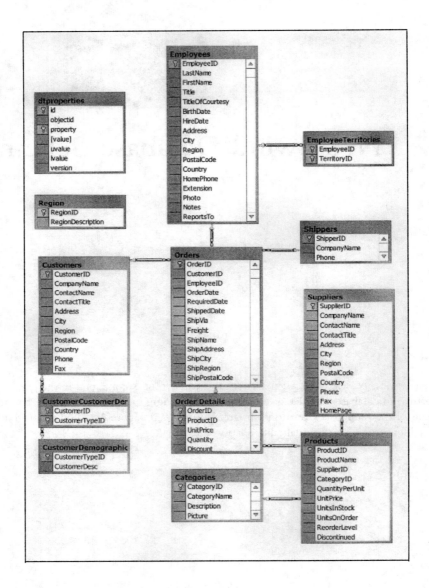

Figure A.1 Northwind Database Tables.

Hopefully, this appendix will save you a ton of time with your coding.

Table Categories

Column Name	Data Type	Length	Allow Nulls
CategoryID	int	4	
CategoryName	nvarchar	15	
Description	ntext	16	✓
Picture	image	16	✓

Figure A.2   Schema for Table Categories.

Index Name	Fields	Clustered	Primary Key
PK_Categories	CategoryID	Y	Y
CategoryName	CategoryName	N	N

Foreign Key Name	Key Field	Related Table	Related Field
FK_Products_Categories	CategoryID	Products	CategoryID

Table CustomerCustomerDemo

Column Name	Data Type	Length	Allow Nulls
CustomerID	nchar	5	
CustomerTypeID	nchar	10	

Figure A.3   Schema for Table CustomerCustomerDemo.

Index Name	Fields	Clustered	Primary Key
PK_Categories	CustomerID+	N	Y
CategoryName	CustomerTypeID		

Foreign Key Name	Key Field	Related Table	Related Field
FK_CustomerCustomerDemo	CustomerTypeID	Customer Demographics	Customer ➡TypeID
FK_CustomerCustomer ➡Demo_Customers	CustomerID	Customers	CustomerID

Table CustomerDemographics

	Column Name	Data Type	Length	Allow Nulls
▶🔑	CustomerTypeID	nchar	10	
	CustomerDesc	ntext	16	✓

Figure A.4   Schema for Table CustomerDemographics.

Index Name	Fields	Clustered	Primary Key
PK_CustomerDemographics	CustomerTypeID	N	Y

Foreign Key Name	Key Field	Related Table	Related Field
FK_CustomerCustomerDemo	CustomerTypeID	CustomerCustomer ➡Demo	Customer ➡TypeID

Table Customers

Column Name	Data Type	Length	Allow Nulls
CustomerID	nchar	5	
CompanyName	nvarchar	40	
ContactName	nvarchar	30	✓
ContactTitle	nvarchar	30	✓
Address	nvarchar	60	✓
City	nvarchar	15	✓
Region	nvarchar	15	✓
PostalCode	nvarchar	10	✓
Country	nvarchar	15	✓
Phone	nvarchar	24	✓
Fax	nvarchar	24	✓

Figure A.5   Schema for Table Customers.

Index Name	Fields	Clustered	Primary Key
PK_Customers	CustomerID	Y	Y
City	City	N	N
CompanyName	CompanyName	N	N
PostalCode	PostalCode	N	N
Region	Region	N	N

Foreign Key Name	Key Field	Related Table	Related Field
FK_Orders_Customers	CustomerID	Orders	CustomerID
FK_CustomerCustomer ⇒Demo_Customers	CustomerID	Customer ⇒CustomerDemo	CustomerID

Table dtproperties

Column Name	Data Type	Length	Allow Nulls
id	int	4	
objectid	int	4	✓
property	varchar	64	
[value]	varchar	255	✓
uvalue	nvarchar	255	✓
lvalue	image	16	✓
version	int	4	

Figure A.6   Schema for Table dtproperties.

Index Name	Fields	Clustered	Primary Key
pk_dtproperties	id+property	Y	Y

Foreign Key Name	Key Field	Related Table	Related Field
none			

Table Employees

Column Name	Data Type	Length	Allow Nulls
EmployeeID	int	4	
LastName	nvarchar	20	
FirstName	nvarchar	10	
Title	nvarchar	30	✓
TitleOfCourtesy	nvarchar	25	✓
BirthDate	datetime	8	✓
HireDate	datetime	8	✓
Address	nvarchar	60	✓
City	nvarchar	15	✓
Region	nvarchar	15	✓
PostalCode	nvarchar	10	✓
Country	nvarchar	15	✓
HomePhone	nvarchar	24	✓
Extension	nvarchar	4	✓
Photo	image	16	✓
Notes	ntext	16	✓
ReportsTo	int	4	✓
PhotoPath	nvarchar	255	✓

Figure A.7 Schema for Table Employees.

Index Name	Fields	Clustered	Primary Key
PK_employees	EmployeeID	Y	Y
LastName	LastName	N	N
PostalCode	PostalCode	N	N

Foreign Key Name	Key Field	Related Table	Related Field
FK_Orders_Employees	EmployeeID	Orders	EmployeeID
FK_Employee Territories_Employees	EmployeeID	Employee Territories	EmployeeID

Table EmployeeTerritories

Column Name	Data Type	Length	Allow Nulls
EmployeeID	int	4	
TerritoryID	nvarchar	20	

Figure A.8 Schema for Table EmployeeTerritories.

Index Name	Fields	Clustered	Primary Key
PK_EmployeeTerritories	EmployeeID+Territory	N	Y

Foreign Key Name	Key Field	Related Table	Related Field
FK_EmployeeTerritories_Employees	EmployeeID	Employee Territories	EmployeeID
FK_EmployeeTerritories_Territories	TerritoryID	Employee Territories	TerritoryID

Table Order Details

Column Name	Data Type	Length	Allow Nulls
OrderID	int	4	
ProductID	int	4	
UnitPrice	money	8	
Quantity	smallint	2	
Discount	real	4	

Figure A.9 Schema for Table Order Details.

Index Name	Fields	Clustered	Primary Key
PK_Order_Details	OrderID+ProductID	Y	Y
OrderID	OrderID	N	N
OrdersOrder_Details	OrderID	N	N
ProductID	ProductID	N	N
ProductsOrder_Details	ProductID	N	N

Foreign Key Name	Key Field	Related Table	Related Field
FK_Order_Details_Orders	OrderID	Orders	OrderID
FK_Order_Details_Products	ProductID	Products	ProductID

Table Orders

Column Name	Data Type	Length	Allow Nulls
OrderID	int	4	
CustomerID	nchar	5	✓
EmployeeID	int	4	✓
OrderDate	datetime	8	✓
RequiredDate	datetime	8	✓
ShippedDate	datetime	8	✓
ShipVia	int	4	✓
Freight	money	8	✓
ShipName	nvarchar	40	✓
ShipAddress	nvarchar	60	✓
ShipCity	nvarchar	15	✓
ShipRegion	nvarchar	15	✓
ShipPostalCode	nvarchar	10	✓
ShipCountry	nvarchar	15	✓

Figure A.10   Schema for Table Orders.

Index Name	Fields	Clustered	Primary Key
PK_Orders	OrderID	Y	Y
OrderDate	OrderDate	N	N
ShippedDate	ShippedDate	N	N
ShippersOrders	ShipVia	N	N
ShipPostalCode	ShipPostalCode	N	N

Foreign Key Name	Key Field	Related Table	Related Field
FK_Orders_Customers	CustomerID	Customers	CustomerID
FK_Order_Details_Orders	OrderID	Order Details	OrderID

Table Products

Column Name	Data Type	Length	Allow Nulls
ProductID	int	4	
ProductName	nvarchar	40	
SupplierID	int	4	✔
CategoryID	int	4	✔
QuantityPerUnit	nvarchar	20	✔
UnitPrice	money	8	✔
UnitsInStock	smallint	2	✔
UnitsOnOrder	smallint	2	✔
ReorderLevel	smallint	2	✔
Discontinued	bit	1	

Figure A.11   Schema for Table Products.

Index Name	Fields	Clustered	Primary Key
PK_Products	ProductID	Y	Y
CategoryID	CategoryID	N	N
ProductName	ProductName	N	N
SupplierID	SupplierID	N	N
SuppliersProducts	SupplierID	N	N

Foreign Key Name	Key Field	Related Table	Related Field
FK_Products_Categories	CategoryID	Categories	CategoryID
FK_Order_Details_Products	ProductID	Order Details	ProductID
FK_Products_Suppliers	SupplierID	Suppliers	SupplierID

Table Region

Column Name	Data Type	Length	Allow Nulls
RegionID	int	4	
RegionDescription	nchar	50	

Figure A.12 Schema for Table Region.

Index Name	Fields	Clustered	Primary Key
PK_Region	RegionID	N	N

Foreign Key Name	Key Field	Related Table	Related Field
FK_Territories_Region	RegionID	Territories	RegionID

Table Shippers

Column Name	Data Type	Length	Allow Nulls
ShipperID	int	4	
CompanyName	nvarchar	40	
Phone	nvarchar	24	✓

Figure A.13 Schema for Table Shippers.

Index Name	Fields	Clustered	Primary Key
PK_Shippers	ShipperID	Y	Y

Foreign Key Name	Key Field	Related Table	Related Field
FK_Orders_Shippers	ShipperID	Orders	ShipVia

Table Suppliers

Column Name	Data Type	Length	Allow Nulls
SupplierID	int	4	
CompanyName	nvarchar	40	
ContactName	nvarchar	30	✓
ContactTitle	nvarchar	30	✓
Address	nvarchar	60	✓
City	nvarchar	15	✓
Region	nvarchar	15	✓
PostalCode	nvarchar	10	✓
Country	nvarchar	15	✓
Phone	nvarchar	24	✓
Fax	nvarchar	24	✓
HomePage	ntext	16	✓

Figure A.14   Schema for Table Suppliers.

Index Name	Fields	Clustered	Primary Key
PK_Suppliers	SupplierID	Y	Y
CompanyName	CompanyName	N	N
PostalCode	PostalCode	N	N

Foreign Key Name	Key Field	Related Table	Related Field
FK_Products_Suppliers	SupplierID	Products	SupplierID

B

XSLT Instructions with Reference to Text Usage

THE FOLLOWING TABLE CONTAINS A BRIEF EXAMPLE, description, and text references to the XSLT elements used in this text. Not all XSLT elements are discussed in this table and I refer you to any of the excellent texts on this subject for further information.

XSL Element	Syntax	Description	Text Reference
xsl:apply-templates	`<xsl:apply-templates select = expression mode = qname> (xsl:sort | xsl:with-param)* </xsl:apply-templates>`	Invokes the best-match template rules against the node-set returned by the select expression.	Page 79
xsl:attribute	`<xsl:attribute name = {qname} namespace = {uri} template-body </xsl:attribute>`	Output an XML attribute whose *local name* is name, whose *name space URI* is namespace and whose *children* are based on template.	Page 85
xsl:choose	`<xsl:choose> <xsl:when> + <xsl:otherwise> ? </xsl choose>`	Operates just like a *switch* or Select statement. Evaluates the first xsl:when template whose test expression evaluates to true. If none evaluate to true, then the xsl:otherwise template clause is evaluated.	Page 92
xsl:comment	`<xsl:comment> template-body </xsl:comment>`	Writes a comment to the current output.	Page 88
xsl:copy	`<xsl:copy use--attribute--sets = qnames> template-body </xsl :copy>`	Copies the current context node (and associated namespace nodes) to the result tree fragment.	Page 86
xsl:decimal-format	`<xsl:decimal-format> character/symbol definitions </xsl:decimal-format>`	Defines the characters and symbols used when converting from strings to numbers.	Page 89
xsl:element	`<xsl:element name = {qname} namespace = {uri} use-attribute-sets=list-of- QNames`	Output an XML attribute whose *local name* is name, whose *name space URI* is namespace and whose *children* are based on template.	Page 84

XSL Element	Syntax	Description	Text Reference
xsl:for-each	template-body </xsl:element>		
	<xsl:for-each select = XPath expression> <xsl:sort> * template-body </xsl:for—each>	Selects a node set via an XPath expression and processes each node identically.	Page 93
xsl:if	<xsl:if test = expression> template body </xsl if>	Evaluates the template body only if the test expression evaluates to true.	Page 92
xsl:import	<xsl:import href=uri/>	Imports the contents of one stylesheet module into another.	Page 72
xsl:include	<xsl:include href=uri/>	Imports the contents of one stylesheet module into another.	Page 72
xsl:otherwise	see xsl:choose		
xsl:output	<xsl:output> format-control-expressions </xsl:output>	Controls the format of the stylesheet output.	Page 94
xsl:processing-instruction	<xsl:processing-instruction name= {QName}> template-body </xsl:processing-instruction>	Write an XML processing instruction whose *target* is name and whose *children* are based on template.	Page 88

continues

XSL Element	Syntax	Description	Text Reference

xsl:stylesheet	`<xsl:stylesheet`
	`stylesheet attributes`
	`</xsl:stylesheet>`
		The outermost element of a stylesheet.	Page 71

xsl:template	`<xsl:template`
	`name=QName`
	`match=Pattern`
	`mode=QName`
	`priority=Number>`
	`<xsl:param> *`
	`template-body`
	`</xsl:template>`
		Defines a template for output.	Page 77

xsl:value-of	`<xsl:value—of select=expression`
	`disable-output-escaping =`
	`"yes"|"no"/>`
		Writes the string value of the expression to the output.	Page 80

xsl:variable	`<xsl:variable name=QName`
	`select=expression>`
	`template-body`
	`</xsl:variable>`
		Declares a variable named name and initializes it using either the select expression or template.	Page 72

xsl:when	*see* xsl:choose		

XPath Functions and Examples

THE FOLLOWING TABLES CONTAIN BRIEF EXAMPLES, DEFINITIONS, and text references to the XPath functions available. No text references are available because functions weren't discussed in the book. Not all functions are discussed in this table. Please refer to any of the excellent texts, such as *XSLT A Programmer's Reference* by Michael Kay, Second Edition, WROX Press, on this subject for further information.

XPath Functions	Example	Description
ARITHMETIC FUNCTIONS		
ceiling	ceiling(14 div 3) = 5	Returns the smallest integer greater than or equal to the numeric value of the argument.
floor	floor(4.5) = 4	Returns the largest integer less than or equal to the numeric value of the argument.
round	round(9.6) = 10	Returns the closest integer to the numeric value of the argument.

XPath Functions	Example	Description
BOOLEAN FUNCTIONS		
false	`xsl:if test=false()`	Returns the Boolean *false*.
true	`xsl:if test=true()`	Returns the Boolean *true*.
not	`not(false()) returns` *true*	Returns the Boolean negation of its argument.
CONTEXT INFORMATION FUNCTIONS		
current	If `@LastName` is the context node `current()` returns a one-node node set of `@LastName`'s value.	Returns the context node.

last	`<xsl:if`
	`   test="position() !=`
	`        last()"`
	`</xsl:if>`
		Returns the number of the last node in the node set.

position	`<xsl:if`
	`   test="position() < 3"`
	`</xsl:if>`
		Returns the number of thecurrent node in the node set.

DATA CONVERSION FUNCTIONS		
boolean	`Boolean(0) returns` *false*	Converts the argument to a Boolean value.
format-number	`format-number` `(value, format)` produces a formatted string.	Converts numbers to strings for display. The format is controlled by *decimal-format*.
number	`number('-32.4')` returns –32.4 as a number.	Converts its argument to a number.
string	`string(-32.4)` returns '–32.4'.	Converts its argument to a string.
PROCESSOR INFORMATION FUNCTIONS		
element-available	`<xsl:element-available` `('xsl:comment')` returns *true*.	Tests whether a specific controlled instruction or extension is available.
function-available	`<xsl:function-available` `('string')` returns *true*.	Tests whether a specific XSLT function or extension is available.
RETRIEVING NAMES AND IDS FUNCTIONS		

name	`<xsl:if`
	`   test="not(@LastName)">`
	`</xsl:if`
		Returns a Qname representing a node name.

XPath Functions	Example	Description
STRING FUNCTIONS		
concat	```<xsl:value-of select="concat('address', 'city', 'state', 'zip')" />```	Joins two or more arguments as strings.
contains	`contains('Winston','ton')` returns *true*.	Tests whether a string is contained within another string.
string-length	`string-length('four score')` returns 10.	Returns the character count in a string.
substring	`substring('four score', 2, 3)` returns 'our'.	Returns a portion of a string based on position attributes starting at 1.
SUMMARY FUNCTIONS		
count	```if test= "count('resume/address [zip]') != 0"```	Returns the number of nodes in a node set.
sum	the node `<tri a='10'                b='20'                c='30'` Returns 60 with the expression `sum(@*)`	Calculates the total of a set of numbers in a node set.

Microsoft XML Data Types

Data Type	Description
bin.base64	MIME-style Base64 encoded binary BLOB
bin.hex	Hexadecimal digits representing octets
boolean	0 (false) or 1 (true)
char	One character length long string
date	Date in a subset ISO 8601 format, without the time data, for example, "1994-11-05." The date itself is not validated. (For example, 2-31-99 will pass validation.)
dateTime	Date in a subset of ISO 8601 format, with optional time and no optional time zone. Fractional seconds can be as precise as nanoseconds, for example, "1988-04-07T18:39:09."
dateTime.tz	Date in a subset ISO 8601 format, with optional time and optional time zone. Fractional seconds can be as precise as nanoseconds, for example, "1988-04-07T18:39:09-08:00."
fixed.14.4	Same as number, but is limited to 14 digits to the left and four to the right of the decimal point.
float	Real number with no limit on digits. Float can have a leading sign, fractional digits, and, optionally, an exponent. Punctuation as in U.S. English. Values range from 1.7976931348623157E+308 to 2.2250738585072014E-308.

continues

Data Type	Description
int	A number with optional sign, no fractions, and no exponent.
number	A number with no limit on digits. It can have a leading sign, fractional digits, and, optionally, an exponent. Punctuation is as in U.S. English. (Values have the same range as R8, 1.7976931348623157E+308 to 2.2250738585072014E–308.)
time	Time in a subset of the ISO 8601 format, with no date and no time zone, for example, "08:15:27."
time.tz	Time in a subset of the ISO 8601 format, with no date, but an optional time zone, for example, "08:1527–05:00."
i1	A one byte integer with an optional sign, no fractions and no exponent, for example, "1 or 127 or –128."
i2	A one-word (two byte) integer with an optional sign, no fractions and no exponent, for example, "1 or 669 or –32768."
i4	A four-byte integer with an optional sign, no fractions and no exponent, for example, "1 or 669 or –32768 or 148343 or –1000000000."
i8	An eight-byte integer with an optional sign, no fractions, no exponent, and 19-digit precision. It ranges from –9,223,372,036,854,775,808 to 9,223,372,036,854,775,807.
r4	A real number with seven-digit precision. It can have a leading sign, fractional digits, and, optionally, an exponent. Punctuation as in U.S. English. Values range from 3.40282347E+38F to 1.17549435E-38F.
r8	This is the same as a float. A real number with 15-digit precision, which can have a leading sign, fractional digits, and, optionally, an exponent. Punctuation as in U.S. English. Values range from 1.7976931348623157E+308 to 2.2250738585072014E–308.
ui1	A one-byte unsigned integer with no fractions and no exponent, for example, "1 or 255."
ui2	A two-byte unsigned integer with no fractions and no exponent, for example, "1 or 255 or 65535."
ui4	A four-byte unsigned integer with no fractions and no exponent, for example, "1 or 669 or 3000000000."
ui8	An eight-byte unsigned integer with no fractions and no exponent. Its range is 0 to 18,446,744,073,709,551,615.
uri	Universal Resource Identifier (URI), for example, "urn:schemas-microsoft-com:Excel4."
uuid	Hexadecimal digits representing octets, optional embedded hyphens that are ignored, for example, "132C7AB4-570E-11D0-FF04-1980E7055F83."

Resources

XML

[XML] Extensible Markup
Language (XML) 1.0

```
http://www.w3.org/TR/1998/REC-
xml-19980210\
```

The definition of XML

[XML-MIME] XML Media Types

```
http://www.ietf.org/rfc/rfc2376.txt
```

The definitive listing of all MIME types

Microsoft's MSDN XML
Developer's Center

```
http://msdn.microsoft.com/xml
/default.asp
```

The starting point for all
things related to Microsoft
XML

XSLT

The W3C XSLT Specification

```
http://www.w3.org/TR/xslt.html
```

An XSLT online tutorial

```
http://www.vbxml.com/xsl/tutorials/
intro/default.asp
```

This is an outstanding starting point
to learn XSLT

Namespaces

Namespaces in XML

`http://www.w3.org/TR/1999/REC-xml-names-19990114/`

W3C recommendation
for namespaces

XML Namespaces

`http://www.jclark.com/xml/xmlns.htm`

An excellent discussion
by James Clark

XML Schema

The W3C XML Schema
Specification primer

`http://www.w3.org/TR/xmlschema-0/`

The W3C XML Schema
Specification for structures

`http://www.w3.org/TR/xmlschema-1/`

The W3C XML Schema
Specification primer for
datatypes

`http://www.w3.org/TR/xmlschema-2/`

Microsoft's MSDN XDR
Schema Developer's Guide

`http://msdn.microsoft.com/library/`
`psdk/xmlsdk/xmlp7k6d.htm`

The place to start for XDR
schema development

A discussion of XDR Schema

`http://www.ltg.ed.ac.uk/~ht/`
`XMLData-Reduced.htm`

Dated from 1998 but still
a good resource

SQL Server 2000

Microsoft's starting point for
SQL server information

`http://www.microsoft.com/sql/default.htm`

Performance.com

`http://www.sql-server-`
`performance.com/default.asp`

Offers performance tuning and
optimization articles and tips

Miscellaneous Resources

[SOAP] Simple Object Access
Protocol (SOAP) Version 1.1

http://www.w3.org/TR/SOAP

[URI] Uniform Resource Identifiers
(URI): Generic Syntax

http://www.ietf.org/rfc/rfc2396.txt

[ISO8601] ISO 8601: Representations
of Dates and Times

http://www.iso.ch/markete/8601.pdf

[HTTP] Hypertext Transfer
Protocol—HTTP/1.1

http://www.ietf.org/rfc/rfc2616.txt

[MULTIPART] The MIME Multipart/
Related Content-Type

http://www.ietf.org/rfc/rfc2387.txt

F

IBM's XSL Editor

IN CHAPTER 2, "XSLT STYLESHEETS," I TOLD you about IBM's Java-based program called XSL Editor. You can download this program from `http://www.alphaworks.ibm.com/tech/xsleditor`. This short appendix will in no way cover everything about this software product. It is only intended to give you some idea as to how it works. As of this writing, IBM had no further plans to enhance this product, but remember that this is to be used as a learning tool, not in a production environment.

In addition to the XSL Editor, you'll need a version of the Java Software Development Kit or the Java runtime environment prior to version 1.2. Sorry, but that is the only way the editor will work. You can obtain these at Sun's Java Web site: `http://java/sun/com`. Those of you who know nothing about Java, don't worry. There's not a lot to this installation.

I highly recommend that you use this software to learn XSL Transformations. It's a very simple program to learn and use, so the tool won't get in the way of what you're trying to learn.

Accept the defaults when installing the Java package. There's no sense in making something harder than necessary. After the Java installation is complete, install the editor. During the installation, you will be asked to pick the version of Java you want the editor to use. If you have more than one Java version installed, be sure to pick a version prior to 1.2.

After you start the program, you'll see what is pictured in Figure F.1. The software presents three separate panes for three separate functions.

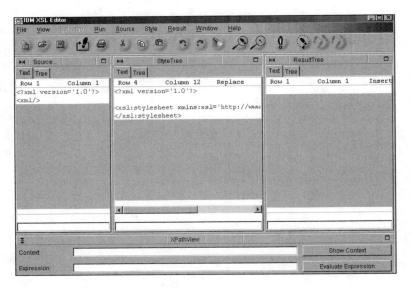

Figure F.1 The XSL Editor's opening screen.

The left pane is used for creating an XML file or loading one you created with some other application. The center pane is for developing or loading an XSLT stylesheet. The right pane shows the results of applying the stylesheet to the XML document.

Figure F.2 shows an XML document, an XSLT stylesheet, and the results.

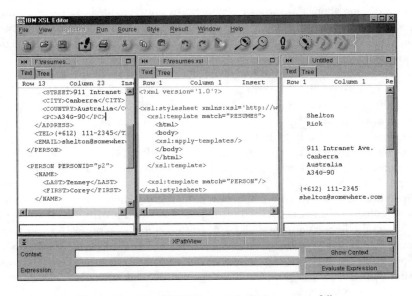

Figure F.2 The XSL Editor with all three panes full.

These results can be saved.

One difference from what you are used to is that files are loaded into the XML and stylesheet panes from their own individual drop-down menus, not from the File menu. See Figure F.3, which shows the drop-down menu for the XML pane.

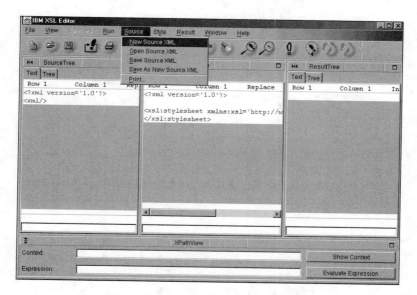

Figure F.3   The XML document drop-down menu.

Tree views of the loaded documents can be examined by selecting the Tree tab in the appropriate window. Figure F.4 shows the tree view selected in both the XML document window and the XSLT stylesheet window.

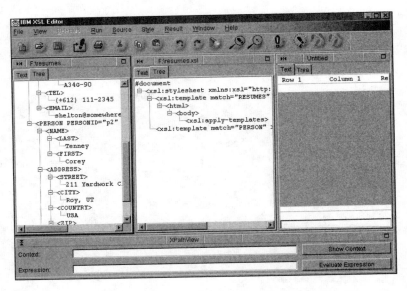

Figure F.4 The XSL Editor showing tree views of documents.

Looking at Figure F.4 once again, clicking the Footprint toolbar icon that looks like an exclamation point will apply the stylesheet to the XML document and will present the results in the results pane. That's really all you need to know for basic operation of this software tool. The rest is easy to figure out.

Oh, and did I mention the price? It's really difficult to beat $0.00, so enjoy.

G

Microsoft's SQL Server XML View Mapper

IN CHAPTER 5, "CREATING XML VIEWS WITH XDR Schemas," I mentioned
Microsoft's XML View Mapper. This program is available free of charge from
Microsoft's Web site:

```
http://msdn.microsoft.com/downloads/default.asp?URL=/code/sample.asp?url=/
MSDN-FILES/027/001/443/msdncompositedoc.xml
```

Sorry about the length of the URL, but that's how deep they have it buried. This
discussion will give a brief overview of this product and an introduction to how it
works.

Overview of XML View Mapper

SQL Server View Mapper enables you to produce an XML View schema file that
relates an XDR schema to a SQL Server schema. SQL Server 2000 uses XML View
schemas to support database access through XML. Creating an XML View schema
by hand can be complex and takes a lot of time. Using XML View Mapper greatly
simplifies this task. It includes tools and a working environment, utilizing drag-and-
drop technology to automate the mechanics of manually merging data from two kinds
of schemas. The product includes a tutorial that will get you started quickly.

How XML View Mapper Works

The following discussion and figures explain the various stages of creating a View schema. Figure G.1 shows View Mapper upon first starting it up.

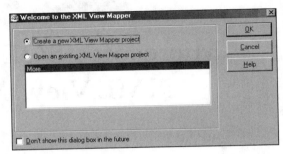

Figure G.1 XML View Mapper's opening screen.

Clicking on the left pane brings up the Data Link dialog box, where you'll fill out the required information to select the Northwind database. Figure G.2 shows the result after selecting Create a New Project.

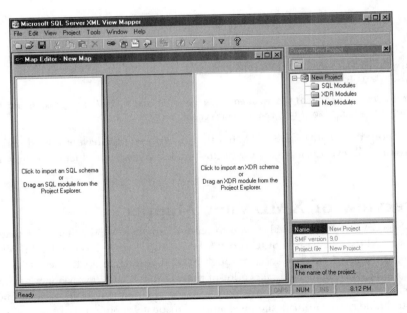

Figure G.2 Creating a new project.

After the information is filled in, you'll be presented with all tables and view components of the Northwind database, as shown in Figure G.3. Clicking the >> button will transfer all the components to the right side of the screen.

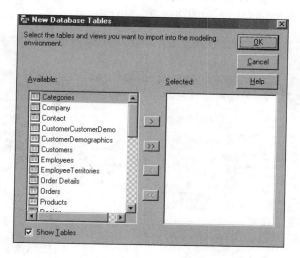

Figure G.3 The table and view selection screen.

Figure G.4 shows the result after clicking OK. The Map Editor lists the tables and views that are included in our project.

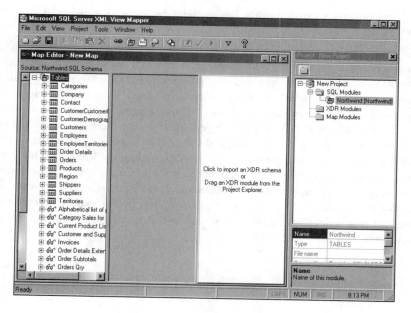

Figure G.4 After loading the SQL schema.

Clicking the right pane of the Map Editor will present a file dialog box that enables you to select a particular XDR schema file to work with. All files in the project are tracked in the right pane. Sample schemas come with the software. Figure G.5 shows the result after selecting the OrderForm.xdr schema.

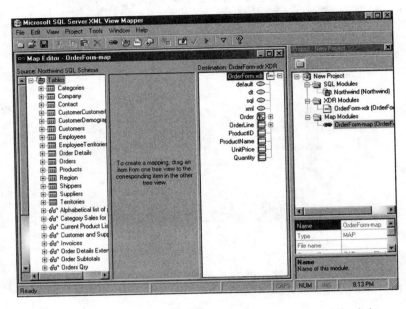

Figure G.5   Both the SQL schema and the XDR schema are loaded.

At this point, you can right-click on the XDR schema pane and select XDR Editor to show the text version of the XDR schema. Figure G.6 shows the text file after calling up the editor. In our example and also in Figure G.8, I've scrolled down a bit to concentrate on the <ElementType name="Orderline" line. That's where obvious changes will occur to show you the addition of annotations.

Let's look at Figure G.7. A lot has changed. After closing the Editor, I clicked on the Order Details table in the left pane and then did a drag-and-drop to the OrderLine element on the right side. Then, after expanding the Products table, I did the same between ProductName elements on both the left and the right. The dotted line between elements of the Order Details and Order Line elements show up after expanding the Order Details table. The important point here is that the lines between the left and right sides (known as the *Mapping Pane*) represent the annotations of a View schema file.

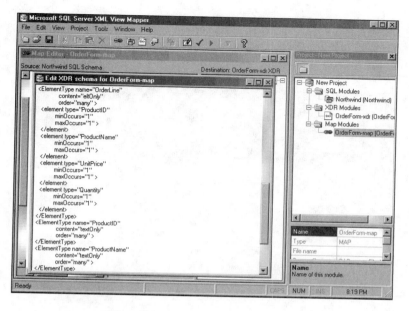

Figure G.6   The starting XDR schema.

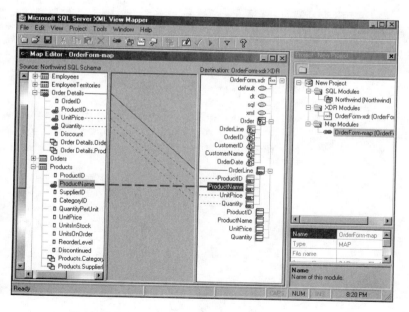

Figure G.7   Dragging and dropping to relate elements.

The last figure, Figure G.8, shows the text version of the View schema file. Did you notice how all the annotations, such as `sql:relation` and `sql:relationship`, have been inserted for you? Isn't that a bit easier than doing so by hand?

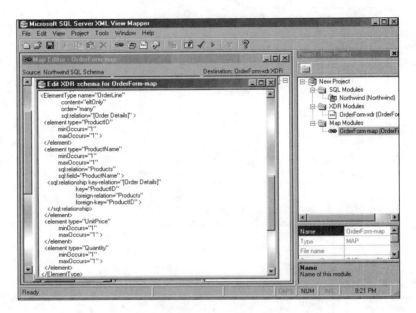

Figure G.8 The XDR schema file after joining tables.

You have the option to modify a schema as you see fit, and there also is built-in schema validation provided for you.

I believe this software will save you a lot of work in the long run (some would say even in the short term), so enjoy using it. And like I said in Appendix F, "IBM's XSL Editor," it's really hard to beat the cost of $0.00.

Glossary

Active Server Pages (ASP)
A Microsoft server-side technology for accepting client Web input, manipulating databases, and returning data results to the client.

aggregate function   A SQL function that returns a single value after performing a column calculation on a rowset in SQL.

alias   An alternative name for a table or column in expressions, an alias often used to shorten the name for subsequent reference in code, to prevent possible ambiguous references, or to provide a more descriptive name in the query output. An alias also can be an alternative name for a server.

ancestor   In XPath, a previous node in a hierarchy that is related through lineage to the current node. See also: *child, parent, descendant, sibling.*

attribute   A data item that provides additional data about its parent element.

axis   In XML, it specifies the tree relationship between the nodes selected by the location step and the context node.

binary large object   A large file, typically an image or sound file, that must be handled (for example, uploaded, downloaded, or stored in a database) in a special way because of its size.

BLOB   See *binary large object.*

Boolean   An operation or expression that can be evaluated only as either true or false.

business rules   The logical rules used to run a business. Business rules can be enforced in a SQL Server database using triggers, stored procedures, and constraints. Usually expressed with conditional logic, such as:

```
if CreditCard = Amex then

    GiveDiscount()
```

calculated column A column in a table that displays the result of an expression rather than stored data—for example:

```
CalcCost = Price * Quantity
```

CDATA An XML document section that defines literal data that will not be interpreted or changed in any way.

character set A character set determines the types of characters that SQL Server recognizes in the `char`, `varchar`, and `text` data types. Each character set is a set of 256 letters, digits, and symbols specific to a country or language. The printable characters of the first 128 values are the same for all character sets. The last 128 characters, sometimes referred to as extended characters, are unique to each character set. A character set is related to, but separate from, Unicode characters.

child In XPath, a node of the immediately subsequent level in a hierarchy that is directly related to the current node. See also: *ancestor, parent, descendant, sibling.*

concatenation Combining two or more character or binary strings or expressions into a single character or binary string or expression. For example, `Name = "John" + "Griffin"`.

context node The current node or the node being tested by an XPath expression.

data type An attribute that specifies what type of information can be stored in a column, parameter, node, or variable. Examples include string and integer.

database A collection of information, tables, and other objects organized and presented to serve a specific purpose, such as searching, sorting, and recombining data. Databases are usually stored in files.

descendant In XPath, a node in a hierarchy that is related to a node of a preceding level within the same hierarchy. See also: *ancestor, child, parent, sibling.*

double-byte character set (dbcs) A character set that generally uses two bytes to represent a character, allowing more than 256 characters to be represented.

element A logical unit within an XML document delimited by start and end tags.

expression A combination of symbols, data, and operators that evaluates to a single data value—for example, $a + b = c$.

float data type A data type that holds floating-point number data from $-1.79E + 308$ through $1.79E + 308$ in SQL Server.

hierarchy A logical tree structure that organizes its nodes so that each node has one parent node and zero or more child nodes.

HTML See *Hypertext Markup Language (HTML).*

HTTP See *Hypertext Transfer Protocol (HTTP).*

Hypertext Markup Language (HTML) A system of marking up, or tagging, a document so that it can be published on the World Wide Web. Documents prepared in HTML include reference graphics and formatting tags. A Web browser is used to view these documents.

Hypertext Transfer Protocol (HTTP)   A set of rules for exchanging files (text, graphic images, sound, video, and other multimedia files) on the World Wide Web. Relative to the TCP/IP suite of protocols (which are the basis for information exchange on the Internet), HTTP is an application protocol.

ID   In XML, an attribute of type ID has a unique value within a document.

IEC   See *International Electrotechnical Commission (IEC)*.

image data type   A SQL Server variable-length binary data type with a maximum length of $2^{31} - 1$ (which equals 2,147,483,647) bytes.

int (integer) data type   In SQL Server 2000, this data type category includes the bigint, int, smallint, and tinyint data types.

International Organization for Standardization (ISO)   One of two international standards bodies responsible for developing international data communications standards. The ISO works closely with the International Electrotechnical Commission (IEC) to define standards for computing. They jointly published the ISO/IEC SQL-92 standard for SQL.

International Electrotechnical Commission (IEC)   One of two international standards bodies responsible for developing international data communications standards. The IEC works closely with the ISO to define

standards for computing. They jointly published the ISO/IEC SQL-92 standard for SQL.

ISO   See *International Organization for Standardization (ISO)*.

ISO-10646   ISO/IEC 10646-1:1993 (published in the first or second quarter of 2000) defines one repertoire of characters and two encoding forms, UCS-4 and UCS-2. The UCS-2 encoding form is related to the UCS-4 encoding form by zero extension; that is, by zero extending the 16-bit form to 32 bits, the equivalent UCS-4 encoding form is created.

literal result element   An element in a template body that is not an XSLT instruction or extension element.

local variable   A variable defined within a template body.

location step   In XPath, this selects a set of nodes relative to a context node.

logical operators   The operators AND, OR, and NOT.

metadata   Information about the properties of data, such as the type of data in a column (numeric, text, and so on) or the length of a column.

N   Causes a string value to be inserted into a database as a Unicode string or a Unicode value to be assigned to a variable. For example, @Name = N'John'. 'John' is converted to a UNICODE string and assigned to Name. See also: *Unicode strings*.

namespace   In XML, a named collection of names. Guarantees that an element name is unique in a collection of documents.

namespace declaration   An XML document construct that defines a prefix used within a part of the document to refer to a namespace with a certain URI.

NCName   A simple name specified to be used in various places of the XML specification.

node   In XML, any object within an XML tree.

node set   A collection of nodes from one or more XML documents.

NULL   An entity that has no explicitly assigned value. NULL is not equivalent to zero or blank. (NULL doesn't equal NULL or any other quantity).

parent   In XML, a node in the immediately preceding level in a hierarchy that is directly related to the current node. See also: *ancestor, child, descendant, sibling*.

parent column   The second column of the Universal table. It indicates the parent tag for the present element.

pattern   An XPath construct that defines a condition met by a node set.

predicate   Part of an XPath expression that selects a subset of a node set.

QName   In XML, a qualified name that is either a simple name (NCName) or a name preceded by a namespace and a colon.

query optimizer   The SQL Server database engine component responsible for generating efficient execution plans for SQL statements. Used exclusively by the SQL Server system.

real data type   A SQL Server system data type that has seven-digit precision. Floating-precision number data from $-3.40E + 38$ through $3.40E + 38$.

record   A group of related columns of information treated as a unit in a SQL table. A record is more commonly called a row.

recursion   A recursive procedure or routine is one that has the capability to call itself. A recursive expression is a function, algorithm, or sequence of instructions (typically, an IF-THEN-ELSE sequence) that loops back to the beginning of itself until it detects that some condition has been satisfied.

result set   The set of rows returned from a SQL SELECT statement. The format of the rows in the result set is defined by the column list of the SELECT statement.

root node   The topmost node in an XML tree.

row   The collection of elements that form a horizontal line in a table. Each row in the table represents a single occurrence of the object modeled by the table and stores the all the object's attribute values.

SGML   See *Standard Generalized Markup Language (SGML)*.

shredding   The process of breaking up an XML document so that its data can be put into database tables.

sibling   A node in a hierarchy that is a child of the same parent as a specified node. See also: *ancestor, child, descendant, parent*.

SQL   See *structured query language (SQL)*.

SQL expression   Any combination of operators, constants, literal values, functions, and names of tables and fields that evaluates to a single value.

SQL statement   A SQL or Transact-SQL command, such as SELECT or DELETE, that performs some action on data in a relational database.

Standard Generalized Markup Language (SGML)   A standard for how to specify a document markup language or tag set. Such a specification is itself a document type definition. SGML is not in itself a document language but a description of how to specify one.

stored procedure   A precompiled collection of SQL statements stored under a name and processed as a unit.

string   A set of bytes that contain a single character-based or binary data value. In character strings, each byte (or pair of bytes) represents a single alphabetic letter, special character, or number.

string functions   Functions that perform operations on character or binary strings. For example, LEN(name) returns the number of characters in the variable name.

structured query language (SQL)   A language used to insert, retrieve, modify, and delete data in a relational database. It also contains statements for defining and administering a database.

table   A two-dimensional object, consisting of rows and columns, used to store data in a relational database.

tag column   The first column of a Universal table. It indicates the level of an element in an XML document, with NULL being the top-level element.

text node   An XML node represented by character data.

top-level element   Elements positioned between the <xsl:stylesheet> element and the root element of the XML document. They perform a variety of functions.

tree   The information content of an XML document in an abstract form. Used by XPath for queries.

trigger   A stored procedure that executes when data in a specific table is modified. A trigger is created like this:

```
CREATE TRIGGER trig1 ON table1 AS...
```

UCS   See *Universal Coded Character Set*

Unicode strings   Unicode strings have a format similar to character strings, but they are preceded by an N identifier (N stands for National Language in the SQL-92 standard). The N prefix must be uppercase. For example, 'Miche[as]l' is a character constant whereas N'Miche[as]l' is a Unicode constant. Unicode constants are interpreted as Unicode data and are not evaluated using a code page. Unicode data is stored using 2 bytes per character, as opposed to 1 byte per character for character data.

uniform resource identifier (URI)   The way you identify points of content on the Internet, whether it's a page of text, a video or sound clip, a still or animated image, or a program. The most common form of URI is the Web page address, which is a particular form or subset of URI called a uniform resource locator (URL). For example, http://www.w3c.org. See RFC 1630 and http://www.w3.org/Addressing/#terms.

uniform resource locator (URL)
Uniform resource identifier used to locate pages on the World Wide Web. For example, `http://www.microsoft.com`. See `http://www.w3.org/Addressing/#terms`.

Universal Coded Character Set A code set containing all characters commonly used in computer applications anywhere in the world. The initial version of 10646 contains approximately 33,000 characters covering a long list of languages including European, Asian ideographic, Middle Eastern, Indian, and others. It also reserves 6,000 code spaces for private use.

Universal Coded Character Set Transformation Format (UTF) UTF-8 is standard ASCII. See also: *Universal Coded Character Set*.

Universal table Used by the FOR XML statement in EXPLICIT mode. It defines the rowset layout of data used to generate an XML document.

URI See *uniform resource identifier (URI)*.

URL See *uniform resource locator (URL)*.

UTF See *Universal Coded Character Set Transformation Format*.

varchar data type A data type that holds variable-length non-Unicode data with a maximum of 8,000 characters.

Size might differ in other relational database management systems (RDBMS).

view A database object that can be referenced the same way as a table in SQL statements. Views are defined using a SELECT statement.

W3C The World Wide Web Consortium, an Internet standards organization located at `http://www.w3c.org`.

XML Extensible Markup Language. XML is a flexible way to create common information formats and share both the format and the data on the World Wide Web, intranets, and elsewhere.

XPath A language that describes a way to locate and process items in Extensible Markup Language (XML) documents by using an addressing syntax based on a path through the document's logical structure or hierarchy.

XSLT (Extensible Stylesheet Language Transformations) XSLT is a standard way to describe how to transform (change) the structure of an XML document into an XML document with a different structure or an HTML document. XSLT is a recommendation of the World Wide Web Consortium (W3C).

Index

G-H

I

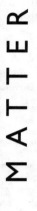
V O I C E S   T H A T   M A T T E R

VISIT OUR WEB SITE

W W W . N E W R I D E R S . C O M

On our web site, you'll find information about our other books, authors, tables of contents, and book errata. You will also find information about book registration and how to purchase our books, both domestically and internationally.

EMAIL US

Contact us at: **nrfeedback@newriders.com**

- If you have comments or questions about this book
- To report errors that you have found in this book
- If you have a book proposal to submit or are interested in writing for New Riders
- If you are an expert in a computer topic or technology and are interested in being a technical editor who reviews manuscripts for technical accuracy

Contact us at: **nreducation@newriders.com**

- If you are an instructor from an educational institution who wants to preview New Riders books for classroom use. Email should include your name, title, school, department, address, phone number, office days/hours, text in use, and enrollment, along with your request for desk/examination copies and/or additional information.

Contact us at: **nrmedia@newriders.com**

- If you are a member of the media who is interested in reviewing copies of New Riders books. Send your name, mailing address, and email address, along with the name of the publication or web site you work for.

BULK PURCHASES/CORPORATE SALES

If you are interested in buying 10 or more copies of a title or want to set up an account for your company to purchase directly from the publisher at a substantial discount, contact us at 800-382-3419 or email your contact information to corpsales@pearsontechgroup.com. A sales representative will contact you with more information.

WRITE TO US

New Riders Publishing
201 W. 103rd St.
Indianapolis, IN 46290-1097

CALL/FAX US

Toll-free (800) 571-5840
If outside U.S. (317) 581-3500
Ask for New Riders
FAX: (317) 581-4663

New Riders

RELATED NEW RIDERS TITLES

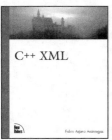

ISBN: 073571052X
with CD-ROM
330 pages
US $39.99

C++ XML

Fabio Arciniegas

The demand for robust solutions is at an all-time high. Developers and programmers are asking the question, "How do I get the power performance found with C++ integrated into my web applications?" Fabio Arciniegas knows how. He has created the best way to bring C++ to the web. Through development with XML and in this book, he shares the secrets developers and programmers worldwide are searching for.

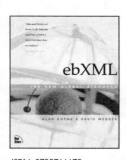

ISBN: 0735711178
300 pages
US $34.99

ebXML: The New Global Standard for Doing Business on the Internet

Alan Kotok
David Webber

To create an e-commerce initiative, managers need to understand that XML is the technology that will take them there. Companies understand that to achieve a successful Internet presence their company needs an e-commerce method-ology implemented. Many department managers (the actual people who design, build, and execute the plan) don't know where to begin. *ebXML* will take them there.

ISBN: 0735710201
1152 pages
US $49.99

ISBN: 0735710899
760 pages with CD-ROM
US $49.99

ISBN: 0735711364
640 pages
US $49.99

Inside XML

Steven Holzner

Inside XML is a foundation boo that covers both the Microsoft and non-Microsoft approach to XML programming. It covers in detail the hot aspects of XML, such as DTDs vs. XML Schema CSS, XSL, XSLT, XLinks, XPointers, XHTML, RDF, CDF, parsing XML in Per and Java, and much more.

XML, XSLT, Java and JSP A Case Study in Develop a Web Application

Westy Rockwell

A practical, hands-on experien in building web applications ba on XML and Java technologies this book is unique because it teaches the technologies by u them to build a web chat pro throughout the book. The project is explained in great detail, after the reader is show how to get and install the necessary tools to be able to tomize this project and build other web applications.

Inside XSLT

Steven Holzner

Inside XSLT is designed to be companion guide to Inside X This example oriented book ers XML to HTML, XML to Music, XML with Java, styles creation and usage, nodes an attributes, sorting data, crea XPath expressions, using XP and XSLT functions, namesp names templates, name varia designing style sheets and us XSLT processor API's, the 5 XSL formatting objects, the DTD, and much much more

Colophon

The image on the cover of this book, captured by photographer R. Strange, is that of Mayan pyramids. These pyramids are said to have served a number of purposes. As a religious symbol they were a place of worship and sacrifice; however, they also served as a landmark for Mayans traveling through the jungle because they were easily seen above the trees. They also served as burial chambers for high-ranking officials.

Ancient Mayan civilizations existed on the Yucatan Peninsula, in the lowland rainforests of Mexico and Belize, on the highlands of Guatemala, and parts of Honduras and El Salvador. Contemporary Mayans continue to populate the Yucatan Peninsula, the Chiapas state in Mexico, and the Guatemalan highlands.[1]

This book was written and edited in Microsoft Word, and laid out in QuarkXPress. The font used for the body text is Bembo and MCPdigital. It was printed on 50# Husky Offset Smooth paper at R.R. Donnelley & Sons in Crawfordsville, Indiana. Prepress consisted of PostScript computer-to-plate technology (filmless process). The cover was printed at Moore Langen Printing in Terre Haute, Indiana, on Carolina, coated on one side.

1. http://www.gorp.com/gorp/location/latamer/arc_maya.htm